Son of a Butcher

By
Reid Matthias

Copyright © Reid Matthias 2022

All rights reserved. Other than for the purposes and subject to the conditions prescribed under the *Copyright Act*, no part of this publication may be reproduced, stored in a retrieval system, or transmitted in any form or by any means, electronic, mechanical, photocopying, recording or otherwise, without the prior permission of the publisher.

ISBN paperback: 978-0-6450472-8-8
ebook: 978-0-6450472-9-5

This edition first published by A 13 in November 2022

Typesetting by Ben Morton

Publication assistance from Immortalise

Back Cover photo – Mr. Xerty on Unsplash

Front Cover photo – Josephine Matthias

For Ryan

Acknowledgements

It has been a work of love to write about an imaginary place like Amicable, populated with imaginary people like Amicableans. Though these stories have all been fictional, the people, like the town, have been derived from the beauty of real places – places with exotic sounding names like Rake and Buffalo Center, Lakota, Titonka and Thompson. They continue the story in real life, while I simply try to remember it.

Throughout this journey, I have been blessed with the extraordinary editing eyes of my wife, Christine, my daughter, Greta, and my mother, Diane. Though not an exhaustive list, I'd also like to add a few others: Bonnie Doty for a keen eye on phrasing and storyline, Ben Morton for his work on typesetting and printing advice, and most joyfully, my sister, Vikki Matthias, whose keen eye for details and ability to streamline the narrative was crucial for this incredible story. Finally, I'd like to thank those small-town people everywhere who enjoy sharing their memories and expressing goodness in a world that seems slightly wonky.

In the pages of this fourth installment of the Amicable Circle, you'll gaze through the perspective of young and old people alike. For those with a keen love of symbolism and metaphor, you'll enjoy searching for both. I hope you'll think deeply about what this story *means* as much as how it *reads*.

Chapter 1.

It wasn't until Murgatroyd MacDonald entered the third-grade classroom of Amicable Elementary School that J.T. Jensen began his return to the real world. After months and months of struggle, attempting to reconcile his father's death and put it into a picture that his nine-year-old mind could understand, that moment, that *exact* moment, was the pivot for him to move forward.

She was short, with curly reddish-brown hair. A pug nose squatted in the middle of her face like a tiny peach. Her eyes, close set and dazzlingly blue, stared around the room with wonder. Decorating the walls were pictures and numbers and galaxies and musical notes. Her mouth dropped as the school secretary deposited her in the doorway and handed her off to the classroom teacher. All the other nine-year-olds, mouths similarly agape, watched Murgatroyd approach Mrs. Brown and hand her a note. This was a rare event. New kids never entered the class. Amicable, even after the elevator's restoration, was still a place most people ignored. But not the MacDonalds. No, most certainly not the MacDonalds.

J.T. watched the strange looking girl turn from Mrs. Brown who had pointed to a chair in the corner of the room. "Murgatroyd, please pull that chair up next to J.T." Mrs. Brown's eyes caught J.T.'s. "Raise your hand, J.T."

He did and Murgatroyd smiled shyly at him. After fetching the chair, she stumbled with it through the other students who snickered as she banged into desks and human legs on the way to J.T.'s desk.

"Murgatroyd," said Mrs. Brown, "we'll get you a desk of your own after lunch today, but this will do for now."

Although the other students masked their giggles regarding her name, Murgatroyd seemed unfazed. Stuffing her legs under the desk, Murgatroyd bumped J.T.'s knees. "I'm Murgatroyd. I know, it's a weird name. Me mum says that it's a fine English name, but I think it sounds like a Transformer." J.T. tilted his head at her strange accent.

Murgatroyd continued with lowered voice. "We moved to Amicable a coupla of weeks ago. Me mum said that it would be good for us to get out of jolly old London, not that we lived there; it was actually a suburb of London, Chigwell. Have you heard of Chigwell?"

J.T. was instantly fascinated by the fact that she changed her l's into w's. 'Chigwell' had become 'Chigwew,' and 'Amicable' was 'Amicabuw.' He shook his head.

"Not much to look at," Murgatroyd said.

Unsure of whether Murgatroyd was speaking of Chigwell, Amicable or herself, J.T. remained impassive. Certainly, this intruder into his personal space was odd: not just her appearance, not simply her accent, but the way she carried herself. Amicablean, she most certainly was not. As she spoke, her hands worried on the desk in front of her; small, thin fingers, designed to play a harp or guitar or something that came from England. J.T. sensed her nervousness and he wondered if she was about to explode.

"You don't talk much, do you?"

Just before he responded, Mrs. Brown interrupted them. "Murgatroyd, I know that this is your first day, but in this class, talking is kept to a minimum until conversation is necessary."

"Sorry, Mum."

The class laughed again.

"My name is Mrs. Brown," she said sternly.

"Sorry, Mrs. Brown."

At recess, Murgatroyd followed J.T. into the hallway where they grabbed their coats. "Dog's bollocks!" she exclaimed as they trekked down the hallway. "You're a big blighter, aintcha?"

Unwilling to turn around, J.T. frowned. He had no idea what she was saying.

"How tall are you? One eighty? One eighty-two?"

"I'm five nine," he finally responded. She was a foot shorter than he.

"Bloody hell."

Opening the door, they strolled out onto the playground where other students were already running and sliding, throwing things, screaming and laughing. From a plastic web hung half a dozen children who looked like a spider's morning snack.

"What do you do for morning tea?"

Chapter 1.

He stopped and turned around, towering over her. "What are you talking about?"

"This," she motioned around the playground and pantomimed running.

"I watch."

"Watch what?"

J.T. frowned at the way she clipped her words. 'What' turned into 'wha' with a guttural stop at the end. "People. Things. I just like to watch." He unconsciously overenunciated the words.

"That's boring." Murgatroyd's face scrunched up into a ball of disbelief. With her hands on her hips, she swiveled her head around the grounds. "You should be playing basketball, or something like that."

"I don't like basketball."

"What?" she repeated, astounded.

"Are you deaf or is that your favorite word?" She frowned. "Why don't *you* go play basketball?"

"Me? I'm too short. And besides, you're my only friend."

Leaning down over her, J.T. brought his face close. "I'm *not* your friend."

"Yes, you are," she replied adamantly. "We already knocked knees."

"That's stupid." J.T. turned and strode quickly across the cushioned ground. When she began to follow him, he started to jog to get away from her. Thinking he was beginning to play, Murgatroyd chased him. Onlookers would have pointed at the odd couple, the lanky boy being accosted by the short, red-haired girl, like an albatross annoyed by a red seagull.

Murgatroyd put her head down and ran after him. His long legs carried him quickly, past the tetherball pole, past the plastic tube slide, beyond the margins of youthful humanity to the boundary of the chain-link fence where J.T. could see his house across the street. His mom was not home. She was never there now that his dad was gone.

"That was fun," Murgatroyd puffed beside him. He was not breathing heavily.

"Do you want me to help you find some other friends? Some girls?" he asked.

Son of a Butcher

"No, that's okay. I'm all right with just the two of us."

J.T. frowned. "Just to let you know, I'm awkward."

"Me too!"

"No, you don't understand. I... well... I can see things."

She covered her eyes and released them in a peekaboo motion. "Two for two!"

Frustrated, he grunted. "What I mean is, I can see everything." She was about to respond again, but he stopped her. "Before you say, 'Me too!' I can see from a long way away. I can see in the dark. I can read people's faces, all that stuff."

"Me too!"

"Aagh," J.T. tried to move away from her, but she grabbed his arm.

"Why don't you want to be my friend?"

"Because..." he responded lamely.

"Me mum says that's not really an answer. She *always* makes me give a reason, even if I have to make something up."

"You lie to her?"

"I'm good at it," Murgatroyd smiled as if competency in lying was an admirable trait.

"You wouldn't be able to lie to me."

"I bet I could." Murgatroyd's jaw jutted out.

"What do you want to bet?"

Screwing up her face, she put her fingers to her chin. "I'll leave you alone for five minutes."

"Make it an hour, and you're on."

"Wait," Murgatroyd said, "what do I get if I win?"

"I'll leave you alone for an hour."

She slapped him on the arm. "No, silly. How about you sit with me at lunchtime?"

J.T. surveyed the playground. Thankfully, no one was watching them. "Deal."

Murgatroyd clapped her hands giddily. "Okay, now, what should I lie to you about?"

"You can't do it that way. If you just start out lying, I'll already know."

Chapter 1.

"Hmm, I didn't think about that."

J.T. leaned against the fence; it bowed against his weight. Crossing his arms, he banged his head against the links. "How about you tell me three truthful things and one lie."

"Good idea." She cleared her throat. "I have two brothers. Me mum has brown hair. In me school in England, the uniform I wore was green. And... me favorite movie is Starman."

Breathing in sharply, J.T. stared down at her. The first three were obvious lies, but the last one she told was true. In her eyes, he had seen the shift, and her pulse had quickened, but with Starman, she held his gaze.

Starman was his favorite movie, too.

"First of all, in America, we use the word 'my' instead of 'me' as a possessive."

"Neat!" she smiled.

"Secondly, I thought you were going to tell me three truths and a lie, not the other way around."

Her eyes widened and her grin beamed. "Blimey! That's bloody brilliant!"

"You talk like you were in the Harry Potter movies."

She laughed. "You say the nicest things. All right, it's your turn. Let me see if I can pick out when you lie. Three truthful things and one lie. Make it a good one, too." Staring up at his face, she ground her teeth. "Come on, don't dilly dally."

"You're supposed to leave me alone for an hour."

"I will, but I didn't say when that had to happen. I'll leave you alone for an hour after school lets out."

"Hey, that's not fair." J.T. complained.

"You've got to learn to negotiate on your terms, my friend. Don't assume anything – that's what me mum says." He frowned. "Sorry! *My* mum says."

J.T. threw up his hands and pushed away from the fence. She followed behind him a step. "Where are you going? It's my turn."

"Wasn't part of the negotiation, Murgatroyd. You shouldn't have assumed anything."

Son of a Butcher

Murgatroyd stood with her hands on her hips, crossly watching the tall boy walk away from her. He was going to be hard work.

* * * *

Since his father's death, life had been difficult for J.T. Jensen. There were memories, pieces of him, stashed in nooks and crannies all around Amicable. The melting sculpture at the cemetery was one, of course, and a second at Peterson's Butchery where Unca Derek and Unca Nash had reconstructed the Leo Jensen Memorial coffee area in the front window. Those who wanted to have a cup of coffee while waiting for their orders could sit in the shade of the awning, leafing through self-help books and chatting about the weather. The reconstructed elevator attached Leo Jensen's name to one of the silos. An artist acquaintance of Demetrius Chandler had painted a life-size silhouette on the concrete. J.T. had seen his mother standing next to it sometimes, touching the shadow's shoulder or hand. She missed him a lot, too.

Georgie, J.T.'s sister, had moved on without their dad. Sometimes, she talked about him, but it was as if she was speaking about one of her stuffed animals. They were real, but not really alive. J.T. did not know if Georgie had a special talent like his and he was not particularly keen to find out. She certainly didn't act like it. She acted like a big pain in the patootie. That's what J.T. thought.

While J.T. stood on the front porch of their house, he turned back to see the line of yellow buses parked in front of the school, swallowing children to take them home and vomit them into their driveways. They were country kids and they were used to the ride. J.T. wished he could ride the bus sometimes, to drive around the countryside along the miles of raised asphalt roads, staring at the oceans of green, undulating corn; to watch the sun turn the stalks golden in the fall and to feel the thrumming of the tires over the gritty ice during the winter. He would sit by himself, lean on the seat in front of him, chin resting on his forearms and be carried far away from his sadness and loneliness.

J.T. missed his father fiercely. On the downslope of ALS, when the disease took his father's mobility and speech, they had become very close. Sitting on his lap while his dad was in the wheelchair, they would

Chapter 1.

watch the movie, *Starman*. When Jeff Bridges spoke with that jaunty robotic voice, J.T.'s dad would laugh and laugh until he would cough. Starman's movements, herky jerky, were a lot like his dad's up until the end of verbal communication.

The last time they watched Starman, J.T.'s head was leaning back against his shoulder. "Hey champ," his dad turned down the sound on his computer monitor which spoke for him. "I need you to do something for me." J.T. nodded, but his eyes were still glued on the television.

"I have to go away pretty soon."

J.T. turned his head to look at his father's face. There were tears in his eyes. Reaching out for the Kleenex in the arm of his wheelchair, J.T. dabbed at them.

"Thanks." Nodding, J.T. followed his father's eyes on the computer screen. "Do you know what it means that I'm going away?"

"Yes. You're dying."

"That's right. Now, I was wondering if you could share some words at the funeral for me when I'm gone."

"Like Unca Dorge's funeral?"

"Yes." He paused. "Where is Mom?"

"In the kitchen."

"Good. Now, I'll write them out, but you can say them, cause I won't be there. Got it?"

"Okay, dad." J.T. focused his eyes on Starman again.

When the funeral took place, J.T. stood at the front and spoke the eulogy his father had prepared. Many, if not all who were in attendance in the school auditorium (the church was not nearly big enough), were crying noisily. J.T. politely asked them to keep the noise down. As he gazed out over those in attendance, he knew most of their faces. Butcher had been a well-respected citizen of Amicable. Universally regarded as one of the saviors of the town, people came from far and wide to pay their last respects. During the funeral service, J.T. memorized those who had come to grieve. For him, it had been a game, like a Where's Waldo picture. If he closed his eyes, he could see exactly where people were sitting: Ms. Nelson, Rodrigo, Mrs. Thompson – everyone. Way in the back though, was someone who surprised him.

Son of a Butcher

His Watcher.

Over the last few years, J.T. had noticed the Watcher come and go. Wondering if the Watcher was a guardian angel (Unca John had told him about those at church), J.T. was afraid to approach. He only saw him infrequently. The Watcher was stout and had a big beard. He was tall, not quite as tall as J.T.'s dad, but tall nonetheless. Not good with guessing age, J.T. assumed the man was old, perhaps his mother's age. His mom had just spoken about getting old – forty was just around the corner, she said – and the man seemed about like that. The Watcher didn't have grey hair, not like his mother's anyway. Because of J.T.'s ability to see details, he memorized the Watcher's details: he had a cane and a limp to go with it as well as a big nose that had lots of little red lines on it. From the top of his shirt, brown hair stuck out in a tuft, like a little bird nest. Strangely, the Watcher always seemed to be wearing sunglasses. Even at the indoor funeral.

J.T. never pointed out the Watcher to anyone else. He didn't want people to think he was a silly little boy, or a weirdo, or that he was seeing things. Granted, the Watcher never stayed around long enough for others really to notice. J.T. had only noticed him around Amicable a few times: when the elevator blew up, when Mr. Johnson's tractor ran into the side of the John Deere Implement building and around the time when Rodrigo's Mexican restaurant started on fire. It never really occurred to J.T. that these inauspicious times would be linked.

* * * *

Gazing back at the schoolyard, J.T. focused in on the red curls of the annoying girl who shared his desk. Murgatroyd would be an interesting addition to his inner monologue, he was certain. As she approached a car, Murgatroyd glanced in his direction. Her face was vacant, serene, as if she was just passing through time without a care in the world. A woman stepped out of the car. She was thin and dressed in a long flowing skirt with a lacy hem, a top that seemed pieced together with various rags, and clompy blue shoes – considered 'hippie clothes' by some of the older ladies around Amicable. Her hair was tied up with a

Chapter 1.

yellow ribbon and she stained her face with bright blue eye shadow and orange lipstick.

Although he couldn't hear what the woman said, he could see that she was impatiently motioning for Murgatroyd to get in the car. Murgatroyd opened the rear door carelessly tossing her schoolbag inside, and then climbed into the front passenger seat. The car, a rusted compact, coughed blue smoke as the woman pulled out into traffic narrowly missing a Ford pickup driving past. The Ford stopped to allow the Omni in. After stalling the car once, the woman stepped on the gas and roared away.

Turning back to the front door of his home, J.T. opened it and stepped inside where he was greeted by the sound of the television. Georgie had positioned herself on the sofa while the movie, *Frozen* began.

J.T. hated that movie.

Meanwhile, his mother, Rhonda Jensen, decompressed in the Human Beans Café with a coffee mug in her hand. Across from her, Leslie Deakins sat primly. Leslie's hair, now recently colored to a mottled brown and blonde which had become so popular with the Midwestern ladies, hung loosely over her shoulders. To Rhonda, she seemed tense.

"Who's watching your kids this afternoon?" Leslie asked.

"J.T. is fine. If he needs anything, he can walk next door to the Andersons to call me."

Leslie nodded. "John has our girls."

They both sipped at the same time.

"I have some news," Leslie said with a smirk.

"I heard."

"You did?" Leslie was shocked.

"Yes. When I was picking up my order at Peterson's this morning, Leona was there. Supposedly she'd seen the new family on their way to school. According to her, they're not from around here."

Leslie's mouth tightened. "Let's hope that Amicable has learned its lesson regarding outsiders."

Rhonda laughed. It felt good to do it. Far too often, since Butcher's death, she'd found herself holding back, bottling up her joy.

Son of a Butcher

She didn't want Amicableans to think she was moving on from Butcher. No, his death was still extremely painful. Every day, Rhonda woke up devastated that he wasn't next to her. Rhonda's wearisome days were punctuated by work at the Mexican restaurant, mentoring the youngest members of the town council and, at times like these, enjoying moments of maternal respite by having coffee with her closest friends.

"I'm sure she'll fit in just fine," Leslie continued. "I heard she has a daughter, too. I think she's around J.T.'s age."

"That's nice," said Rhonda distractedly as she peered out the front window towards Carley's X-Er-Size Studio. A few women were exiting in their bright Spandex sweatsuits. "It would be nice if we could welcome outsiders without running them through the gauntlet of suspicion."

"Hmmm," Leslie folded her hands primly in front of her. "The news is not about *those* newcomers." Rhonda's eyebrows arched. "I'm pregnant."

"What?"

"Ten weeks. I know, it's a shock, for you and me. I thought I was done, but here we go again."

Speechless, Rhonda's mouth bounced up and down. A hurricane of emotions swirled around her – giddiness, shock, sadness, anxiousness, excitement.

"Well, say something," Leslie said.

"I'm… I'm…" Feeling tears begin in her eyes, Rhonda reached out for her best friend. She and Butcher had talked about having more, but it wasn't to be. Another child in the Deakins household would mean less time for her. Guiltily, she absorbed the last thought, stood and hugged Leslie. "Oh, that's so wonderful, right?"

Leslie's own tears appeared as she nodded. "We're hoping for a boy, but we'll take either."

"Could be twins again?" Rhonda said over her head. The rest of the café stopped what they were doing to watch the two women embracing.

"I certainly hope not," Leslie answered as they separated.

Sitting back down, Rhonda asked quietly. "Who else knows?"

"No one. Just you and John, now."

Chapter 1.

"Your secret is safe with me."

After returning home, Rhonda sighed as she pulled the car in the garage and perused the contents. The boat they had purchased years ago sat under a tarpaulin covered with dust and bird droppings. Rusting cans of stain and paint sat along the shelf in front of the boat. These were projects left undone once Butcher had passed away. The garage smelled of grime and grease, gasoline and mouse droppings. During the summer those smells were overpowering, but now that late September had rolled around, they were muted. Even so, the sights and smells of the building left her feeling empty.

As the car's engine ticked quietly, Rhonda rested her hands on the steering wheel musing over Leslie's news. How would their relationship change? When Leslie became a new mother again, would she spend more time with other young mothers? Would she have time for Rhonda?

John would be overjoyed, of course. He loved the girls, and another child would be welcomed, but neither of them were spring chickens anymore.

The car door groaned as she opened it. When her eyes fell on the boat again, she felt a twinge of guilt. Maybe it was time to take the kids fishing. They loved doing that when they were smaller and Butcher was able. Now that J.T. was nine and almost her height, he might like to do some more adultish things. Georgie would go along with anything.

She closed the garage door and climbed the front steps to the porch. When she entered the house, the TV blared a song from *Frozen*. J.T. sat hunched over a bowl of cereal at the kitchen table. To his left was a book.

Dropping the keys into the bowl by the front door, her attention was arrested by a photo hanging on the wall above the bowl. It was a picture of her and Butcher after they were first married. As the sun set over Lake Ikmakota, someone had snapped the picture as they were holding hands. Even in silhouette, the viewer could see that they were smiling.

"How was your day?" she asked Georgie.

Georgie poked her head above the sofa and launched into a complete, exhaustive recap of her day. Her wide eyes and expressive

Son of a Butcher

mouth verbalized with glee. Though she communicated like Rhonda, Georgie looked much more like Butcher. She, too, would be tall, with sandy brown hair and long, nimble fingers. Rhonda attempted to focus on them but was distracted by the television behind her daughter's head. Once Georgie reached the climax of her day, a video about butterflies, Rhonda was nearly worn out listening. "That was really nice, sweetheart."

Sensing that her time with her mother was done, Georgie slid back down the sofa and went back to watching the movie.

"And you?" Rhonda asked J.T.

Morosely, he took a bite of his cereal and closed his book. "It was okay. Different, but okay."

"How so?"

Pushing back his chair, he stood and placed his cereal bowl in the sink. Rhonda was again shocked at how much he'd grown. "There's a new girl in our class. Very weird."

"What do you mean?"

"Her name is Murgatroyd."

"What?"

He rolled his eyes. "I know. And she's got a funny accent. They moved from England."

"Why did they come to Amicable?"

He shrugged. "I didn't ask that question. I was trying to get away from her."

"Why?"

"She's a girl."

"Ah."

"Besides, she's awkward. I know, because I'm like that too."

"You're not awkward." He stared at her. "Okay, maybe a little… but you're kind and funny and…"

"I'm not funny." He walked past her and down the hallway to his room.

"I think you're funny," she called out to his retreating form.

Later, during dinner, Rhonda watched J.T. push his spaghetti around his bowl. It was his third serving. His hair, bleached during the summer, had turned a dirty brown; and the freckles which dotted his

Chapter 1.

cheeks had now faded. Georgie's wavy hair kept falling into her spaghetti sauce. She would need a bath.

"What do you guys think about going fishing?"

"Yay!" Georgie shouted.

J.T. looked up over his bowl. "When? Where?"

Rhonda stopped twirling her noodles on the fork. "I don't know. Lake Ikmakota? We'll take the boat out, maybe ask Unca John and Aunt Leslie if they want to come. I'm sure Grandma and Grandpa would love to spend some time outdoors with you."

"It would be kind of cold, wouldn't it?"

Rhonda shook her head. "We're not going swimming, J.T. Just some fishing. It will be fun."

He scooped a meatball into his mouth and wiped his chin with the back of his hand. "Do you know how to run the boat?"

She sniffed. "Of course."

"You're lying," J.T. said.

"Don't be rude."

"Sorry. I'm not trying to be rude."

"So, we'll go fishing next weekend. Great." She tapped the table with her hands. "Now, tell me about this Margaret or whatever her name was."

"Murgatroyd. Murgatroyd MacDonald. I think that's what Mrs. Brown said. She's about this tall," he held up a hand to his chest, "she's got blue eyes and dirty red hair. Like sludgy red. And she talks a lot."

"She sounds wonderful. Maybe we should invite them over for dinner sometime."

"Please no, Mom. It's bad enough that she's in my class…" J.T. responded testily.

"All right, all right, don't get snippy."

They finished the meal in respective silence, although Georgie continued to hum. When the dishes had been packed into the dishwasher, J.T. trudged into the living room. "J.T.," his mother stopped him, "I hope that you can find a friend, even if it's not the MacDonald girl." He didn't respond.

Chapter 2.

Gustav Keller rubbed his aching calf muscle. For most of the day, just like many of the days beforehand, he had been working up his strength. At some point soon, he would shed the cane and his rehabilitation would be complete. Tired of what the cane represented – incarceration and a nightmarish existence – he was ready to move on.

As Gustav opened his computer and pored over news articles, photos and anything that might benefit his plans, he was subtly aware that behind him, cutouts of newspapers were pinned to the corkboard. Staring down at him was the grinning face of Rhonda Redman and the tall man she married. And, photos of a rebuilt grain elevator (Gustav smirked at that).

The headlights of a car flashed through the slats of his blinds and moved quickly across the faded photographs. He looked up, irritated, then stretched his fingers.

Gustav thought back to that fateful day so many years ago, a cabin in the Wisconsin woods, a beautiful young woman, naïve and fresh faced from Shitsville, Iowa, who had come to the big smoke of Chicago to escape. Everything had been going so well. She was pliant, fun and engaging, but cautious. Her father had abandoned them when she was little; her mother was psychotic. A true opportunity for him to step in and become the very thing she was missing.

Although they had gotten hot and steamy pretty quickly, he hadn't pressured her. He had been brought up right – don't mistreat women. No meant no, so he had stopped. Even though frustrated, he had let her run from the house. Somehow, though, his good deed had not gone unpunished. When the police showed up that night and rapped on his door, he was surprised when they shone the light into his eyes and threw him to the floor. Much of that night had been lost in the subsequent horror of days. Unfortunately, during the trial, Rhonda had lied about everything. Whatever had happened in her past had suddenly become his reality. Sentenced to ten years in prison, he had done his time. Three years on good behavior. Three years to plan his vengeance.

Chapter 2.

More than once he had wanted to end it all, but the only thing that kept him going was the thought of revenge. Just to make her life a little more like what he'd experienced. *That* was what he lived for.

While in prison, he suffered endless atrocities. The guards broke his right kneecap while he was 'attempting' an escape. As he recovered, other inmates made it their duty to continue his miserable existence. Once out of the infirmary, a particularly nasty inmate named Jacob Reinhold, a convicted armed felon, sent Gustav back to the emergency ward.

Jacob Reinhold took his right eye, too.

Left with a cane and an eyepatch, Gustav seethed.

Since his parole, Gustav had lived five years in Iowa. Five *excruciatingly* long years in Clancy. Surrounded by nice, boring (but surprisingly easily offended) people, Gustav had gone about his business of plotting his payback. Earning a salary as an information specialist, Gustav spent his days parked behind a computer solving computer 'issues' for senior citizens: lost passwords, inabilities to pay online, confusion as to how to solve the most basic issues. It was incredibly dull, but it paid his bills to prepare for that one specific moment when Rhonda Redman's world would come crashing down around her.

Once he had been imprisoned, she had fled back to Amicable while he rotted away in a Wisconsin prison cell. She fell in love, had kids and enjoyed life. Now that she had suffered the death of both love and life, he smiled sadistically at her ill-fortune. Gustav remembered her wild keening as she watched her husband's wheelchair being dredged from the lake with the dead man still strapped into it. The sight of Rhonda's endless funeral tears and the son's eulogy affected him even more. He had to hold back his laughter.

Now in his forties, Gustav had no sympathy for Rhonda, nor her children, nor any of these small-town residents. He had lost eight of the best years of his life because of her lie and now it was time to return the favor.

Stretching his arms above his head he groaned. Pushing himself up from the chair, he adjusted his eyepatch and limped toward the front door. Taking his light jacket from the coat hook and his cane leaning against the jamb, he opened the door and headed into the darkness.

Son of a Butcher

Gustav Keller was used to darkness. It had become an old, trusted friend to help him cope with the tragic events of his life. As he walked, rubber tip of the cane thumping methodically on the sidewalk, he smirked at what was about to happen. Though he wanted to do this alone, he needed help with a few things. Thus, he had enlisted a local Clancyvite, Danny Thul, who labored at the hardware store during the day and inhabited Rusty's Pub and Grub by night. Danny called himself a 'frequent fryer' because of his intense love of buffalo wings. This adoration of wings showed up fully in his ever-expanding waistline. Danny was about three hundred and ten pounds of solid excess.

Opening the door to Rusty's, Barnaby inhaled the ancient aromas of deep-fried things which clung to the carpet and upholstery. A hint of cigarette smoke still lingered among the other scents. For Barnaby, the overwhelming smells of Rusty's were welcome. They reminded him of long ago.

A bar stretched along the left side of the room. Black padded stools were positioned underneath the overhang. Above, beer and wineglasses hung between patrons and bartenders. Behind the bar, a heavily bearded man with tattooed neck and arms smiled contentedly at two men arguing good-naturedly over some kind of sporting event. Above the bartender's head, two televisions displayed two different games.

Noticing Barnaby's entrance, the bartender raised a hand. "Barney. How are you?"

Faking his best smile, Barnaby moved into the bar area and laid a hand on the wooden top. "Fine, fine, Tony. And you?"

"Peachy. How about a beer?" Barnaby nodded and Anthony poured a Milwaukee's Best from the tap. While he waited for the drink, Barnaby glanced around the room. Some locals were leaning back in booths engaged in light conversation. Their hands cuddled sweating beer glasses in front of them, while their heads were illuminated by neon beer lights above. A few nodded their acknowledgement. Barnaby was almost considered a local now. *Almost.*

With beer in hand, Barnaby took a sip and wiped his mouth with his cane hand. The froth clung to his skin and he wiped it on his pants. Crossing Rusty's to the back, he pulled out a chair giving him a full

Chapter 2.

panorama of who was coming and going. Laying his cane on the floor, he sat and waited.

Ten minutes later, Danny Thul arrived. Even from across the room, Barnaby could see that Danny was breathing heavily. Although he had driven to Rusty's and walked only twenty or thirty steps, his gasps bespoke a man who stood on the knife's edge of a coronary. Barnaby shook his head. It was one thing to gain a few pounds to fit in and disguise oneself; it was another to plot a course for Type 2 Diabetes.

Barnaby heard Danny shout at Tony to fry up a Cowboy Basket of buffalo wings. The bartender smiled and retreated into the kitchen through swinging doors to fire up the fryer and set a basket of boiling angina into the oil.

Danny raised a hand and waddled towards Gustav. "Yo, BarNEY!" he shouted accenting the second syllable.

"Hello, Danny," Barnaby responded as the other patrons watched him pull out a chair and plop into it. The chair complained loudly.

"How's it hangin?" Danny, too, greeted the others who smiled and held up their beers to him. A few hearty *How are yas?* were tossed in his general direction.

"'Bout the same," Barnaby said predictably.

"Long, low and to the left?" Danny laughed raucously and pounded the table with his hand. Most assuredly, Barnaby found Danny disagreeable, but he needed him.

"Whatever you say, Danny."

Folding his hands on his generous gut, Danny leaned back in his chair. "What are we talkin' about tonight? The thing?" He waggled his eyebrows.

"Danny, please."

"Sorry."

Barnaby cleared his throat. "It's been a long week. So many things to do and to arrange. We're just about ready for go hour."

"It sounds like a tactical strike, doesn't it?"

Ignoring the statement, Barnaby leaned in closer to Danny. "When can we take the next drive?"

"You're really excited about this, aren't you?"

Son of a Butcher

"Yes, of course. I've waited a long time."

Danny shook his head. "It feels like we've been to Amicable fifty times. Are you sure you don't want to go somewhere else exciting? Council Bluffs? Jeez, Des Moines even?"

"No, I like Amicable. There's something really comfortable about it."

"Yeah, but we just drive through. We stop in front of the park, the cemetery – that's pretty creepy if you ask me – the elevator; we've got those things in Clancy, ya know."

"I know."

"All right," Danny sighed, "we'll go to Amicable."

Tony came out from behind the bar holding a sizzling basket of buffalo wings. They left a barbecue scented trail behind him, and by the time he had set them in front of Danny Thul, three others had called out an order.

"Now," Danny said as he dug his fingers into the basket. Taking a bite, his eyes rolled back in ecstasy. Barbecue sauce clung to his fingers and lips. "Why did you want to meet tonight?"

"I need a few things from the hardware store."

Danny frowned between his bites. "Why don't you come to the store and get them?"

"I'm too busy during the day. I can't get away to buy things."

Grunting, Danny grabbed another wing. "Too important, huh?"

"No, just necessary." He pushed a list across the table which Danny glanced at.

"Why do you need these things?"

Barnaby looked around. "I'm doing some cleaning."

"These are industrial chemicals, most of them. You must have a really rough house."

"Let's just say I need to do a total transformation." Barnaby's eyes glinted in the pale light of the beer signs.

* * * * *

Glory MacDonald watched her daughter bounce from the garage to the house. Stopping at the mailbox (Murgatroyd *loved* the new mailbox – not

Chapter 2.

a slot in the door, but an actual *BOX* with a red flag and everything!) she checked to see what the mailman had brought. The day before, Glory had met the mailman in a chance encounter. His name was Jim and he drove a car with the steering wheel on the righthand side of the car. Glory felt a brief stab of homesickness as Jim's mail car drove just like hers in England. He waved at her and yelled out from his rolled down window.

"Hello, neighbor! How are ya today?"

Surprised by his exuberance, Glory stepped down from the stoop and strolled out to his car. His smiling face grinned up at her from the righthand side of the car. His right arm lolled out the window hanging down over the door like a drooping dog tongue.

"Hello, Mr. Postman. How are you?"

His eyes registered shock. "Well, you're not from around here. Where's that accent from?"

"Great Britain."

"I think it's absolutely beautiful." He continued to grin.

"Yes, well, me daughter, Murgatroyd, and I journeyed from jolly old England about a month ago. It was time to make a change. You see…"

As she spoke, Jim's eyes glazed over. A few times, his eyebrows scrunched, trying to parse the words and the accent, the tone of her voice carrying most of the meaning. By the time she ended her story, Jim's mouth had dropped open. He had no idea what she had just said.

"Well, for sure, that's some story ya got. Okay, then. You have a good day, now." He blinked rapidly and stared forward through the dusty windshield, driving off slowly towards the next house on Peppertree Lane.

Murgatroyd held up a letter triumphantly. "We've got mail, Mum!" Racing towards Glory, feet flying, she held the envelopes up to her face.

Flipping through them, Glory shook her head. "All junk mail. What do you notice, though?"

Murgatroyd took the letters and read the names. "They're all addressed to different people. I wonder if they had a party of people here." *Leo Jensen, Stedman Boswell, Jennifer Adams.*

Son of a Butcher

"Just a rental, luv. Most people forget to change their addresses."
The pair made their way into the house. Glory laid her car keys on the small wooden desk near the front door. Murgatroyd tossed her backpack on the floor halfway across the living room and walked into the kitchen. Singing a song from *Frozen*, she opened the refrigerator and yelled out to her mother inquiring what there was to eat.

"Use your eyes," Glory responded as she picked up the backpack and laid it on a chair. Following Murgatroyd into the kitchen, she found that her daughter had located the cheese and pickles and was cutting them up into pieces to put on crackers.

"How was your day?"

Murgatroyd munched her snack and bounced up and down on her seat. "It was good. Very strange, though. It took me a while to meet some new friends, but eventually I did."

"What were their names?"

She shrugged and ate another bite. "Well, actually only one. His name is J.T. He's very tall. Like a giraffe."

"Was he nice?"

"Not sure. Different."

"What does that mean?" Glory asked.

"He didn't say much, but he seems to be pretty good at picking out lies. We did a little experiment and it was amazing."

"You lied to him?"

She nodded. "Yup. He told me to."

"Why would he do that?"

"So I'd leave him alone."

Glory's face tightened. "That's not very nice."

"I know," she responded brightly, "but I don't think he has many friends either. At least I didn't see him playing with anyone else. I think he's got some issues."

"He's weird then?"

Once again, Murgatroyd shrugged while she chewed.

Glory walked to the cupboard and pulled out a coffee mug. Wanting a cup of tea, she had already been frustrated by the dearth in Amicable. The grocery store had a few boxes of Lipton which proclaimed, 'Best for Iced Tea.' Glory thought the idea of iced tea was

Chapter 2.

an abomination, and not for the first time did she wish for a few bags of English Breakfast. Instead of tea, she filled the stained coffee pot with water and poured it into the receptacle. Flipping the switch, she waited for the percolation to start before she turned back to her daughter, who was still bouncing.

"Did you want to hear about my day?" Murgatroyd nodded. "It was highly enthralling," she rolled her eyes and straightened the ribbon in her hair. "I walked down the street wanting to do a little bit of shopping. No one here walks, and I can see why. The smell! I used to think sheep were bad, but truckloads of pigs. Ugh. And then, after crossing the road, the people stared at me as if I was some kind of alien. They were friendly enough. A smile, hello, a few of the older fellows nodded to me, but even in the grocery store, the only talk I heard was about the weather. Ghastly. Where are the gossips? How am I supposed to know anything if I'm not in on the goss?"

Murgatroyd's head bobbed back and forth and she made a *mmmuhmmm* sound, her way of saying *I don't know*.

"What I wouldn't give for a couple of ladies who like to talk about other people." Glory smirked and turned back to her coffeemaker. "Anyway, after shopping, I popped in the butchery where these two fine looking twins were working. Good breeding stock, those boys," she winked at Murgatroyd. "Then, just for the fun of it, I toted my groceries across the street to the café and had a cuppa. There was a lady there, a tall one, who was hugging a short one. Very affectionate, these people."

Murgatroyd finished her snack and brushed the crumbs onto the floor. She put the cheese and pickles back into the fridge while her mother watched her. She was a good girl, decent and kind. Surprisingly so. Of all the things that happened back across the pond, Murgatroyd was the best.

There were times when Murgatroyd asked about her father. Glory's answer was always the same. "You were miraculously conceived, luv. A true angel." Only in the last year had Murgatroyd begun to doubt the veracity of her heavenly creation. Soon, as the curriculum included sexual education, they'd be having the 'discussion' as Glory's own mother called it. Then, Murgatroyd would be asking questions other than when her wings were going to arrive.

Son of a Butcher

Glory shook her head remembering Murgatroyd's conception. There was rock music, some alcohol and a disposable moment which changed her life. Glory couldn't remember his name or even his look, only that he was short with peach fuzz on the underside of his chin. Certainly, the young man was not her type, not that Glory truly knew what her type was – something between hippie and yuppie, she thought. Glory had always wanted security, but could never really settle into it. She wasn't designed that way.

Their move to America had been spurred on by a moment of spontaneity. As Murgatroyd's schooling became harder because of bullies, Glory knew that it was time to get out. Murgatroyd was becoming more and more confused about everything, and her anxiety grew daily. Glory applied for a visa and six months later, they arrived in Amicable. Soon, Glory would have to find work, something at one of the local restaurants or café, perhaps.

Glory followed Murgatroyd into the living room where her daughter had picked up her phone and began to watch videos. Glory sighed. Why couldn't life be that easy for her?

Glory cupped her chin in her hand and turned on the television.

Chapter 3.

Leslie Deakins felt different. It wasn't just the vomiting, and it wasn't just body aches and mood swings. She felt sad. During her pregnancy with the twins, she had felt a glow of contentedness. Life had been good to her: a doting husband, a nice little town with helpful people, a stately old home. Upon the girls' arrival, twins being a harbinger of goodwill amongst Amicableans, she felt joyful.

Since Leo's death, though, it had taken the Deakins family a long time to adjust to the Butcher-sized hole in their lives. They had done so many things together as families, whether camping or fishing, playdates in the park, even attending municipal plays.

John had worn the pain much more than Leslie. Even as he preached, there was a deadened ember that refused to light. When they went to a movie or for a walk, he was quiet, not himself. They had talked about the loss, but John often stared off into the horizon. He seemed to be waiting for his best friend to reappear.

On that particular Saturday morning, one that would resonate for a long time, Leslie closed the door behind the parsonage and clomped down the front steps in her exercise gear. Every Saturday morning, Carley now opened the X-Er-Size studio for 'extra workouts' as she called them. After a great outcry from many of the constituents, Carley had removed the 'stripper poles' as so many called them, and instead inserted free weights. When asked where the poles went, Carley said she sold them to a farmer near Clancy. Supposedly he was going to put them in his hogbarn as railings, but people had their doubts.

The day was fresh. Fall was approaching rapidly and the farmers were nervously itching to get out into the corn and soybean fields. Dust and pollen swirled in the air. After walking west from the parsonage, Leslie approached Main Street and turned to her right to survey a two-block stretch of one-way road half full of pickups, domestic sedans, an SUV or two and lots of minivans. Awnings and American flags had been unfurled and flapped lazily in the late summer breeze. Across the street, a few younger mothers stood idly outside Human Beans Café at wrought iron tables grasping coffee cups and chatting happily about kids and all things school related. Certainly, Leslie was just on the edge of being young enough to be conversant in that language, but she smiled wryly at the thought that legitimately, she was almost old enough to be their mother.

Almost.

While John took the girls on a walk to do some Saturday morning visiting, Leslie's exercise group provided a good distraction. The women, although much older than she, were great company and the exertion, however little there was, kept her mind from the other, more depressing things.

Opening the door to the studio, she saw a few had already gathered. Linda, who was still in remission from her cancer, was talking to Carley. Leona and Jeannie were stretching lightly near the front stage. Angela Chandler was sitting with Penny Reynolds chatting loudly. Even from this distance, she could hear that they were talking about Stedman and Summer Boswell.

A tremor of sadness passed seeing the solitary walker positioned in the corner of the room. Anne Johnson had died six months before. In her will, she asked that the walker be donated to the exercise studio with a stuffed pigeon affixed to the handles.

Life was always changing yet not always for the better.

Leona waved to Leslie. "Hello!" she shouted across the room.

Leslie waved back. Dropping her bag on a plastic chair, Leslie moved towards the tornado of gossip.

"We're so glad you're here." Leona started. "We were hoping you could give us a yes or no about a certain thing." She looked to the others. Linda shrugged apologetically.

"Um, are you… er… have you…?"

"Have I what?"

"Have you fallen… jeepers, I don't know if this is appropriate, but…" Leona's face had turned red, and she nudged Jeannie who jumped forward.

"Are you preggers?"

Leslie's mouth tightened. "Do I look pregnant to you?"

The others looked ashamedly sideways at her. Mumbled apologies ensued. None dared answer the question.

Chapter 3.

"Well, I'm sorry that you've all been rumoring behind my back without just asking me personally, but the answer is yes, I'm pregnant." She smiled.

A few of the ladies threw up their hands and laughed loudly. Penny reached out to hug Leslie gently and Carley went right in to rub her stomach. Knowing that social protocols would be difficult for these women, especially Carley, Leslie put up with it. For now.

"Such wonderful news! And here I thought you were getting a little long in the tooth for getting knocked up," Jeannie stated awkwardly.

"Jeannie!" Angela chided. "That's no way to talk to a woman in her state."

"Good Lord, ladies," Leslie responded. "It's not like I'm the first woman to have children a little later in life. How about we move on and exercise."

"Do you know if it's a boy or a girl?" Linda asked.

Leslie shook her head. "No, not yet. We'd rather be surprised."

"Twins?" Angela asked.

"No, thankfully."

"Well," Carley clapped her hands in front of her daintily, "this is cause for celebration. Maybe we should forego exercise today and head directly over to Human Beans for a cup of coffee!"

"No!" Leslie laughed, "I didn't get out of the house to have a cup of coffee. Come on, let's dance." She reached down for a set of small hand weights. Leona stopped her.

"Are you sure you should be lifting those?"

Leslie rolled her eyes. "How much do you think my ten-year-old twins weigh?"

"Good point."

The women hooted delightedly at the news, all thoughts of rumormongering left. As the sweat started, the ladies continued to talk over the music. When Men Without Hats finished their dance of safety, they grabbed white towels and moved to the chairs.

As they sat, the front door opened without warning and two unexpected faces peeked through.

"Hello," Carley called out. It sounded like a question.

"Are you open?"

Carley put a hand in front of her mouth and giggled. "I don't know what you said, but I think you were asking if we were open. Of course! Who are you?"

"We're the MacDonalds. I'm Glory and this is Murgatroyd."

Jeannie blinked rapidly. "Hello Glory, I'm Jeannie. And you said... Margaret?"

"No, Murgatroyd." she pushed the child in front of her, a little girl of about eight or nine, with red hair and curls. Her skin was very white, much lighter than normal. She looked like an ice cream cone with a layer of cherry syrup on top.

"Murgatroyd? I've never heard that name before." Jeannie looked around at the others who were nodding in agreement.

"It's English."

"Aaaah," Jeannie replied as if that meant something to her, but it didn't.

"May we come in?"

"Of course, of course!" Carley replied stepping in front of the others. "This is my studio and it's suited for women who are remembering how to exercise."

"What does that mean?" Glory asked.

Carley held a hand up to the side of her face as if sharing a secret. "Mostly old women who want to bounce and gossip."

"I heard that," Leona's face and voice frowned.

"So anyway..." Carley continued, "where are you from?"

"England."

The women tittered.

"And what are you doing in Amicable?" Linda asked.

"We've moved here. Something different. A new start. Do any of those work?"

Angela frowned. "But to Amicable? England is one thing, but Iowa? It is gorgeous and all, but..." she raised her hands and shrugged.

"Let's just say the change will do both of us good."

"That's quite the exercise outfit," said Leona. Glory wore a maroon velvet sweat suit and a striped headband. Murgatroyd's outfit, although slightly less flamboyant, was bright and colorful. "Is that how you exercise there?"

Chapter 3.

Glory smiled through her irritation. She had noticed that people spoke loudly when around her, as if somehow increasing the volume would help her to understand better. She responded in kind. "No," she said slowly, "but these are the clothes I brought from Great Britain."

"I love how you talk," Carley said.

"Thank you." Raising her eyebrows, Glory moved her head towards the rest of the women.

"Oh right!" Carley said as she grabbed both of their arms. "Come on in and make yourselves at home."

The group gathered at the front of the studio and faced the mirrors. Turning the music back on and up, Carley helped the women attach straps to their ankles and gave them small weights. The women began to move slowly in time to the music. Lifting their legs and pumping their arms, they gyrated and flounced. Carley, with great exuberance, called out the moves.

Glory watched the women around her and noticed that they had all subconsciously spaced themselves away from her and Murgatroyd. Glory knew that it would take some time to ingratiate herself. She glanced over at the youngest of the women. She had dark hair and slight cheekbones, elfin ears and tired eyes. She was the short one from the café. Glory wondered if she was pregnant. She'd seen lots of women with that 'look,' the tired, baby carrying/thinking-about-six-months-later look. The woman was probably not that much older than she was. Certainly, the other women were nice, but quite a bit older. Old enough to be her mother, certainly.

She did not want another mother.

As they were wiping the sweat from their faces – the older women had exercised more than they had in months, maybe years, because someone new and young had joined – they settled in their plastic chairs sipping deeply from their fluorescent, scratched waterbottles.

"All right everyone, how are we feeling?" Carley's face was red with exertion.

Thumbs up around. Murgatroyd smiled at Carley who giggled. "Say, kiddo, how do you like Amicable?"

Son of a Butcher

Murgatroyd nodded and bounced on her stool. "It's just wonderful. So much space, and I've met a friend at school, he's interesting and tall."

"Was it J.T.?"

"You know him?" Murgatroyd's mouth dropped open.

"Yes, of course," Carley responded as a droplet of sweat clung to her nose. "He's the son of our former butcher. Tragic story, that one."

"What happened?" Glory asked.

Carley delicately related the story knowing that Butcher's relationship with many of the exercise group had been close. Especially Linda's. Giving an overview of his time in Amicable, she finished with the funeral and the statue in the cemetery.

"You mean there is a monument made of wax?"

Linda nodded. "A young man from our town, Angela's son, Demetrius, is quite an accomplished artist. As the years pass, the wax continues to melt. It's a pretty amazing thing." Angela grinned.

"Why did he make it out of wax? Why not stone?"

"Because," Angela responded, "Demetrius wanted to show the slow, melting effect of the disease that Butcher died from." She paused and looked around at the other women. "But we all still miss him."

Leslie's eyes misted over. She was surprised at the surfacing emotion.

"You said that he could read people. What does that mean?" Glory asked.

Leona patted Glory's arm. "He could look at you and immediately know who you were, where you've been and where you were going."

"That sounds like science fiction," Glory said honestly.

Nodding, Leona smiled. "He was our big bundle of science fiction, that's for sure. He helped everyone – even at the end..." Her voice trailed off.

"Can anyone else do that in Amicable?"

Jeannie laughed. "No, not really. I mean, Louise, Amicable's police officer, got some tips, and maybe the twins have figured out a few things, but nobody else has any special gifts except..."

"Except who?"

Chapter 3.

"Well, I don't like to talk out of turn," Jeannie continued, obviously meaning the opposite, "but some say that J.T. has inherited some, how shall we say, special tendencies."

Leslie frowned. "Now Jeannie, just because J.T. has good vision doesn't mean he is a savant."

"What's a savant?" Murgatroyd asked.

"A person who is very gifted in a specific way," Leslie answered.

"But he is gifted, then, isn't he?" Murgatroyd's face scrunched up.

"I guess he is," Leslie said slowly, "but he's not weird or strange or anything."

"I think he's weird," Murgatroyd answered.

"Murgatroyd!" Glory interjected. "I'm so sorry," she apologized to the frowning women.

Murgatroyd could tell from them that they were very protective of J.T. and it was probably best that she didn't let them know about J.T.'s ability to read her lies. "What I meant was that I think he's weird, but it's very cool. That's how we do it in England."

Their faces relaxed. Everything was going to be all right.

Penny blew the hair from her face and then leaned in. "How about you, Glory. Tell us a little bit about you? How did you end up in Amicable? What's your story?"

Glory MacDonald sighed and glanced at the surrounding women. It was too early to trust. Far too early. The scars were still too raw.

* * * * *

When Glory Stockman turned seven years old, what she really wanted was a unicorn. Though she was firmly positioned on the fence whether the horned horse was real or not, she chose to go with hope. When she went to bed on the night before her seventh birthday, she asked the gods to lower her own Pegasus from the heavens by ropes of gold. Her father had told her that Pegasus was a flying horse, one with immense wings that could take her far, far, up, up and away towards the moon where, she was sure, unicorns were born.

Son of a Butcher

Glory's father, Bartholomew Stockman (Barty to almost everyone except his mother), told her the great myths.

But he did not stay long. Delaney, her mother, had the supernatural gift of alienating almost everyone she met. With her acerbic tongue and constant nagginess, Barty flew off into the night to ride unicorns when Glory was five and a half years old. To make matters worse, Glory no longer had her father's presence, nor his stories, to buffer her from Delaney's personality. Nagged for everything, from her hair to her clothes, the way she cleaned her teeth to her slouching gait, Glory found that the only way she could escape her mother's clutches was to enter into a series of unprofitable relationships which scored her soul and annoyed her mother to no end.

But it was the night before her birthday when Glory most poignantly felt the sting of her mother's wrath.

"Where is Daddy?"

Delaney turned on her from decorating her cake. "He's off with the fairies."

"Really?"

Her mother pointed the icing knife at her. "You listen to me, Glory Stockman," she spit out the last name. "If you start believing in imaginary things like fairies, unicorns and true love, you're going to end up in a world of pain. Mark my words." She emphasized each word with the knife.

"But I want a unicorn for my birthday."

"There's no such thing as unicorns, luv."

"But Mum, I saw them on television. They run on rainbows."

She snorted. "You shouldn't be watchin' them shows." Delaney set the icing knife down and lit a cigarette. She inhaled deeply and blew the smoke upwards past her nose to create a halo around her head. "Maybe it's time for you to get a job." Her eyes rolled out over the cake and into the slag heap in the back yard.

"I don't want to get a job. I want to eat cake and play with dolls."

"Tough," Delaney answered. "You don't often get watchya want in life." She glanced down at the cake. It was a unicorn. She picked up the side to show her daughter who smiled and laughed.

Chapter 3.

"It's so beautiful, Mummy!"

"You think so?" For a moment, Delaney pondered her artwork. The white horned horse seemed to be swayback and the one visible eye sagged in the middle. The horn, which twirled up and away from the head, was twisted into bright colors. "Too bad this unicorn is about to be dehorned."

"What do you mean, Mummy?"

Delaney picked up the knife again and proceeded to amputate the horn. To her daughter's horror, Delaney grabbed it in her fist and stuffed it in her mouth. "See? Unicorns aren't real, but they taste good."

Glory screamed at her mother and pounded her with her fists. It wasn't fair. Why couldn't she have a nice mummy like all her miserable classmates? Why couldn't her mummy buy her presents and take her to the zoo? Why couldn't her mummy be nice?

"I'll never forgive you," Glory cried as she left the room screaming.

Delaney shrugged and picked up the remnants of the horn and deposited them in the rubbish. With one quick motion, she stabbed the unicorn cake in the guts. "Welcome to hell, Uni."

That seminal birthday, the first of a slew of disappointments, marked the pointed change in Glory's life. From then on, Glory, even though she disliked her mother, did everything that she could to please her, to make her feel loved and important. Whenever Delaney would pick at her, Glory would smile and run to her mother, wrap her arms around her generously growing middle and say, "I'm so sorry, Mummy. I will do whatever you want."

Yet, when the time came, somewhere in the middle of her fourteenth year, when Glory found out that she was on the right side of attractive, Glory turned her attention towards boys. Instead of coming home after school to tell her mummy how much she loved her, Glory instead let the boys tell her the same thing.

As the distance expanded between Delaney and Glory, the tightness to which each held apron strings grew. Delaney wanted to be the only one receiving love and praise, and Glory wanted a mother. Any mother.

Or any father, for that fact.

Son of a Butcher

On the night Murgatroyd was conceived, at the rock concert, Glory told most people who she semi-trusted that she didn't remember much other than the young boy who impregnated her. But she never would have gotten to that point if Barty had not also been in attendance.

After twenty years, Glory was surprised that she recognized him, but he hadn't changed much. Now, pushing fifty, Barty had less hair, and what was left was mostly grey. He hadn't shaved in a while and when she approached him, he smelled of beer and sweat. He was lifting a drink to the thumping bass and synthesized music.

When she spotted this posture, she shook her head. Surely, this couldn't be her father, her rock, her mythmaker, her unicorn storyteller. No, he should have made his way into parliament, or at the very least, a reasonably high-priced attorney waging war on drug dealers and pimps.

But it was. It was her father, Barty Stockman, and he was not looking good.

"Hey!" she shouted above the music.

Barty scanned her. He obviously liked what he saw: a young woman wearing tight clothes, heavy makeup, fishnet stockings and hair that danced six inches above her head. "Hey to you!" He took a sip of his drink and extended his hand.

"Barty."

"I know," she said.

"Have we met before?"

Surprisingly, tears welled up in her eyes. Glory wanted to turn. She wanted to run away and go back to her father myths. She wanted him to be the unicorn.

"Yes," she said loudly. "I think I saw you about twenty-years ago."

He laughed. "Yeah, right. You would have been three or four!"

"I was six."

Suddenly, Barty stopped and stared. "No…"

"Yes. It's me, Dad."

"But… how…?"

"Life is full of ironies, right?"

He still looked confused. "How did you find me? How did you know I'd be here?"

Chapter 3.

"I didn't. I saw you across the room and... well, I couldn't believe it myself."

"But you're all grown up and you dress like..." He didn't finish the sentence.

"So are you, Dad. All grown up and dress like..." She pointed to his jeans and sweaty white t-shirt. He was wearing a headband.

Barty Stockman was ashamed.

"I don't know what to say."

"How about, 'I'm sorry.'"

As the music blared, their words fought for survival. Floating just above the heavy melody, like swimmers, swamped from a boat, nearing exhaustion, these words threatened to go under. "You didn't know your mother back then. She was horrible."

"What are you stupid?" Glory felt her anger rising. "You left me with her! You left me to absorb all of what was rightly yours."

"She was killing me," he said. His words finally went under. She had to read his lips.

"And now she's doing the same to me." At that moment, Glory wanted to turn away, to leave her father, but he grabbed her arm.

"I'd go back and change it if I could."

"You're a coward," she said.

"I am. I'm a coward." Suddenly, he was grabbed by a mob of younger men. Each one was drunk, or well on their way. "I have to go," he shouted.

"Have fun," she waved and watched his retreating face as the boys tugged at his arms.

It was only after she could no longer see his face that Glory turned and saw the sad looking, scruffy faced young boy standing disconsolately on the edge of the floor.

He would do as well as any.

* * * * *

Derek Peterson reclined in the butchery 'café' chair. His hair, lanky and badly in need of a cut, hung just below the jutting bones under his

Son of a Butcher

eyebrows. Though he had taken off his apron, his sleeves and pantlegs retained traces of gore, but he didn't care.

As he sat in the chair, he listened to Nash using the saw in the back room. Generally, he ignored the sound, but for some reason, his mind flashed back to Butcher. His face seemed to resurrect at the strangest of times...

The front door of the shop opened and the bell above tinkled. A stranger walked in. Struggling up the stairs, his cane leading the way, the man spotted Derek. He wore large, black sunglasses and a dark blue Yankees baseball cap. Blue jeans, just a bit too tight, pushed out an ample gut which was nearly covered by a black sweatshirt.

"Good morning," Derek said.

"Hello." The man's voice was slightly raspy, but empty. Derek found it strange that he hadn't taken off his sunglasses inside the building.

"What can I do for you today?"

"I've heard about this butcher shop."

Derek smiled. "Well, we like to think our fame is circulating, Mr...?"

"Koppel," he responded shortly. "I'm looking for the butcher."

"That's me," Derek said with a smile.

"No, the tall one. You know, the guy who can read people's minds."

"Uh, I'm sorry to tell you this, but Butcher died a while ago."

"Oh, gosh, that's terrible." Barnaby's cane tapped nervously.

"What did you want to talk to him about?" Derek asked.

"I just wanted to see if the stories were true."

"They're true. He was the best."

Gustav's lips pursed. "What about you? Did he show you how to do it?"

"Me?" Derek laughed. "Are you kidding? I can't even tell when my wife is making fun of me."

"You seem pretty young to be married."

Derek rolled his eyes. "You should see my brother. He's the one with the baby face."

"Maybe some other time."

Chapter 3.

"Is there anything else I can help you with?"

"What about the butcher's wife?" he asked rudely. "How is she taking it?"

"What, Rhonda? I... um... well, she's making progress." Derek began to get a funny feeling about the stranger. "How do you know Rhonda?"

"I don't," he said hastily, perhaps too. "I just assumed."

At that moment, Nash appeared from the back room. "Derek where are the... Oh," he stopped as his eyes fell on Gustav. "I'm sorry."

"Nash, this is Mr. Koppel. He was looking for Butcher. I've filled him in."

"Okay," Gustav said as he began to turn away from them back to the door. "Maybe I'll get going then."

"Wait," Derek stopped him, "why did you need to see Butcher?"

Gustav's hand trembled as he raised it to his sunglasses to push them up farther onto his nose. "We have a connection from years ago," he mumbled, "and I was hoping he could help me find a job."

"Here at the butchery?" Nash asked.

"Do you have a job opening?" Gustav asked.

Nash and Derek's eyes caught. "Not at the moment, but if something opens up, we'll give you a call."

"I'm happy for casual work. I do have skills in the area."

Nash wondered what skills this man might have but didn't say it.

"If you give me a minute of your time, I can show you what I can do."

Derek shrugged. "Okay, I guess. As long as you're here." Derek held his hand out to the fliptop counter and Nash lifted it. Gustav walked robotically towards the back. Although his body ached, the adrenaline kept the searing pain at bay.

As Gustav approached the stainless-steel table, the smell of the meat was reassuring. Over the last few years he'd been practicing his carving skills in his home in preparation for just this moment. Although he couldn't walk quickly, his ability to cut was second to none.

Taking the knife in his hands, he tested the sharpness with his thumb and smiled at the twins.

"Do you want a glove?" Derek asked.

Son of a Butcher

"Unnecessary."

"All right. Why don't you cut up that pig there and give us a rundown of what you're doing while you do it."

Gustav nodded. Being left-handed, he grabbed the pig with his right and proceeded to amaze the Peterson's with his knife skills. Effortlessly, he cut and stacked the meat on the table. The running commentary caused the twins to nod their heads in unison, and at the end of his skillful display, they looked at each other.

"Okay, Mr. Koppel," Nash said, "how about you leave us your name and phone number and we'll see what we can do."

Nodding, Gustav produced a business card from his pants pocket. Struggling to pull it out from his tight pants, he eventually placed it in Nash's hand.

Barnaby Koppel
Butcher
barnabycutups@gmail.com

"Do you have a pen?" he asked.

Derek patted his front pocket and handed one to Gustav who wrote his cell phone number on it.

"I'll expect your call in the next day or so."

"We'll have to talk it over. We're not really…"

"Don't worry, I can work casually, like I said."

Nash looked past Gustav to see his brother shrugging. "You can't wear your sunglasses while you're working."

Gustav sneered. "I'm afraid I'll have to."

Nash shook his head.

Pausing, Gustav reached up for the frames and pulled them from his face. The boys couldn't hold back their revulsion at Gustav Keller's empty right eye socket and his disfigured left eyebrow. "I've had a hard life, boys," he said, "but I work hard." He put his glasses back on. Turning on his heel, Gustav caned his way out of the work area, lifted the counter and left the butchery.

After he had left, Nash raised his eyebrows. "Ever feel like you're walking over someone's grave?"

Chapter 3.

"No," Derek said, "but that guy cuts meat like only one other person."

Butcher.

Chapter 4.

She was still following him.
    As the week progressed, Murgatroyd continued her third-grade stalking. Gradually, J.T. had grown used to her, somewhat like a person getting used to having a wart or a mole. Her presence was not essentially offensive, just noisy. Murgatroyd MacDonald had no pause button for her outer monologue. She spoke whatever came to her mind: her joy at the wide expanse of the sky, squirrels, the number 14, other children on the playground, even a description of the bathroom at the rental house. Though he didn't want to tell her, he was amused by the thought of the overwhelming scent of poop (or poo, as she called it) emanating from some mysterious crack in the septic sewer of the universe.
    At lunchtime, they sat near the edge of the playground, just the two of them. Murgatroyd, a garden gnome to J.T.'s giant, munched on the crustless part of a sandwich. Chicken and cheese, she told him, as she handed the crust over which he accepted with gratefulness. Perpetually hungry, he shoved the crust into his mouth and took a swig from his apple juice box.
    "I think we're going to get married someday."
    J.T. choked on the juice filled crust and spit it out onto the concrete between them. It lay like a dead white mouse.
    "That's gross," she said as she poked at it with her toe.
    "Not as gross as what you just said."
    "What? That we're going to get married someday? That's not gross. Just reality. Get used to it."
    "How did you get to be so weird?" he asked as his eyes played on the rodent like regurgitated bread.
    "I'm not weird," she responded stuffing the other inner half of her sandwich into her mouth. "Just different." Her words were muffled by the food.
    "I can't understand you."
    "Different."
    He shook his head. "Just swallow first, Purgatroid."

Chapter 4.

She snorted and spit the sandwich onto the ground beside J.T.'s. "It's funny when you call me that."

He had been doing it for a few days. When he had talked to Unca John about the MacDonald's, John struggled. He didn't have sons, but he was as much a father to J.T. as anyone since Butcher died. After J.T. had said her name, John asked him if he had said her name was Purgatory. J.T. set him straight, but then asked him what purgatory was.

"It's a place after you die where your sins are purged from you. Like a place of suffering."

"That's definitely her name then."

A conversation about purgatory ensued to which John Deakins put J.T.'s mind at ease. "There is no such thing as purgatory, J.T. Even the Catholics have taken a vote against it." J.T. was confused about voting over the existence of a place, but he didn't push. "Either way, J.T., your dad would never have gone there. He did enough suffering while he was alive."

Unca John's eyes went far away, way back into himself. They frosted over like the car windows in winter, and it took a while before they defogged.

J.T. knew that his father would not suffer. They had talked about it before he died. His dad told him that it would be a lot like Starman; he would just go away. J.T. wasn't sure if he liked that kind of talk, but it did pacify him knowing that his dad was flying around space with aliens.

"We're not getting married. We have to at least get through seventh-grade, first."

Solemnly, Murgatroyd nodded. "By the time we reach high school, we'll know everything about each other. Like, what our favorite colors are, who our favorite bands are, what our favorite kind of peanut paste is."

"It's peanut butter."

She smiled at him. "I know. I just like hearing you talk."

Confounded by her reasoning, he went back to staring at the two dead mice on the ground. "I watched Starman last night," she said.

His eyes stayed on hers. "So?"

"I always cry. The movie makes me cry."

Son of a Butcher

J.T. didn't want to tell her that he felt the same way, but not for the same reason. Everything about Jeff Bridges' portrayal was eerily similar to his father. J.T. hadn't watched the movie since his dad's death.

"I'll bet you cry a lot. Do people cry a lot in England?"

She raised her eyebrows. "Don't really know. I suppose the ones who are sad do. What do you cry about?"

He shrugged. "Nothing."

She made a *psh* noise. "Stop being such a boy."

Digging through her lunch box, she extricated a Snickers. He watched her open it, his mouth watering. Noticing this, she grasped it in the middle and split it. Licking one half, she giggled and put a section in both hands. "All right, let's do a test. If I close my eyes, can you tell which hand the unlicked half is in?" She moved her hands behind her back.

"I don't know."

"If you guess the correct hand, I'll give it to you. If not, I'm eating both."

His stomach rumbled. "You're on."

"Okay," she said as she closed her eyes, "which hand."

J.T. tried to do what his father used to do, to read her, to find the signs. Unfortunately, J.T.'s main source of information was from the eyes. Heart pounding, he tapped her right hand. "That one."

She opened her eyes and handed it to him. "You're good."

Watching her, he put the chocolate to his mouth and took a bite. She exploded with laughter. "You chose the wrong one! I slobbered all over that one!"

Gagging, J.T. spit the chocolate onto the ground next to the sandwiches. A whole family of mixed-race dead mice now was waiting for burial. "You're sick," he said and pulled himself up from the ground. Mostly, he was annoyed that he couldn't tell the lie. For him, it was all in the eyes.

"Don't be sore, Johnny Boyo, I was just joshin."

He ignored her.

Back in the classroom, as Mrs. Brown prepared to deliver a lesson on Iowa history, Murgatroyd caught his eye. Mouthing the words, *I wrote you a note*, she held up a piece of paper. He shook his head and

Chapter 4.

frowned. When Mrs. Brown turned back to the whiteboard, Murgatroyd flicked the folded up paper at him. It landed at the foot of his desk. For a moment, J.T. was quite sure it looked like another dead mouse.

Surreptitiously reaching down, J.T. was able to grab it without Mrs. Brown's noticing. With one eye on the teacher and the other on the task of opening a note which had been folded at least five times, he finally finished.

> *I still think we're going to get married.*
> *What color should my flowers be?*
> *I was thinking plaid, like Starman's flannel.*

The note was followed with an assortment of love hearts and x's and o's. J.T. shook his head, held the sheet up in Murgatroyd's direction, and slowly ripped the paper vertically. Murgatroyd's mouth dropped and she blushed. Now angry, her mouth screwed up and she crossed her arms as she leaned back in her chair.

"What are you doing, J.T.?" Mrs. Brown asked.

Startled, his face turned towards the front. Confronted by the choice of telling the truth or tinting it a different color, he chose the second. "I just needed to separate my notes into sections."

Knowing that J.T. was not usually one for disruption, Mrs. Brown frowned and nodded. "Just keep the noise to a minimum."

"Yes, Mrs. Brown."

As the last bell rang, Murgatroyd stopped in front of J.T.'s desk and planted her hands in front of him. Her curly reddish-brown hair hung over her face, but she was the same height as him seated. "Let's get one thing straight, Johnny Boyo. If this marriage is going to work, you've got a lot of growing up to do."

J.T. was flustered. "We're not getting married, you moron." His voice was loud enough for a few others to hear. They whispered into their hands. Now he was embarrassed.

Murgatroyd stepped back and folded her arms. "I realize that this is going to take some getting used to, but just know that time heals everything. That's what me mum says."

Son of a Butcher

As if happy just to have the last word, Murgatroyd spun away from him and stomped out the room. J.T. glanced at the other kids, some who were giggling. "It's not... I don't... Agh!" He grabbed his pencil case and headed for the door. Never before had he been so thankful for a weekend.

* * * * *

Leslie picked up her twin daughters from the front doors of the school. Fortunately, the Deakins family lived just across the street so Leslie did not have to fight the 'traffic' to pick up her kids.

The girls were chatty, excited that the first month of fourth grade had already passed. Now ten years of age, the two were growing up quickly. When they found out that they were going to have a baby brother or sister, they alternated between happiness and consternation. It had always been just the two of them.

When they entered the house, the girls hung their bags and coats on the hooks by the front door and pounded up the stairs to their bedrooms. As they clomped upwards, their hands grasping the wooden railing to make the turn above her, Leslie was suddenly aware how big their hands were. Briefly, she harkened back to the days when their little fingers tentatively reached for the top of the banister.

Sighing, Leslie walked through the living room and into the kitchen where the refrigerator hummed contentedly. The window overlooked the school. It was dirty. Fall cleaning was not her favorite thing, but it was something that had to be done. John was usually good with domestic activities, but recently, he had been more distracted.

When Leslie told him about the baby, he had smiled and clapped his hands. His hug, although warm, was half-hearted. It was not that he wasn't happy, just vacant, as if pregnancy and another baby had just been one more thing to think about. His work with the church seemed to be less fulfilling: visiting shut-ins, preparing sermons, working with the desperate seemed to be getting him down. Leslie was sure that he just needed another friend, but they were hard to come by. Amicable was a friendly place, but not a place for making friends.

Chapter 4.

Noticing the dirty afternoon dishes, Leslie walked to the sink and began to wash. The mundanity was comforting. As she scrubbed, she watched humanity walk past her window. Carefree parents gathering their children, an aging couple bent on getting last walks in before the cold crept in, and a few high school students loitering on the front steps of the school, checking their phones and laughing. They seemed so happy, so content to be outside and moving. Life was but a dream.

From the east, movement caught her eye. It was almost 4:00 and many of the teachers were now leaving school for their well-deserved weekend. But the person who had captured her attention was new. It was a man, tall, but not overly so, with a bushy dark beard and large gut. He walked with a cane. This was odd. Not many people in Amicable under the age of eighty used a cane, and certainly if they did, she would know about it. No, this man seemed to shuffle, cane, shuffle, cane. Leslie couldn't place him. Then, it came to her. Jeanie had mentioned there was a new butcher in town, a man named Barnaby Koppel. Leslie frowned. The news had hit Rhonda hard, as if the twins were replacing her beloved husband. They had visited her personally to let her know what they were doing. Rhonda said she was fine with it, but Leslie was not so sure.

Leslie frowned as the limping man stopped in front of her house, facing the school. From her vantage point, she noticed he was balding and had scars on the top of his head. Obviously, he struggled physically, but for the Peterson twins to hire him, he must have been capable, especially with the high standards set by Butcher.

As he stared at the school, Leslie grew more uncomfortable. The news was chock full of pedophiles who lingered around schools and places where kids congregate. As the outer world closed in around them, Leslie felt a surge of fear that Amicable might no longer be safe. She shook her head, chastising herself not to judge too quickly, or even at all. First impressions were rarely correct, and how could she possibly stereotype a stranger like that? Hadn't enough lives been ruined by the imaginations of a moment?

Leslie's thoughts went to her daughters. What would she feel if that man was staring at them? What would she feel if he was plotting to do something terrible?

Son of a Butcher

As if reading her thoughts, the man turned slowly and looked in her direction. Shocked, Leslie attempted to look away quickly, but not before seeing the scar above his eye and over his sunglasses. He smiled at her which, despite the appearance, seemed less creepy. Transforming his face, the smile almost took away her discomfort. She raised a hand. He did the same.

After lowering his hand, he gritted his teeth. Over the last five years of watching these parochial people of Amicable, Gustav knew Leslie was Rhonda Redman's best friend. Not just friends, but sisters. They were women who shared everything together – mothering, babysitting, social engagements, and the occasional volunteer work. Gustav turned back towards the school just long enough for Leslie to wonder what he was doing.

She had no idea what he was capable of.

As he walked towards the sinking sun, now two-thirds through its journey across the sky, Gustav stepped through his plan. His walk to the school had been helpful. The timing would have to be perfect. But he had no doubt everything would be so.

Leslie watched him limp away.

Behind her, the front door opened and John entered. In earlier days, he would hum as he approached her, but his recent despondency was draining for both of them. Sometimes she wanted to shake him, squeeze his arms and tell him to snap out of it, but grief seemed to have its own hourglass.

"John," she called out wiping her hands on the dish towel. "I'm in the kitchen."

He rounded the corner. His haggard face appeared even more careworn than the day before. Deep crevices began at his eyes and towards his temples. Grey hairs multiplied daily.

"Sweetheart." Eyes tired, he focused on her and then smiled. "How was your day?" He moved in to kiss her.

She shrugged and leaned against the countertop. "Same as always. Kids, errands, catching up with a few people, kids…"

"Regular Groundhog Day, isn't it?"

As he moved to the refrigerator, she watched his body clench. He'd been sore, part of the aging process, he said, but she was not so

Chapter 4.

sure. Leslie wanted him to go to the doctor just to be certain. He had told her not to be a worrywart, but his words did not alleviate her concern.

"Yes. How was your day?"

Grabbing a piece of chocolate cake, he took it to the small nook and table and sat down to eat it. "Same as always. People in need. Mostly they're in need of time, not things, you know?" She nodded. "The old folks want more time; the young folks want more attention. Us in-betweens, we want time to relax. It all adds up to a lot of brokenness."

"It must be hard."

"It's exhausting. I don't know when the world changed, whether it was the pandemic, riots and racial theories, or just a plain spiritual battle that feels like we're losing badly." He pushed his plate forward and scratched his head. "When are the angels going to show up?"

"I guess God's the only one who's got those answers."

"Be nice to get a bulletin every once in a while."

"Not to change the subject, but I saw a strange man out in front of our house not too long ago. He might have been the new butcher."

John raised his eyebrows. "I talked to Derek and Nash about that. Supposedly the guy is a wizard with the knife."

"Did you find out anything else about him?"

He snorted. "Not much. The boys said he wasn't much of a talker, but did tell them about his scars. Car accident, supposedly."

"Poor guy."

"Yeah, well…" *Life is hard for everyone.*

"Are you going to catch up with him?"

John shrugged. "I suppose I will sooner or later. He lives in Clancy and commutes, or so the boys said. Someone drives him."

"Maybe he'll want to move here eventually. Isn't Liam's place available?"

Shaking his head, John picked up the plate and deposited it into the sink. "No, the new lady from England is there. Didn't you and the exercise group meet her?"

"Yes, but we didn't talk about where she was living. She and her daughter are certainly interesting people."

"How so?"

Son of a Butcher

"Their names, for one thing. Glory and Murgatroyd. Have you ever heard such a thing? They seem nice enough though. Rhonda said the little girl has been tailing J.T. around. I'm sure he's loving that."
"He's got to get used to it. We all do."
"Yes, John Thomas, you really had to beat them off with a stick, didn't you?" She wrapped her arms around him and kissed his neck.
"You know it."
Suddenly, Gabi and Michelle burst into the room. They were quite excited about letting their parents know the plans they'd already made for the weekend.
A look passed between Leslie and John. *Oh, to be young again.*

* * * * *

After retreating from the parsonage, Gustav turned right and limped past the front doors of St. Clements. In the arched stained glass windows backlit by the setting sun, he saw the primitive faith of Christianity reflected in the colors. A lamb seemed to be digging in a ravine and a man stood below it cradling a cup catching the water. An anchor hung to the side of his neck. Unsure of what these symbols meant (and apathy to match), Keller rolled his eyes and searched the church grounds. His eyes alit on the bell tower. *Now isn't that interesting? Possibly...*
Not wanting to draw attention to himself, he turned and continued southwards looking to his left where the bowling alley was. A few young people approached the front door. The sign above it carrying the emblem of both a bowling ball, bowling pins and a particularly large rooster standing erectly above them, held the words, GRAB A BITE, ROLL A BALL, TAKE OUT YOUR FRUSTRATIONS FOR THE NIGHT! DON'T FORGET – HALLOWEEN COMING!
Gustav would have liked nothing better than to take out his frustrations, but he had other work to do. Waiting at home were the supplies he'd ordered from Danny who would be picking him up from Casey's gas station four blocks in the distance. Gustav would rather have not walked that far, but he realized that he still needed to get fitter. And, he did not want people in Amicable to see Danny.

Chapter 4.

Hearing the raucous noise from inside the bowling alley, Gustav ground his teeth. The sound of happiness grated on his nerves. Before the Incident, Gus had been a relatively happy-go-lucky-life-of-the-party kind of young man. Now when he experienced joy, he had to fight back the urge for rage. A few younger men entered the bowling alley clapping each other on the back. It had been a long time since that had happened to him. People didn't touch him. It didn't bother him though. To be an outcast fueled his resentment and ire.

Later that evening, the town gossips arrived at the Bowling Alley for a recap of the day's events. When 7:30 rolled around, the group sat at the bar in the Greedy Pecker perched behind an assortment of cocktails that Shania Peterson wanted to learn how to make. Each of them had a small umbrella, including Jeannie's Bud Light.

"I saw him at Peterson's," Leona said with her mouth hovering over the straw. A purple umbrella fixed a pineapple in the piña colada.

"Who?" Jeannie asked.

"The guy. You know, the limper."

"You shouldn't judge someone by their outer appearance," Penny inserted.

"Like you're one to talk," Jeannie laughed. "Remember when Butcher showed up and we almost had to put a bib on you for your drooling."

"Oh, for heaven's sake," Penny reddened and waved away the statement, "I did no such thing."

"You did!" The rest of the women started laughing.

"Gosh, I miss Butcher," Linda said.

"We all do," Leona insisted, "but now there is a new one and he's definitely not the same. He wears sunglasses and it looks like his head is full of scars. Do you think he's been in a war?"

"Or a car accident," Penny added.

"What if he is in the Witness Protection Program?" Jeannie lowered her voice and sipped her beer through the straw.

"In Amicable?" Angela rolled her eyes.

"Well, he'd certainly be protected."

"Has anyone spoken to him?" Linda asked.

Son of a Butcher

"Not *to* him," Leona's eyes scanned the room, "but I heard his voice from the back room. It sounded freaky. Nothing like Butcher's."

"No one is going to be like Butcher, but we can let him be his own butcher."

"I heard he lives in Clancy and he commutes to work. Have you ever heard of such a silly thing?" Penny wondered.

"Imagine driving all that way to go to work. Fifteen minutes *one way!* I think I'd go crazy if I had to spend that much time in the car." Leona and her husband lived five minutes east on Highway 10.

"Well, we should do something to make him feel welcome, don't you think?" Penny asked.

Linda cleared her throat. "Not that I don't think that's a good idea, but we might be a little more gentle than previously."

"How about we bring him something to eat – he's probably single." Jeannie was nodding as she spoke.

"Because he's scarred and limps?" Angela said.

"That's not what I meant," Jeannie frowned, knowing that's exactly what she meant.

"I can make a pumpkin pie. It's almost pumpkin pie season," Leona volunteered.

"I've got cookies," Jeannie said.

"Anybody up for a bundt cake, or some peanut brittle?" Penny and Angela raised their hands.

"Okay," Leona brushed her hands, "that should welcome him real good. Now, on to the next business. Did anyone talk to Glory? Is she still going to meet us here tonight?"

Angela nodded. "I spoke with her about two o'clock. She said she'd drop Murgatrix off with a friend. I don't know who that is yet, but she's quick to make friends."

"Her name is 'Murgatroyd,'" Jeannie corrected. "Murgatroyd."

"Sorry, it's just not a name I'm familiar with."

"Glory seems very friendly," Leona nodded and smiled, "uh, eccentric, though."

"I think she's wonderful," Linda countered.

"Of course!" Leona said. "I'm just saying… with that hair, and her clothes and her accent. We'll have to help her fit in a little bit."

Chapter 4.

For the women who gathered in the bar that day, various strategies for 'fitting in' flitted through their minds. It wasn't that they, or Amicableans by nature, viewed outsiders in a particularly pejorative sense, but the fear of difference created a need for conformity so that they didn't have to feel that fear. Whether people from different places, cultures or worldviews, Amicable wanted uniformity, if not conformity. Those who stayed were reluctantly accepted, but those that left often brushed the dust from their feet and good-riddanced it. Thus was the delicate balance of life in the small town.

These women, advocates of goodness and justice and hopefulness, were at the same time vigilantes of tradition. Gossip was not simply about passing on information, but it was also about protecting the interests of those who had lived in Amicable for generations. Gradually, as the world changed and shifted, these women felt intense, personal pressure to guard that which kept them comfortable. Yet when outside influences encroached, they encountered new perspectives which naturally made them question their preconceived ideas.

And Glory MacDonald certainly had new perspectives.

From the beginnings of Amicable, pioneers had arrived from the east. For two hundred years, Amicableans could trace their roots to Scandinavia, Prussia, Germany and a smattering of Southern Europeans – Eye-talians, as the older ones called them. But the British? Very few, and those that did arrive in this wide-open prairie were viewed with suspicion as if they were a new form of human being. In any case, the melting pot of the Midwest remained just warm enough for niceness, but melting rarely happened.

When Glory appeared at the front door of the bowling alley on that Friday night, she was nervous. Mixing with people had never been difficult for her, but she had already sensed something polarizing about the small town. There were 'in-people' and 'out-people' and it took some work to be allowed into the former. She was fairly certain this was no different than any other town.

Accents were funny things, especially in small towns. Back in England, languages from all over the globe were spoken: Arabic, French, Russian, Chinese. In such a multi-cultural society, it was natural to accept without asking questions, but here in Iowa, she was taken aback by the questions already asked. Even though posed altruistically, it felt as if people were prying, as if knowing the answers *about* someone was 'knowing' them. When they asked about where she lived, why she had come to Amicable, how did she like the United States? – these were probing but judgmental questions. To know *about* Chigwell, was to compare it *to* Amicable. For them, Amicable was the center of the universe and a heaven unto earth. To know why she had come helped them understand what Chigwell was missing. Obviously, Amicable was far better than anywhere else. To help her learn the dialect and the customs, to help her identify with the superiority of Midwestern life, was to reconfigure her perspectives.

But the questions unnerved Glory. Did they really want to know her? Did they ask because they wanted to bring her into a circle of trust, or did they just want to know 'about' her, so that they could control her? She shivered. That was her history. Many people only wanted to control her, how she looked, how she spoke and how she thought.

Which was why she went to such great lengths to be nonconforming.

At the front door of the bowling alley, Glory bent down to Murgatroyd and straightened her coat collar.

"You'll be all right then?"

"Yes, Mum. I know how to get there."

"It's dark out."

"I have my phone. I'll call you if I get worried."

Glory smiled at her daughter. "You won't."

"I will," Murgatroyd insisted.

Ruffling her daughter's head, Glory stood. "You won't get worried."

"Oh," Murgatroyd smiled. "I suppose not."

Turning her, Glory patted her on the backside. "Off you go."

Glory watched her daughter merge with the darkness, past the streetlights to the north. As every mother did, she swallowed her worry and allowed her daughter to stretch the tether.

Sighing deeply, Glory crossed her arms and waited for Murgatroyd to cross the next street. The reflectors on her backpack

Chapter 4.

looked like cat's eyes in the dimness.

Opening the door to the bowling alley, Glory reveled in the sounds of community. Voices were raised in good-natured disagreement about the skill of the bowler. In the background, ancient pinball machines pinged and dinged. Balls dropped and slid down the lane. There were crashing of pins and the dropping of the gate to reset them.

At the front desk, a teenage girl was studying her phone. Looking up, she smiled. "Hello." Her greeting sounded like a question.

"I'm looking for the pub."

"What?"

"The pub."

"The what?"

"The bar. The saloon. The watering hole."

"Oh," the girl responded with a smile. "I *love* your accent. Where are you from?"

"Peppertree Lane, actually."

"I've never heard of that place before."

"It's about three blocks that way." She pointed southwards.

"Oh," the girl repeated. It was the most popular response, Glory had found.

"The pub?"

"What? Oh, yes. Just that way. About fifteen steps and then to the left. Right before you get to the Indiana Jones pinball machine."

Glory thanked the young girl and began her march past the colored bowling balls, behind the shoe changing area to the far end of the building. A few bowlers stopped to watch her. When she caught their eyes and waved, they quickly turned away, but not without waving first.

When she entered the Greedy Pecker, a young woman in a black shirt with the logo of a red rooster stood behind the bar. Her arms were crossed and she was intently watching the gaggle of women in front of her. Glory recognized them from the exercise club.

Jeannie saw her first and waved wildly. "Glory! Oh, hi!"

Glory tilted her head back, took a deep breath and walked towards them. "Hullo. Nice to see you all."

Leona pulled another stool close to her and patted it. "We're so glad you could make it. Now we can get to know each other a little better."

Glory sat down. "Interesting place."

"It's been a real community center for a long time." Penny said.

"The pub?"

"No, the bowling alley in general. Gosh, the stories." She paused. "Goodness, where are my manners. What would you like to drink, Glory?"

"What's good?"

All of them answered at the same time; their responses ranged from *nothing*, to *everything*, *beer* and *anything but beer*. Glory smiled while the bartender approached.

"I'm Shania."

"Like the singer."

Shania smiled. "Yes, but I don't sing. What can I get you?"

"How about a cider?"

Blinking twice and then glancing at the ladies, Shania scrunched up her face. "You want apple cider?"

"Sure," Glory nodded, "Or pear, whichever you have."

Shania turned towards the fridge knowing that they had nothing of the sort. "Um, I don't think we have that."

"You don't have cider? I thought this was a pub." Glory leaned to look into the cooler.

"It is, but... well, we don't get many kids in here, and I suppose we get some apple cider at Christmas, but to be honest, most people don't like cinnamon that much."

"Or licorice," Jeannie interjected.

"I don't understand. I'll just have a bottle of cold cider."

The women wondered between each other what the English woman was talking about. Then, Angela leaned forward. "How about a beer instead?" she said kindly.

"I'm a bit cheesed off about that, but when in Rome..." She smiled and noticed the women staring at her. "What did I say?"

Jeannie plucked up the courage to speak. "I have no idea what you said, but it sounded so exotic. Did you really say something about cheese in Rome?"

Chapter 4.

For a moment, Glory was quite certain that these women surrounding her were insane. At the same time, though, they were intrigued by her. She was something of an enigma, an unopened box. Glory nodded and explained herself – slowly, and loudly – they might not be able to understand her otherwise.

"You know what? I'll have a G & T?" She looked up at Shania expectantly who once again looked like a deer caught in headlights. "You do have that, don't you?"

Shania shook her head quickly. "No, we've got a Ford pickup."

"What?"

"2010. Nash bought it last year. Real nice, too."

"Are you all mad?"

"Not even upset," Leona responded. The women had all leaned away from Glory. "We're just trying to speak the same language."

"What does a Ford… what did you call it?… pickup have to do with a gin and tonic?"

The penny dropped. "Oh," Shania smiled. "I thought you were asking if I had a GTO – you know, a Pontiac. Jim Beemer has got one of those – shiny red, stunning car. Yes, we have gin and tonic and I can mix them."

She leaned forward. "I'm so happy for you."

"So," Jeannie's face was wide-eyed wonder, "tell us more about yourself."

"What would you like to know?"

"What about… where does the name Murgatroyd come from? I mean, I've never heard anything like that before."

"It's a generational name. My great grandmother was named Murgatroyd."

Jeannie frowned. "But, um, does it have a special meaning?"

"It means 'breath of heaven.'" Glory knew that it did *not* mean 'breath of heaven,' but it sounded good.

"That's beautiful," Jeannie grinned.

"She is a beautiful young lady."

"What about you? How did you get your name?"

Glory shrugged and accepted her drink from Shania who had also put an umbrella in it to pair with the small piece of out-of-season lime, which looked rusty instead of a pretty green. "I'm not sure why my mother gave me that name. I guess I'm just lucky."

"Sure are," Linda agreed.

"Why don't you tell me about yourselves?" Glory responded. "You all know so much about each other, but I know nothing."

Penny sipped her drink and then spoke. "There's not really much to say. We're Iowa ladies, split right down the middle Hawkeye and Cyclone supporters; mostly Republicans with a few radicals sitting on the fringe, but we love 'em anyway," she winked as if this was a joke, but it wasn't. "We're famous, I guess, for the way we've handled the elevator explosion. Don't you think, girls?"

Glory looked confused so Linda took over. "A few years ago, the elevator exploded and the town rebuilt it. Together. But then, well, we've all had some personal tough times."

"Linda had cancer," Leona lowered her voice as if it was a secret. Glory searched their faces trying to remember which one was Linda.

"That's me."

"Thank you. And you're right as rain now?"

"Yes."

"And then there's Angela who has the most famous son in Amicable," Leona continued as Angela raised her hand proudly. "Demetrius Chandler. His artwork is everywhere." They all nodded again. "Even in here." She pointed at a rooster sculpture perched behind the bar in front of the glass. It was winking.

"Amazing."

"If you go to the cemetery, you'll see the melting grave marker. It's Butcher's."

"I keep hearing about this Butcher," Glory checked their eyes. "What's so special about him? Who is he?"

"He was a wonderful man and friend. He married Rhonda, you know, J.T.'s mother. The boy that you said Murgatroyd was hanging out with."

"Oh, goodness. What happened to him?"

"He had motor neuron disease."

"That's terrible."

Chapter 4.

"He had a special gift of reading people," Penny added. "It was almost like he could read people's past and future."

Glory's eyes narrowed. "That sounds a bit far-fetched."

"If only you could have met him," Penny said wistfully.

"But now we have a new butcher, isn't that right?"

Leona leaned in. "Yes, that's right. We've been trying to get some… information about him, but so far, nothing has come up. It is really helpful to know who is moving into Amicable. You know, to keep us safe."

Glory knew about wanting to be safe. There was no greater desire for her, but just like acceptance, safety had been a stranger. Flashing back to episodes in her life, she frowned, but quickly regained her smile.

"How do you find things out?"

Jeannie snickered. "The grapevine is very connected here in Amicable."

"It seems like I've come to the right people then. If I want to know anything, I just ask you?"

"That's right," Leona said. "Anything at all you want to know about anyone at all, we're your women."

Chapter 5.

Murgatroyd adjusted her orange backpack and climbed the porch stairs. They weren't steep, but she still stumbled in the dark. Murgatroyd did worry, though, that she might have ended up at the wrong house. But when she peered through the window, she saw the television and J.T.'s sister sitting on the sofa.

Pushing the doorbell, Murgatroyd waited. She heard J.T.'s mum say, "Who could that be?" Soon, footsteps echoed towards the front door. The light flipped on above her and the door opened.

"Oh," the tall woman said quizzically. "Hello."

"Hello, Mrs. Jensen. I'm Murgatroyd MacDonald. I'm J.T.'s friend."

"Nice to meet you, Murgatroyd. Uh, what can we do for you?"

Murgatroyd tried to look around the woman towards where she hoped J.T. was. He stood in the hallway, motionless. "Can J.T. come out and play?"

Mrs. Jensen frowned. "It's awfully dark, Murgatroyd." She glanced out the door and around the street. "Is your mother with you?"

"No, she's at the bowling alley."

The frown deepened. "Did you walk here by yourself?"

"Yes, of course."

Once again checking the street for a responsible adult, Rhonda put her hand behind Murgatroyd's head and guided her through the door and into the house. By the time she had shut it behind her, Murgatroyd had rushed into the house, dropped her backpack on the floor by the sofa and was standing in front of J.T. Arms hanging limply, J.T. stared down at his diminutive 'friend,' unimpressed by her interruption.

"Hi, J.T.!"

"Purgatroyd."

"Me mum is at the bowling alley with her new friends, and she said I could come over here and hang out with you."

"Murgatroyd," Rhonda interrupted, "if you could tell your mom that the best way for playdates to happen is if she calls ahead and we can organize a time. Maybe we could meet at a park, or…"

Chapter 5.

Murgatroyd's face fell. "You don't want me here."

"No, no," Rhonda held up her hands, inwardly agreeing with her assessment, but outwardly not wanting to seem rude. "It's just that surprise visits aren't socially acceptable."

"Unless you're an adult," Murgatroyd added desultorily.

"What do you mean?"

"It's all right for adults to 'pop by for a chin wag,'" Murgatroyd changed her voice to be that of an adult and used quote fingers, "but for us kids, we have to wait for you to get your diaries organized, pick an acceptable time, and tell us exactly what we're going to do and watch us do it."

Rhonda finally smiled. "I've never thought about it in that way."

Murgatroyd nodded and crossed her arms. Staring up at the much taller Jensens, she held her ground. "Look, imagine that you want to go see your best friend, but your mother says, 'It's not really a good time dear,' and you say, 'but I'm fifty years old...'"

"I'm barely forty."

"Okay, whatever, but your mum controls your life, every piece of it to keep you 'safe' and then she tells you that she'll 'ave to come with you to prepare the playground and make sure there are no razor blades on the slippery dip, enough wood chips at the bottom so you don't get a boo boo – imagine 'ow frustrated you'd be."

Rhonda couldn't help but laugh. "My mother used to be like that."

"Now multiply that for us kids now. John Boyo and me, we just want to do stuff."

Rhonda glanced at J.T. who was slowly shaking his head. "What is this 'John Boyo' thing? Is that your nickname for him?"

Murgatroyd moved to stand next to J.T. Facing Rhonda, she smiled. There were gaps in her teeth and her freckles sparkled in the overhead lights. "Yes – all best friends need nicknames. He calls me Purgatroyd."

"Don't you find that... offensive?" Rhonda asked.

"Sheesh no," she scrunched up her face. "He could call me Arse Whisew and I wouldn't be offended. It's just what best friends do."

Son of a Butcher

Rhonda hiccupped a laugh and thought about calling Leslie 'Ass Whistle.' "Do you know what purgatory is?"

Nodding, Murgatroyd peeked up at J.T. whose head leaned back slightly. He was staring at the ceiling. "Boyo told me. It's a place where souls go to pay their penance. It's like a prison for people who die."

Rhonda raised an eyebrow. "Where did you hear that, J.T.?"

"Unca John."

"So, can we go play now?"

Rhonda glanced around the house. The place was a mess. Toys and books were scattered everywhere. The light cover above was layered with dead bugs. No one really came over anymore, not even her mother.

"Yes," she acceded, "go play."

Murgatroyd grabbed J.T.'s hand. "Come on! Let's go outside! We can build a fort or something."

"Isn't it kind of late to be playing outside? You could trip... or," seeing Murgatroyd's face, Rhonda added, "never mind."

J.T. allowed himself to be led outdoors to their backyard. As they walked, Murgatroyd gave a running commentary of what they would be doing and what they would *not* be doing. Dutifully, J.T. followed her instructions and picked up sticks. As he bent down, J.T. noticed how short the sleeves were on the arms of his jacket. He'd been growing so fast. Soon, he would be wearing his father's clothes. Murgatroyd, on the other hand, nearly stumbled over her coat. The hood kept flopping down and covering her face.

"Bollocks," she shouted as she finally flung back the hood.

"What does that even mean?" J.T. asked.

"What do you mean, what does it mean? It means just that."

J.T. rolled his eyes. "That makes no sense."

"Just go get those pieces of wood over there." She motioned at some unused siding lying alongside the garage.

"What exactly are we doing?"

"Are you deaf? 'Aven't you been listening? We're going to build a treehouse."

"What, right now?"

"Do you have any other plans for the night?" Exasperatedly, she dropped the small twigs in her arms at her feet.

Chapter 5.

J.T. followed suit with the larger branches. "No. But I don't see what the hurry is. Why don't we do this during the day?"

"I thought you didn't have a problem with the dark…"

"I don't. It makes no difference to me, but how long will we have until your mom gets here? We need a plan."

"I *have* a plan," she protested.

"Do you think you could let *me* know about *your* plan?"

"You're on a need-to-know basis." Murgatroyd ambled over to him and stood looking up into his face.

"You don't even know what that means."

Harrumphing, Murgatroyd turned away from him and changed the subject. "So you really can see in the dark?"

"Everyone can see in the dark," he corrected.

"Yes, but I suppose not like you."

He shrugged. "I guess not."

"Prove it."

"What do you want me to do?"

"Hmmm," she glanced around her. "How many boards of siding are there on the back of the garage?"

J.T. turned and counted them from the bottom up using his finger to keep track of his progress. "Twenty-three."

Murgatroyd traipsed to the garage to count. "Impressive, but you could have counted before."

"Do you think I go around counting siding everywhere?"

"Maybe. You told me you were awkward socially."

"Counting siding?"

She ignored him. "What about… what's written on my jacket?" She covered up her lapel.

"Purg – how am I supposed to see if you cover it with your hand."

"Oh, yeah," she uncovered it but cupped her hands around it.

"From what you've left uncovered, it says *ore Than Magi*, so I guess that's *More Than Magic*."

"Wow, that's right!" she frowned. "But you could have seen that when I walked in the house."

Son of a Butcher

He was quiet. "You've fifty-seven eyelashes in your right eye. There is a smudge of something dark on your left hand. And, I'm assuming you haven't noticed, but there's a little piece of booger in your right nostril."

Instinctively, she raised her hand to her nose and wiped.

"Just kidding," he said as he laughed. She smacked him which made him double over.

"Hey! You don't have to get abusive."

"You listen to me, Boyo, I don't suffer fools lightly."

He rubbed his stomach. "Jeez, chill out."

She smirked. "It means don't mess with me, Buttsniffer."

Finally, he laughed with her. There was something good and comfortable about it, an appeal to a long-buried emotion which had been interred with his father. Murgatroyd's smile was broad and obstinate. Her small chin jutted out as if daring him to retort.

After a comfortable time of mutual admiration, J.T. rubbed his own nose with his hand. "I'll show you how good I can see. Do you want to see him?"

"Who?"

"My watcher."

"What?"

"I have a guardian an... er, a person who is always around."

Frowning, Murgatroyd looked behind him. "Is he here? Your guardian aneraperson?"

"What?"

"That's what you said."

"No, just... aagh, never mind. Come with me." He tugged on her arm.

"Where are we going?"

"I'll show you."

Sneaking past the garage and between the front yards of Unca George's house (he'd never been able to think of it belonging to anyone else) and their own house, J.T. felt a thrill that he was breaking out, or stepping out, from a long dormancy. To be able to play with someone else, even if it was Murgatroyd MacDonald, was cathartic. To find a friend, that was worth its weight in gold.

Chapter 5.

When they hit the streetlights, they pretended to be spies as they slid along the front of George's house. Murgatroyd held up her fingers in the shape of a gun. "Is this going to be dangerous?"

"Probably," J.T. said. "What are you doing with your hands?"

"It's a gun, silly. We might need them. Come on," she motioned with her gun to copy her. "What kind of heat are you packing?"

Momentarily, he stared at her, but then, wondering what it would be like to play, he stooped down to grab a small twig from a tree. "It's a pistol."

She switched her hands. "I've got a machine gun now."

"Oh yeah," he put his hands on top of his shoulders. "Bazooka."

Laughing, she pushed ahead of him and then leaned against a tree. "What's the mission?"

His eyes narrowed. "Are you afraid?"

"Not with my guns."

"Okay, Purgatroyd. We're on our way to the cemetery."

Her eyes widened slightly. Looking back to the safety of the house, she briefly considered turning around. Instead, though, she called his bluff. "No problem, Captain."

Nodding, he began to run towards the street and then, after looking both directions, he ran across. When he turned back, he saw Murgatroyd pausing at the curb.

"I thought you said you weren't afraid?"

"I'm not," she whispered loudly stopping to pick something up from the ground. "But if we're going to the land of the dead, I'm getting some of these?" She held up some rocks in her hands.

"Why do you need rocks?"

"They're not rocks," she said conspiratorially. "Grenades."

* * * * *

Gustav Keller sat rigidly in the dark on the park bench. Although the unforgiving wood hurt his back and caused his legs to ache, he remained. The pain was motivational. He had been to this spot many times before. If one didn't know Gustav, they would have thought him a bereaved

Son of a Butcher

family member unable to move past his grief. But he was not grieving. He was summoning the rage to go through with his plans.

The terminus of his hatred approached. Though the last minute details needed to be worked out, the overarching plan was brilliant. For Rhonda to suffer hell and all of its torments, each particular piece of the revenge needed managing. Danny and his hardware had been helpful, but the large man knew nothing of the final event.

Eventually, Rhonda would feel nothing but pain, for it was she who had brought this upon herself, her family, her community. And he would be there in his anonymous glory reveling in her pain.

As Gustav peered through the darkness at the monument, he was galvanized with power. He had memorized the engraving at the foot of the grave –

> Leopold 'Butcher' Jensen,
> Beloved Amicablean,
> husband, father and friend
> He loved everyone

Every time Gustav read the last line, he snorted. No one loved everyone. It was hard enough loving just one other person, but everyone? One of those ridiculously hyperbolic platitudes that inevitably showed up on gravestones. Granted, even what little the Peterson brothers said about him, it would be easy enough to imagine the guy was a likable fellow, but there were limits to altruism. There were always limits to kindness.

Gustav had been a kind person. A long time ago in a land far away, Gustav had concerned himself with working hard, paying his taxes, taking care of his parents, attending church occasionally. In Wisconsin, he had been a confident, yet average young man, not excelling in many things, but good-enough at most. After graduating from college, he took a job as a bookkeeper in a local newspaper. Though not enough money to get rich, he was happy, and certainly he had plenty of time to run around in the woods. His passion was the outdoors. Hunting, fishing, cross country skiing, anything but staring at his computer.

Chapter 5.

When he purchased the little cabin in the woods, Gustav felt that at least one piece of his dream had come true. To own property, even at his young age, was a sign of his independence and status in society. At the age of twenty-nine, he was socially and fiscally responsible, a real 'catch' for any woman.

For Rhonda Redman, this had been part of his allure. She had been used to the farm boys, the pigherds, the corn rangers, but he had been different – a big city boy. Granted, Beloit, Wisconsin was not exactly Metropolis, but it was certainly much larger than Amicable. Arriving in Chicago one weekend (he had been there on a day trip), she had fallen for him, and then...

He shook his head not wanting to remember and yet needing to be reminded of why he was here in Amicable. The pain of his prison experience, the loss of his eye, the all-consuming agony of his limp, his vile treatment fueled his rage, and now as he stared at the half-melted statue across from him, he knew that everything was almost ready.

The statue had been sculpted by a nationally known local artist. Whatever it looked like before it started melting, must have been incredible. It was an amazing replication of Michelangelo's *Pieta*. The sight of Rhonda holding her melting husband in her arms must have cut her every time she saw it. Now that much of his torso had dripped onto the ground by the power of the sun, the sculpture was nearly unrecognizable. Placing his hands on the cane in front of him, Gustav sucked in a lungful of air and focused his thoughts on anger and resentment summoning the wherewithal to take the next important steps.

Hating was hard for him. He had to work at it. Especially now, since he had ingratiated himself in Amicable. Even though he'd been working at the locker for just a week, people were getting used to him. At first, he worried about being recognized. That Rhonda would enter the shop and see and remember him was frightening. But he needed to have access to various places in the town. People were far too vigilant for him to show up as a stranger. Thus, the job at Peterson's.

Except... the brothers were extraordinarily hard to dislike. Genial and good-natured, hard-working and a gritty niceness, Nash and Derek treated him as an equal and partner. It had been such a long time

Son of a Butcher

since that had happened. To be treated like a human was chipping hatred from his stone heart. It needed to stop.

The twins had nicknames for everyone: farmers, shopkeepers, kids, parents, it didn't matter. They knew everyone. Gustav called them 'Boss.' The first time he did this, Nash's face went white. When Nash told him that Butcher used to call him that, Gustav was determined to keep doing it.

But then they had given him a nickname. *Hoot*, they called him. When he asked them why, they responded with cross-armed laughter. "Your name is Barnaby. We," Derek tapped his brother's chest, "thought we should call you 'Barn owl,' but Nash came up with 'Hoot.' What do you think about that, Hoot?"

Barnaby shrugged. He was perturbed and honored at the same time. Perturbed, that the name seemed demeaning, yet honored, that they would give him one. He was becoming part of the community. Yet the moniker seemed counterfeit. His name was not Barnaby, but Gustav. He cared nothing for Amicable and his only desire was for its destruction.

Oh yes, for a long time he had watched from a distance. From the burning of the house on Peppertree Lane to the elevator explosion. How he had loved watching them burn. The heat from each had seared his face, not enough to char, but enough to *burn*. Then, of course he watched…

Behind him he heard a noise. Turning quickly, he squinted into the darkness for the source of the sound, but he couldn't see anything. A cat or bird or something. A short time later, he rose from his perch and staggered to the melting sculpture. Taking a knife from his pocket, he stepped on Leopold Jensen's gravestone, the Man Who Loved Everyone, and leaned forward. With intense glee, he viciously scratched madly around Rhonda's stone heart. If she would have been made out of wax, he would have stabbed her. The grating noise was cathartic for Gustav – each scratch was release, as if a steam valve on his anger.

Halfway through another mark to Rhonda's heart, he heard the noise again. It sounded like a voice. Heart beating quickly, he turned but still couldn't see into the night. Satisfied that it was simply a passing car of kids, he moved away from the statue and towards the grassy path

Chapter 5.

between gravestones. When he reached Dennis Keslo's grave marker he paused. More noise.

Suddenly, he felt a thud on his collarbone. Pain shot through him and he fell to the ground. Cane gone, he moaned as he searched for it. Each movement was excruciating, but he had to leave. He couldn't be found in the graveyard after dark.

* * * * *

"What did you do?" Murgatroyd shrieked a whisper.
"I threw a grenade at him!"
"Who?"
"Him." He pointed. "At the Watcher. Didn't you see him?"
"I don't see anyone." She looked back towards the cemetery but saw nothing.

Angry, J.T. watched the Watcher writhe on the ground. He had seen everything. The sitting, the mumbling, the scratching of his mother's stone heart.

Yet, could he have imagined it?

They had walked towards the cemetery to see the Watcher. It wasn't the first time J.T. had seen him there. Sometimes when J.T. couldn't sleep, he snuck out and came here to be with his dad. But the first time he saw the Watcher guarding his parents, he felt comfort. But now?

J.T. glanced down worriedly at Murgatroyd. "So you didn't see him?"

"No. You must be seeing things."

He shook his head. The Watcher was still lying on the ground, motionless. Maybe he'd just wounded an angel? Maybe the Watcher had stabbed a demon in front of the sculpture? Maybe the Watcher was protecting his parents, especially his father. All that J.T. needed was a positive perspective. *Of course* that's what had happened. The heavenly Watcher was simply doing what he had been asked to do. And J.T. had stoned him.

J.T. suddenly wanted to go help the Watcher. As he stepped towards him, Murgatroyd grabbed his arm. "Where are you going?"

Son of a Butcher

"Over there."

"Let's get out of here. This is creepy."

Staring down at her, he saw the scared lines around her eyes. "Okay," he said quickly, hoping that the Watcher would be able to pin his wings back on and float back to heaven.

With one last look, the kids turned and ran back across the grass, down the street to J.T.'s house. When they rounded the last corner, Murgatroyd gasped as she saw her mother's car approach the house. Dropping their 'weapons,' J.T. and Murgatroyd sprinted the last fifty yards to the backyard. Stealthily, they made their way between the houses and panted when they reached their dropped twigs and branches.

J.T. looked down at Murgatroyd who was smiling broadly at him. "That was awesome," she said. "Can we do that again some other time?"

His mind spun back to the cemetery. "Well, maybe we'll do something different next time, okay."

Murgatroyd unexpectedly rushed him and hugged his body, arms trapped by his sides. Her head barely reached his chestbone.

"What are you doing?" he whispered.

"Thanking you, Buttsniffer."

The back door to the house opened. J.T. gazed up at his mother who was frowning. Obviously, she and Mrs. MacDonald's discussion had centered on something particularly un-positive. "Murgatroyd, your mother's here."

"Thanks, Mrs. J." Murgatroyd ran up to the back step where Rhonda was holding the door open. "Are you coming, J.T.?"

Without speaking, he nodded and followed Murgatroyd into the house. When they reached the front door, Mrs. MacDonald waved at the boy. Her smile was forced. "Thank you, J.T. for spending some time with Murgatroyd. She really appreciates that. *I* really appreciate it."

He shrugged and put his hands in his pockets. "It was fun."

Rhonda stared at him and her mouth dropped open. *Fun? When did he ever say that?*

"Bye J.T." Murgatroyd plowed past Glory. Before the front door had shut behind them, Murgatroyd was already reaching into her vast array of words to describe the treehouse that they were building. In the dim light of the porch, Rhonda stared out at the single mother and her

Chapter 5.

daughter. Suddenly, she realized that both were paddling the same canoe and she felt guilty about her words of frustration. Almost preemptively she had accused Glory of being a neglectful parent (but in a very nice way) and that if their kids were going to spend time together, appropriate measure should be taken to organize their time. Perhaps an afternoon at the park where they could meet and watch the kids play.

Rhonda glanced at her son. He was looking at a speck on the ceiling. "What do you see?"

"A spider."

"What color is it?"

His eyes adjusted. It was eerie how his lenses worked. "Brown with black on its back."

"What's so interesting?"

"It's got a broken leg, but she is making the web really fast."

Rhonda looked up to search for the spider but couldn't see it. "I guess she's hoping to catch a fly. Hungry, maybe?"

"Yeah, I guess so."

"Did you have a good time?"

His eyes refocused on hers. "Yes."

"What did you do?"

"We started building a treehouse."

"You mean, like up in a tree?"

Somehow, J.T. was able to hold her gaze through his little white lie. "Yeah, like up in a tree."

"You didn't get very far then, did you?"

Without turning around, J.T. thought about the episode in the graveyard.

"Far enough, Mom."

Chapter 6.

For Barnaby Koppel, life moved glacially slow. Each meticulous step of his plan was written out carefully in his little black book which sat on the edge of his table. A rubber band held the covers together, and when he was done recording his days, his conversations and the reflections from them, he stuffed the book into the library of other books on his living room shelf. Any casual observer would never choose to look at the ratty tome stuck between Philip Pullman's series and Immanuel Kant's cryptic observations. Barnaby, as he was now remembering to call himself, felt edgy – fidgety – and endlessly impatient to get on with it. But there was a right time and wrong time for everything. Thus, the hour hand crept rather than ran.

As his hand left the little black book, he reflected on what he had written tonight.

His own gravestone.

While he had been imprisoned, he shared a cell with a man named Lonzo Coleman. For the first month of their incarceration together, they had spoken very little. By the end of Lonzo's time – two years and seven months (assault and battery) – Gustav and Lonzo would have considered each other good friends.

Roughly a year after the loss of his eye, Gustav revealed his crime. Lonzo listened with appreciative awe. Certainly, the man sitting in front of him, crippled and half-blind, did not seem the type for rape, yet appearances didn't always matter. As Gustav retold the story through the lenses of his hatred, they began to concoct a plan which would allow him vengeance – a prisoner's Golden Fleece.

"*Lonzo,*" *Gustav whispered.*
"*What?*" *Lonzo was doing pushups in the middle of the floor.*
"*I need some help.*"
"*Later.*"
"*Can you take a break now?*"
Lonzo held his pushup. His triceps quivered from effort. "*Man, one of these days...*" *He stood up.* "*Whatchoo want?*"

Chapter 6.

"I figured out how I'm going to pay her back."

"You gotta give that dream up, Boy. The only thing that will happen if you go after her when you get out is that you'll get right back in."

"It's fool proof, Lonz."

Lonzo shook his head. "Plans that are fool proof only prove the fools who make them."

"Where did you hear that?"

"Just made it up," Lonzo smirked.

"You're smarter than you look." Lonzo bowed at the backhanded compliment. "Anyway, here's how it's going to go down."

From the top bunk, Gustav plotted the direction for his post-incarceration future. He still had two more years to go.

"When I get out, Gustav Keller is going to be dead."

"Excuse me?"

"I need you to do something for me, cause you're going to get out way before me." Lonzo waited. "In Beloit, there is a gravestone maker on the southwest side of town. Don't worry, he doesn't know me. I want you to buy a headstone for me."

"What the hell for?"

"For me." Gustav smiled wickedly. "I want this engraved into the stone: Gustav Keller, May 15, 1991 – October 17, 2022. Life was hard."

"You want me to buy you a headstone?"

"That's right. And I want you to take it to my family's cemetery. It's out in the country. You're going to place the headstone right next to my parents' markers."

"But why?"

"I have this sneaking suspicion that Rhonda will come looking for it someday – you know, closure. Seeking forgiveness from a headstone for ruining my life. Some people find that easier than asking forgiveness in real life."

"How will she know you're dead?"

"Because I'm sending the suicide note directly to her."

Lonzo rubbed his hands. "Ooh, that's good. Real good. Then what?"

"I'm going to move to her stupid little town and ruin her life."

"But won't she recognize you?"

Gustav frowned. "I didn't wear these scars when I knew her."

"How are you going to ruin her life?"

Lonzo was alarmed when he saw the look in his eyes.

"I'm going to set her world on fire…"

Son of a Butcher

* * * * *

A strange thing happened to Glory after the night at the Greedy Pecker. She learned to assimilate. Before she knew it, she was wearing blue jeans and t-shirts with American flags; her once eclectic leather shoes were replaced by responsible, white New Balance sneakers. Where her long, dyed red hair had marked her as different, she now had it cut just below her ears.

Murgatroyd noticed the change and queried her mother about it, but Glory shushed her saying that fitting in was the first step towards happiness.

Murgatroyd, though, had not taken that first step and gave no indication of doing so. It wasn't that she didn't want to find a groove, make new friends and wend her way through third grade, but she had no role models to do so. Her mother's acceptance of the culture only hardened Murgatroyd's resolve not to sell out. Though she did not know the reasons for doing this, there was a sense of purpose. She was English for a reason, and it was neither embarrassing nor in need of evolution (or revolution).

Nervously, Glory paced around the house searching through various drawers looking for something. "Murg, have you seen my cat ears?"

"No, Mum." Murgatroyd was standing in the front doorway, plastic pumpkin in her hand. Where her mother had decided to dress as Catwoman for Halloween, stuffed into a patent leather jumpsuit with mask to match, Murgatroyd fell on the other side of the holiday festivity. Dressed as a life-sized pine tree car freshener, she dangled a string from the Styrofoam triangle around her head. To complete the ensemble, she had liberally doused herself with Pine-Sol.

"I thought I put them on the bench."

"Maybe you can go without the ears?" Murgatroyd played with the string.

Glory pouted as she stomped through the living room. "I don't want to go without the ears. Catwoman needs ears."

Chapter 6.

Murgatroyd lifted her arm and smelled her armpit. Perfect pine scent. Nice. "Whatever you do, get a move on it. We're supposed to be at the Halloween party at seven." The clock above the kitchen sink read 6:52.

"Hold your horses." Rushing through the next room, Murgatroyd heard her mother shout *Eureka* and storm back into the living area almost running into the sofa. "Here they are! They were on the bed."

"Put them on and let's go!"

Ten minutes later, Catwoman and Car Freshener stopped outside the Traveler's Choice, a retired restaurant which had been transformed into a community center. Leona and Jeannie organized the yearly event. When it had been revealed that England didn't celebrate Halloween (something similar, but certainly not to the degree to which Halloween was recognized in the U.S.), they had thrown the party together. Although the Traveler's Choice could not hold more than two hundred people, some would come and go. Others would protest such a heathen spectacle in a nice town like Amicable (those poor Clancy Baptists). Glory and Murgatroyd would be the guests of honor.

Whatever that meant.

The small alcove outside Traveler's Choice was strung with fake cobwebs and oversized spiders. A tiny ghoul poked its face from the corner. Murgatroyd, unafraid of the objects, looked up at her mother with a puzzled expression. "What's the point of Halloween, anyway?"

Glory patted the tip of her pine tree. "No idea. But, we're about to find out."

As they stepped through the door, the 'scary' sounds, creaking doors, footsteps, howling wolves, and hooting owls alternated in the background. Around the room were pockets of people dressed in costume. In one corner was a football player and a werewolf; Darth Vader and Marvin the Martian were conversing by the punch bowl. Linda Harmsen had dressed up in what Glory assumed to be a nurse's outfit while her husband appeared uncomfortable, tugging at the collar of his ill-fitting (and oh-so-tight) Spiderman suit.

"There's J.T." Murgatroyd pointed and released her mother's hand to run to him.

Son of a Butcher

As Glory watched her go, she felt a stab of pain. Her daughter was growing up and fitting in. J.T. and Murgatroyd had become inseparable. Most afternoons, Murg traipsed across the schoolyard with J.T. to his house. They had continued building their treehouse, or mansion-in-the-branches as Murg was calling it. As of yet, Glory had not seen the progress because Murgatroyd didn't want to spoil the surprise. Either way, Glory was pleased that she had found someone.

Murgatroyd pulled up just short of J.T. They had coordinated their costumes. He was a much taller yellow version of a car freshener. As she leaned back, he reached a stubby hand out from his tree which she slapped. The duo left Rhonda and headed for the snacks. Rhonda raised her hand to Glory and smiled.

After their first misunderstanding, Rhonda and Glory had figured out a way to make 'co-parenting' work. Glory had convinced her of the safety of allowing the two children to walk around town. Murgatroyd had her phone (which she rarely used) and J.T. could see danger from at least a mile away. Still, Rhonda grew nervous when he said he was walking to Purgatroyd's house after dinner.

Though both women found it difficult to watch their kids grow up and to give them more freedom, the more trust they showed, the happier the children became.

Glory felt a hand touch her arm. "What do you think of the party?" Leona, as Freddie Krueger, asked.

"Good God!" Glory exclaimed as she jumped away from her.

"Nice, isn't it?" Leona clicked her blade-like fingers. "I bought it online. Seventeen dollars."

"Quite an unexpected gift to nearly be eviscerated on Halloween."

Leona pulled her scarred mask up over her head and beamed. "You're welcome."

"Does every town do this?" Glory asked.

Shrugging, Leona scanned the room. "Probably not. But we've been doing it since the early 2000's. There was a scare that people were putting razor blades in apples, so we decided to have a community party instead."

"Were people actually putting razor blades in apples?"

Chapter 6.

"Not in Amicable."

"So you changed it just in case?"

"There are crazies in every town."

Glory smirked. "Are there any here tonight?"

"What? Here? Of course. We're all crazy in our own certain way." She laughed and pulled the mask back down. "Come on, let's go scare some kids."

As they wandered between hay bales, scarecrows, a cattle tank for apple bobbing and various caskets full of dusty skeletons, Glory was amused to see most of those in attendance really enjoying the opportunity to be something/someone they were not.

Once Glory had donned the Catwoman costume, she felt a little bit like her old self. A woman who could hide in plain sight. As her eyes strayed across farmers dressed up as older farmers, replete with straw sticking out of their mouths, she wondered if all people needed this diversion. Maybe Halloween was less about tricks and treats as it was about community and laughter.

At the cattle trough, a few children were getting soaked from head to toe. After shoving their faces into the water, very few had been able to wrest an apple from the water. Giggling with glee, yet much to their parents' chagrin, these children went back time after time. A couple teenagers sat in the corner, one dressed as a teddy bear and another as a ninja, taking pictures of each other on their phones.

Rhonda, dressed in a sleek black outfit like Sandy from Grease, sauntered over to her. The two women, similar in many respects, seemed like twins, but one with cat ears.

"You look sexy," Glory said.

"What, this old thing?"

"Hmm, I'd die for a body like yours."

"You look purrfect in that Catwoman suit."

"Very funny."

Their eyes strayed to the car fresheners on the other side of the room. Murgatroyd was eating cotton candy while J.T. was stuffing a homemade caramel popcorn ball into his mouth. Both were laughing about something.

"J.T. is very tall for his age, isn't he?"

Son of a Butcher

Rhonda nodded and took a sip of her apple cider. "Yes, his father was very tall."

"You're not so short yourself," Glory looked up at her.

"No, not in height, only in patience."

"I heard that your husband… died." Though they had spent some time together, Rhonda had never brought up Butcher's death and Glory had avoided the subject. Until this moment.

Rhonda turned slightly but still spoke into the noise around them. Cavorting on the 'dance' floor were a mummy, a vampire and a Teletubby. "Being a widow at my age brings a lot of pity."

"I'm sorry for your loss."

Rhonda nodded. "So am I. He was a kind, wonderful, infuriating, beautiful man. I miss him like crazy."

"How do you get by?"

"I don't. Every part of me is stuck where he was. I hear him everywhere. His presence still speaks to me in the corners of the bedroom, underneath the covers, in the bathtub. I can smell him and hear him, but I can't see him. That's the hardest part."

"It must be difficult for you to get out to something like this." Glory motioned to where Dr. Spock was line dancing with a lumberjack and a football player. They were all women.

"Yes, but good," Rhonda responded. "If I continued to hide myself in the house, I'd go crazy. People don't expect me to be happy, but they want me to be seen."

"Do you think you can find happiness again?"

Rhonda sighed and ignored the question. "What about you? How do you get by?"

Glory's eyes were drawn to Murgatroyd where she and J.T. were making cotton candy ghosts. "My daughter is everything." Glory was surprised by the tears which stung the corners of her eyes.

Little Bo Peep herded multiple Ewoks across the floor to the far end of the building where a Halloween petting zoo had been constructed. In small pens, cats, rabbits and a solitary miniature pig cowered from the overly affectionate children. "We came here to escape Chigwell and everything that went with it. But I didn't realize that we'd

Chapter 6.

fall in love with the place so quickly. It's so different, yet the people seem so familiar. Do you know what I mean?"

"No matter where you go," Rhonda said, "you'll always find friends and enemies, just with different names and addresses."

"I like that."

"Were you married?" Rhonda asked.

"No. Never married. I think I'm allergic to it. Murgatroyd is the product of a mistaken relationship, but she is certainly not a mistake. She's an incredibly talented, smart young lady."

"Does she know her father?"

Glory snorted. "God, no."

"Does he know her?"

A strange look crossed Glory's face, one of annoyance and wistfulness. "I tried contacting him once. He told me to bugger off."

"I assume that's not a pleasant thing?"

Glory laughed. "You've got that right."

"Any thoughts about finding anyone else?" Rhonda's question was almost drowned out by the sound of Michael Jackson's *Thriller*. More and more dancers streaked for the floor. A few of the farmers raised their eyebrows because they had no idea what the song was.

"Let's just say, finding a man who could put up with me would be a miracle in itself."

"I don't think you're half bad."

Smiling, Glory placed her hand on Rhonda's arm as a gesture of solidarity. "My less than half bad is worse than fully bad of many others. Let's just say I can be particularly difficult to put up with sometimes."

As Glory was talking, Leslie Deakins caught Rhonda's eye and waved. She had been talking to some young mothers who were toting their babies dressed up in saccharinely sweet flowers or ladybugs. The Deakins twins were enmeshed with J.T. and Murgatroyd as they played cornhole with beanbags that looked like spiders.

Leslie approached. She was wearing a nun's habit.

"Ironic, isn't it?" she laughed.

"Why is that?" Glory asked.

"I'm pregnant. A pregnant nun, you know?"

Son of a Butcher

Glory caught on and her loud bray caused the crowd to stop and stare. "Sorry!" she yelled out and raised a hand.

"Are you having a good time?" Leslie asked both of them.

Rhonda smiled at her friend. "I suppose. It brings out the child in all of us, doesn't it?"

Leslie nodded. "I remember walking around Amicable when I was a kid. My parents would drop us off at the edge of town and we would walk in packs to every old person's house. They'd open up the door, drop a cheap candy in the basket and tell us, 'Ooh, so scary.' It seems kind of weird, now."

"I heard in Clancy people were getting upset because kids were truly getting scared. Some of the residents were setting up their front yards to look like murder scenes."

"That is kind of strange," Glory said.

"Well, thank God we have this event. It's safe."

Each one of the women wondered exactly at the same time, *but who knows for how long.*

* * * * *

While Leslie, Rhonda and Glory waxed nostalgic about the way things used to be, Barnaby Koppel worked at his dining table. Because of his injuries, motor function, especially for small things, (amazingly not butchering) was difficult. The immense patience it took was enervating for him, though. Putting the pieces together was like assembling a model car or airplane. Checking and rechecking the plans and making sure each piece was correct took a great deal of concentration.

Stretching his back, he reached towards the ceiling and yawned. It was 9:00. Suddenly, there was a knock at his front door. Frowning, he knew who it was. Stupid kids wanting candy. Strangers and their brats begging for sugared refuse. Even though he had posted a large sign on his front door (I DON'T DO HALLOWEEN!), it didn't seem to make a great deal of difference. Frustratingly, it seemed to encourage the little urchins.

The doorbell rang again.

Chapter 6.

Gustav swore under his breath and rose from his chair. Caning his way across the wooden floor, he approached the entry. "Go away! No trick or treating here!"

The bell sounded.

"Damnit!" He grasped the door handle. As he opened it, he was about to shout at the kids, maybe scare them a little bit by raising his eyepatch. A good pirate welcome might do them some good. Instead, he encountered Danny Thul dressed as Spongebob Squarepants panting on his steps.

"Trick or Treat!"

"What are you doing, Danny?"

"I thought you could use some company. I haven't seen you for a while at the bar and I wanted to make sure you're not dead." His broad face beamed.

"Not dead."

They stood awkwardly.

"Can I come in?" Danny asked.

"No."

"Why not?"

"Because I'm tired. I've got a job, you know? I get up early, work for a living. Pay the bills and taxes. A model citizen."

Snorting, Danny looked to the neighbor's house where a group of children were extending their treasure sacks. "Oh, come on. It's Halloween. Let's have a beer."

"What do Halloween and beer have to do with each other?" Gustav asked.

"The better question is, 'What *don't* Halloween and beer have to do with each other?' I'm sure you've got some pumpkin ale stashed in your fridge."

"I don't, actually."

"Well, come over to my house then, because I do."

Gustav shook his head. "Your wife won't like that."

"I don't have a wife, Barnaby. I thought we talked about that."

"Well, you can please yourself and have all the beer to yourself. I'm tired."

Danny looked hurt. "You don't want to spend time with me?"

"Not tonight, Danny. Maybe some other time."

Sighing, Danny was about to turn when he glanced into Barnaby's living room. "Wait, what are you doing in there? Are you building something?"

"It's nothing, Danny," Gustav's jaw clenched as he closed the door.

"I can help. I'm handy."

"I'm sure you are. Good night."

As the door clicked in Danny's face, he scratched his head and turned away. What in the world was Barnaby putting together in his dining room? It looked like a… Suddenly, there were screams across the street. At a particularly gruesome fake murder scene, a man was holding a severed hand and chasing children.

Danny was quite sure Halloween was one of his favorite holidays of the year.

Chapter 7.

On the first Monday of November, Barnaby Koppel arose early. For the first time in a very long time, he whistled as he put on his work uniform. He was getting stronger, his fingers more dexterous. His legs more muscular. The consistent work and the stimulation of conversation was helpful. But it was also suppressing his anger. To stoke the fuel of his rage he would reread the details of his trial and wrongful imprisonment every night. By the time he was ready to go to sleep, Gustav was back in black.

Barnaby adjusted his work shirt so that it didn't snag his thick black beard. The facial hair continued to be a mask against any minute possible recognition by Rhonda. He had seen her a few times as she passed on the street. He wondered if she'd stop in. He asked Derek about it, but Derek shook his head. Rhonda didn't come in anymore. It was too hard for her.

Grateful for that, Barnaby felt like there was some supernatural blessing on his plans. Not that he needed God's help (in fact, if there was a God, Barnaby was pretty sure this was not on the list of things to bless), but it was a nice feeling.

Pushing up his sunglasses, Barnaby checked his good eye, or as-good-as-it-could-be eye. The pupil remained perpetually dilated. The trauma of the blow had stunned it open, thus leaving Barnaby susceptible to bright lights. Blinking was difficult due to the scar, so he had drops that he placed in his eye at various times during the day. Whenever he did it, the twins would surreptitiously watch. They were fascinated by it.

He rubbed his shoulder. It was still sore where something had hit him in the cemetery. Whatever it was, it scared him. Needless to say, Barnaby had not been back there since.

Tapping the black patch on his other eye, Barnaby spun away from the mirror and walked caneless into the living area. Strength finally returning, he still limped, but he could walk for most of a day. He still took the cane, but it was more of a pacifier than anything else.

Son of a Butcher

After work, Danny was going to take Barnaby car shopping. Not needing much, he just wanted to be able to drive from Clancy to Amicable each day. Whether or not he made it farther, to Des Moines or Council Bluffs, made no difference to him. This was not going to end as a sightseeing trip. Of that, he was sure.

Barnaby's phone buzzed. He grabbed it and saw that Danny was at the front of his house. Although Danny was nosy, he was patently useful.

Grabbing his coat and cane, Barnaby locked the house behind him, but only after glancing at his covered creations on the table.

He smiled.

* * * * *

"Good morning, Hoot!" Derek welcomed Barnaby. Lifting the bench, Barnaby moved past Derek with a quiet 'Morning, Boss,' and hung his coat on a hook. Striding into the back, he prepared himself for the day.

Around lunchtime, the doorbell rang. Derek's voice could be heard over the butchery sounds.

"Well, if it isn't our favorite Mrs. Carl."

"I didn't lose my name when I married him, Nash," she snipped.

"Me either, Connie," he snorted. "I'm Derek."

"Oh, you!"

"How are we feeling today?"

She paused, but then said something that caused Barnaby's ears to prick up. "I'm fine, but I'm worried about Rhonda. She seems to be pulling into herself."

"We saw her at the Halloween party. She seemed fine then."

"That's just a mask, Derek."

Silence. "What about J.T. and Georgie? How are they?"

"Well, that's going pretty well. Rhonda told me that J.T. has a new little friend, Margaret, or something like that. They spend a lot of time together."

"He's got a girlfriend?"

"Don't be ridiculous. He's nine."

"Yeah, but he's almost our height."

Chapter 7.

Connie made a noise. "What did you expect?"
"You never know. Hey, Connie, did you meet Hoot?"
"Who is that?"
"No, Hoot."
"Very funny. No, I have not met *Hoot*."
Barnaby's skin tingled. He was going to meet the mother of his mortal enemy.
"Hoot!" Derek called out. "We need you."
Taking his time, Barnaby set down the knife and took a deep breath. Limping slowly from the back, he inched his head around the corner.
"Hoot, this is Connie, Rhonda's Jensen's mother. You know, Butcher's mother-in-law."
At Butcher's name, Connie flushed.
Barnaby reached out his hand. "Nice to meet you, Connie," he said congenially. "I'm Barnaby Koppel."
Connie stared curiously at her reflection in his sunglasses. She'd heard the rumors.
"Connie Jacobsen."
"They've told me about your son-in-law and your daughter. I'm sorry for your loss." He hoped his words sounded empathetic.
"Thank you. It's still hard to believe."
There was a gap in conversation and Barnaby cleared his throat.
"So, where are you from, Hoot?" Derek asked.
Connie frowned and glanced toward Derek. "I'm able to carry on my own conversation, Derek. I'm also quick enough to pick up the fact that Barnaby would like to get back to work."
Barnaby nodded, but just as he was about to turn, he saw a young boy and girl walking outside the butcher shop. The boy, blonde and quite tall, was measuring his steps next to the red-haired doll next to him. She looked up at him adoringly, gesturing wildly with her hands while the boy smiled and pointed at the shop.
"There's J.T. now," Derek said.
Barnaby's eye fell on the young boy who paused to look through the window. Suddenly, the boy's face transformed into a mask of terror.

Son of a Butcher

Grabbing Murgatroyd by the hand, he pointed, said something and they raced off towards Main Street.

"What got into them?" Derek asked Connie.

"I have no idea, but that was very strange."

Barnaby, too, was puzzled by the boy's reaction.

* * * * *

"It was him, Murg. The Watcher!"

They panted beneath the bank sign, which alternated between the temperature and interest rates in blinking, bright lights.

"Are you serious?"

"Yeah, the Watcher is real. And I thought I was imagining it."

"But… what about the cemetery the other night? You… you threw a grenade at him."

"I know," he said as his eyes widened in fright. "But, how can he be real?"

"Oh, blimey, this is insane."

"You know what this means, though, don't you?"

She shook her head.

"It means," he stretched out the word and leaned down to her, emphasizing the importance of what was coming next, "that he's been watching us for a long time. Years."

"What, like a stalker?"

"Exactly."

She put her hands on his shoulders. "Just because he's been watching doesn't mean he's been *watching*, like a peeping Tom."

"No," J.T. agreed, "but why hasn't he appeared before? Why has he just been hanging around?"

"I have no idea."

"Let's go back and talk to him."

"Are you totally nuts?"

She smiled. "Not *totally*."

"We can't go back there and talk to him. Then he would know…"

Chapter 7.

"Know what? Look, Boyo, you either confront your problems or they bite your pooper pumper while you run away from them."

"Huh? What? They're going to bite my what?"

She patted her rump. "Your twin biscuits; your badonkadonk; your fart box."

J.T.'s eyes widened. Suddenly, he cracked up laughing. "Fart box. I love it."

A few passersby gave a wide berth to them. "Now, Boyo, are we going back there, or what?"

J.T. thought about it. "Or what."

"What?"

"You gave me a choice and I chose." He pulled on her arm. "Come on, we're going to talk to Unca John."

"I don't know," Murgatroyd answered doubtfully. "We've met a few priests over the years and they always seem to be full of answers that don't answer anything."

"Don't worry," J.T. now placed his hands on Murgatroyd's shoulders, "he's not like any priest you've ever met before."

The kids did not find Reverend John Deakins at his home. Instead, they went to the church. It was Monday, his day off, but sometimes he had a lot to do. This annoyed Aunt Leslie a lot, but she *said* she understood.

Opening the front doors of St. Clements, the two climbed the back stairs and into the sanctuary.

"Wowie," Murgatroyd whispered in the dim, large room. "It's been a long time since I've been in a church."

"Really? We come every week."

"What for?" Murgatroyd asked him as they wandered slowly down the center aisle. Her head swiveled as she took in the stained glass windows and the large wooden pews lined with red padding.

"What do you mean, 'What for?' That's what we do on Sundays."

"Yeah, but why? What's the point? The time that I went, it was a bunch of boring songs sung by a bunch of old people, all warbly and stuff." She mimicked the vibrato which echoed in the church. Hearing the resonance, they both began to sing like miniature opera stars.

Son of a Butcher

A door opened near the front of the church and the children's voices shut off like a spigot. John Deakins stepped through the door of his office and into the sacred space where J.T. and Murgatroyd stood transfixed in the middle aisle.

"It's something else when it's empty, isn't it?" John said.

"Yeah," J.T. agreed.

"Sometimes I come in here to pray or just to sit. It always feels like I'm closer to God."

Murgatroyd's eyes narrowed. "You're Unca John?"

He laughed. "J.T. told you my name, I take it."

"He tells me everything."

Once again, John snickered. "I'll reserve judgement on that one."

"You don't look like a priest."

John approached them. "And how is a priest supposed to look?"

"Old and crusty. Scowly and jowly, you know." She put up her hands like claws and barred her fangs.

"Had some bad experiences with church, have you?"

"Just one." Murgatroyd's eyes didn't waver from John's.

"Sometimes that's all it takes." He paused. "You must be Murgatroyd. I'm sorry we haven't met sooner. Other things just…" He didn't know how to finish the sentence.

"Got in the way?" Murgatroyd asked and John nodded. "That's what me mum says sometimes too."

"I'd like to meet your mother."

"Hmmm." Murgatroyd remembered hearing her mother's reflections regarding the clergy and it was not something that could be repeated in church. "Anyway, we're here to talk about angels."

John's eyebrows raised. "Really?"

J.T. pushed his friend backwards slightly. "What she means is, do you remember when we had that conversation about guardian angels and how they watch over us?"

"Vaguely," John replied honestly.

"Well, my guardian angel just showed up."

Frowning, John tilted his head. "Where?"

"At the butchery. He's the new butcher."

Chapter 7.

"Barnaby?"

"Is that his name?" J.T. tried out the man's name on his lips silently. So did Murgatroyd.

"You're saying that the new butcher is your guardian angel."

"Well, yes and no. It's complicated." He scrunched up his face trying to find the right words. He could see care and curiosity reflected in John's eyes. The eyes always told the truth. "I've been seeing him around Amicable for a few years. He's always a long way off."

"Which is not a problem for you," John answered.

"No."

"Where do you see him then?"

J.T. snuck a look at Murgatroyd who encouraged him to speak with her hands. "The other night a few weeks ago, we saw him in the cemetery."

John's face was troubled. "Was he at your dad's grave?"

"Yes."

John was confused. "What did you do?"

"I don't want to tell you."

Now John was concerned. "Why not?"

"Because you'll get mad at me."

"What did you do?"

"He made me do it. I only threw the rock after…" his voice fell away. If J.T. would have been able to shed tears, they would have stung his eyes.

"After…" John momentarily set aside the information that J.T. had thrown a rock at Barnaby.

"He was scratching the statue. He was scratching Mom."

"Are you sure?"

"Unca John, I can see across the alley into the school. On the second floor, there is a teacher with a green swatter chasing a fly. In the corner of his room is a spider, an angry daddy longlegs. His leg is twitching because the teacher ran his meal out of the room." He paused. "You don't think I could see a man doing bad things to my mom's statue from thirty feet away?"

"Point taken. So, you've come to me for advice?"

Son of a Butcher

"That's right, your holiness," Murgatroyd interjected. "We were going to talk to him at the butcher shop, but we got freaked out."

"As you would," John agreed.

"So what do I do?"

"How about we talk to him together?"

J.T.'s eyes lit up. "That's good. But we're not going to tell Mom about this, right?"

"Not yet, J.T. Not yet."

Chapter 8.

The 'meeting' didn't take place for two weeks. Inherent scheduling conflicts (pastoral visits, school, doctor's appointments) stood in the way. After the first week, the conversation faded from John's mind. Although he wanted J.T. to feel comfortable, there seemed to be more pressing matters than a nine-year-old connecting with his 'guardian angel.'

When J.T. showed up at his office after school, little friend by his side, John suddenly remembered that he had promised to go with them.

"Oh, hi, J.T. and Murgatroyd. It's good to see you."

"Your holiness," Murgatroyd bowed.

"Oh, for heaven's sake," he laughed, "I'm just John."

Solemnly, she bowed again. "Just John."

He snorted and turned his attention again to J.T. "I suppose you're ready to meet your guardian angel."

"I don't know. I feel kind of nervous."

"What are you nervous about?"

Murgatroyd moved in. "What if his guardian angel is like the Angel of Death, or something?"

John's eyebrows raised. "Who works as a butcher?"

"Same thing, isn't it?" Murgatroyd copied his eyebrows.

"Fair enough," John responded as he stood from his desk. "How about we go talk to Barnaby and see if he isn't a real person?"

J.T. looked at Murgatroyd for permission. She nodded.

Stepping out from St. Clements' front door, the trio turned right. The cold autumn breeze, full of winter's threat, bit at the backs of their necks. The cold north wind swirled brittle, broken leaves around their feet. Murgatroyd pointed to a squirrel hopping in the branches of a bare tree preparing its home for the change of seasons.

A few intrepid citizens were walking to the library. John stopped to say hello, which was the nice thing to do, but the two kids bounced anxiously behind him. After what seemed a stretch too long of visiting for the kids, they forced their way past John and walked slowly towards the butcher shop. John apologized for the brevity of the visit. The library attenders told him not to worry and he caught up with the kids.

Son of a Butcher

Nearing the shop, J.T. stopped.

"What's wrong?" John asked.

"I don't know. It just feels like... something weird is going to happen."

John felt the hair raise on the back of his neck. Knowing Butcher's ability to see future events, John wondered if J.T. was following in his father's footsteps. "Easy, J.T. We're just going to talk, okay?"

"Okay."

Climbing the steps, John opened the door and allowed the children to enter first. Derek was standing at the counter chatting with Mrs. Larson about the size of the Iowa chops. Nash was writing something in a book. Barnaby was nowhere to be seen.

"Hey, you guys," Nash beamed. "How are ya?"

J.T. mumbled something.

"What's that?" he leaned in.

"Can we talk to the other guy. The butcher?"

Nash turned. "You mean Hoot?"

J.T. shrugged.

"Yeah, sure." Stepping back, he poked his head behind the wall to the back of the shop. "Hoot. You've got more visitors."

Moments later, Barnaby appeared. His sunglasses sparkled brilliantly in the shop lights. They seemed like dark onyxes hiding his identity. J.T. involuntarily took a step back. Barnaby noticed, but he had this effect on most children.

"Hi there, kid," he said.

"Can we talk to you, Mr....?"

"Barnaby. My name is Barnaby."

"Yes, Mr. Barnaby."

His smile was forced, fake. This was Rhonda Redman's son.

Lifting the counter, Barnaby limped over to the coffee area. John Deakins watched from a distance as J.T. sat opposite the butcher. Murgatroyd pulled her chair to sit next to J.T. They were so close their arms almost touched.

"What can I do for you, kids?" Barnaby asked.

"Where do you come from?" J.T.'s voice was low.

"Nice to meet you, too." He looked around, smirking.

88

Chapter 8.

The children were not amused. J.T.'s gift was heightened. He noticed everything about the butcher, from the lines in his scars, the throbbing pulse – he was nervous, too. Why was that? There seemed to be electricity in the air, a gathering of charge. J.T. wished that he could see the man's eyes. They would tell the story.

Sensing J.T.'s discomfort, Murgatroyd reached out and touched his arm, which diffused his tension. Something about her presence, her touch, was calming.

"I'm sorry," J.T. said. "I'm not very good with people."

"Me either, kid."

"His name is J.T., mister," Murgatroyd interjected.

Barnaby's black glasses turned to the little girl. "And what's your name?"

Shifting in her seat, she sat up straight. "Murgatroyd Mary MacDonald."

"Wow, that's a mouthful."

"What's your full name, Barnaby?"

Startled, he tilted his head. He never expected to have to produce a middle name. J.T. caught the reservation. He stared at his throat where his pulse was pounding. "Uh, Barnaby... Kevin Koppel."

"Who was Kevin? Who are you named after?"

Her interrogation unnerved Barnaby, who sat back in his chair. "What, uh, what does it matter? Why the third degree? Have I done something wrong?"

Barnaby's heart jumped. J.T. noticed it. He frowned. "She just likes to know everything."

"Obviously," he attempted another smile.

John Deakins watched like a protective hawk. He couldn't hear everything they were saying, but he did smirk at the sight of two third-graders interviewing a grown man.

"I just had this..." J.T. searched for the right words.

"He thinks you might be a guardian angel," Murgatroyd blurted out. J.T.'s face turned a shade of crimson.

"What?" Barnaby was definitely not expecting that. "Why in the world would you think that? Especially the way I look."

Son of a Butcher

Murgatroyd rested both of her elbows on the small table. "What difference does it make what you look like? He's just seen you around before, but always at a distance."

Barnaby swallowed. Behind the dark glasses, he took in the children with his one eye. Without depth perception, they appeared as two-dimensional cutouts. He wondered how the boy had seen him. He had taken so many precautions. Leaning forward, mimicking Murgatroyd's posture, he said, "Have you ever heard of the word 'impertinent?'"

She shrugged. "Of course. It means, like, something major, or awesome."

He smiled. "Not *important*, impertinent. It means 'impolite,' or rude.' It's usually associated with children."

Murgatroyd frowned. "'Ave you ever heard of the word 'wanker.' It's usually associated with butchers."

Barnaby felt Gustav rising to the surface. Breathing deeply, he calmed his inner anger. "That's pretty funny. You're quick."

"I try my best."

"What do you want to know, really?"

"Where did you come from?" J.T. asked again.

"Ohio."

"What happened to your face?" Murgatroyd asked.

"None of your business, actually."

"Why do you wear sunglasses?"

"Also, none of your business."

Murgatroyd was on a roll. "What are you doing here in Amicable? Are you protecting someone?"

Gustav couldn't be contained any longer and he ground his teeth. Slowly, he reached up and removed his sunglasses revealing his one remaining eye and the patch over the other. Murgatroyd gasped and recoiled from the sight.

"I've come," he said quietly, "to settle down and have a different life than the one I had. So, Murgatroyd Mary MacDonald, I'd appreciate it if you would lay off the questions. I'm not a guardian angel, okay?"

"Bloody hell, I'm sorry."

Chapter 8.

John Deakins could see the mood changing. He, too, was aghast at the sight of the grizzly wounds, but hid his revulsion. "Okay, kids, Barnaby here has probably got to get back to work."

Gustav glanced up at the pastor but did not smile.

"Hey, Hoot, you okay?" Nash asked.

"Fine, Boss," he responded as he put his glasses back over his eyes. "Just fine."

Murgatroyd slid off the chair but J.T. was transfixed. The sight of Barnaby's scar and missing eye replayed in his head. He saw something that sent shivers up and down his spine. He didn't like that feeling one bit. Behind Barnaby's eye, J.T. caught a flash of something – something strange and frightening. It seemed like another face, a snarling, outraged mask of fury which was screaming at the children. When Barnaby put his glasses back on, J.T. was thankful. He hoped that face never made an appearance in real life.

* * * * *

John Deakins hung his coat on the hook just inside the door and stamped his feet. There was no snow yet, thankfully, but his body seemed to be preparing for the eventuality. Setting his keys on the desk, he surveyed the house. As of yet, the only occupant was the smell wafting from the crockpot. Chili. His favorite. The living room was neat and tidy, though the furniture was becoming threadbare. Leslie had wanted to upgrade, but the effort that it took to drive to Clancy seemed too much. They could probably get another year or two out of it before the girls started to complain. The television was mounted on the wall on the dark side of the room. Bookending the television were dusty novels, books which hadn't been read for many months, maybe years. Leslie often asked if he was going to donate them, but John's response was a skipping record. *It would be like getting rid of their children.* Her response was equally repetitive. She'd throw her hands in the air exclaiming, 'All children have to leave the house someday, John.'

To the left of the bookshelf was a 20 x 20 picture of John and Butcher drinking a beer by Lake Ikmakota. It was taken before Butcher's imprisonment in the wheelchair. The sun was soft and setting; the pine

Son of a Butcher

trees filtered the light perfectly. Butcher, in his large way, dominated the picture, but in a very good way. Every time John's gaze fell on the photo, he winced.

Hearing the name *Butcher* echo inside his head, John recalled the interaction at Peterson's just an hour beforehand. The children had left in a huff. Without thanking Barnaby, they had hustled out. Just beyond the door, Murgatroyd tugged on J.T.'s arm urging him to say something. Although John couldn't hear what was said, he could tell J.T. was disturbed. They ran away before he could get to them.

When John glanced back at Barnaby, he had already readjusted his glasses and was making his way back to the cutting area.

"I'm sorry about that," John said lamely. "They're inquisitive kids."

Barnaby shrugged. "It's okay. I'm just a little sensitive about my scars."

John, embarrassed, did not know what to say. Reaching out his hand, he said, "I'm John Deakins, the pastor at St. Clements."

Tentatively, Barnaby shook John's hand and released it quickly. John felt something dead, a despair, emanate from him. Immediately, he felt a sense of pity. Suffering in that form did not usually find a quick recovery. "How long have you been in Amicable?"

"I live in Clancy."

It was obvious that Barnaby wanted to get back to his station, away from any more conversation. More questions. John waited for him but he stepped away and through the counter instead.

Once in the back, Nash shook his head. "I haven't seen him like that for a while. At first, it was like, how do I explain it, like a man who was surfacing from underwater. He seemed to be drowning in something. But now," Nash put a hand on John's shoulder and turned him away from the cutting area, "he seems to be on the verge of actual friendliness. I think he's taken a shining to us even if he struggles with the... human relations side of things."

"He's a butcher after all."

Nash scrunched up his face. "What's that supposed to mean?"

"Not everyone is like you and Derek and..." his voice didn't continue.

Chapter 8.

Nash squeezed his shoulder. "I know," he said softly. "We miss him, too." Their eyes strayed to a plaque on the wall. It read. *World Record Beef Cutting* award – *Dr. Leo 'Butcher' Jensen.* The date and time were scrawled on a sticky pad underneath. He had broken his own 'record' quite a few times before he cut off his finger. Butcher didn't really like the plaque, but the intent was what he loved.

Surfacing from the afternoon's memory, John made his way into the kitchen and saw a note on the table. In Leslie's delicate handwriting, she drew his attention to a few things.

Hello Sweetheart,

Dinner will be ready when we get home. I've just taken the girls to piano lessons. If you could please take out the trash, set the table and open a bottle of wine (for you) for dinner, that would be great. Let's have a nice night together as a family. It's nearly Thanksgiving, so let's give some thanks.

The mother of your three children :)

It was still a strange thing, John admitted to himself, that he was going to be the father of a third child. They thought they were done. The congregation had reacted with applause, which had embarrassed the Deakins family. The girls had sunk lower in their seats, while Leslie's face had turned red. It wasn't as if they cheered when any other woman fell pregnant, but that was the life of an Amicablean public figure.

John followed his wife's directions. By the time they arrived home from piano lessons in a bustle of frantic energy, John had taken out the trash and set the table (even lighting a few grumpy old candles with curlicues of ancient wax stuck to the sides) and opened a bottle of wine. Sniffing it brought up a painfully poignant memory of Butcher.

Son of a Butcher

"Where is this wine from?" John asked already slurring his words. The four of them were on their second bottle of red wine. Rhonda and Leslie had had one glass each, and both women were watching their husbands closely. Neither Butcher nor John was a particularly heavy drinker.

"It's from a place called Spain." Butcher giggled as he drew out the word and pronounced it 'Schpayn.' "Perhaps you've heard of it before."

"What? Schpayn?"

"It's one of the places I want to go before I die," Butcher said, his eyes still mirthful.

"Where in Schpayn do you want to go? On the plains to see the rains?" John believed at that moment he might be the funniest human on the planet. Leslie was quite convinced that he was not.

"Okay, schweetheart, maybe it's time to put the vino down and pick up the agua."

He pulled his wine glass away from her and sloshed wine on the front of his shirt. "Oops," he giggled and then frowned. "I think it's time that you relaxed."

By the look on her face, John knew that he had uttered exactly the wrong thing. Tension filled the room until Butcher leaned forward. Suddenly, he was sober as a nun during Lent. "I've been to Spain before, you know?"

Rhonda tilted her head. She obviously hadn't known this.

"It was back in the early '90's. Barcelona. I had a friend who wanted to travel, see Europe, to meet rich and exotic people. To get sunburnt and besotted on wine and wildness." His eyes melted into a memory of his own, but his words took them with him. "It was a fine, late-summer afternoon, and my friend, I can't remember her... er, I mean, his... name." Butcher giggled and coughed. Finally, the others smiled, too. "We drank a bottle of wine that I'd won in a poker game." He laughed at the thought.

"Somebody dared play poker with you?" John asked.

"Weird, I know. But I hadn't been there long enough to make enemies." He took another sip of his wine and swished it around in his mouth. They waited for him to continue. "So in the last hand of poker, this Spanish fellow, who only spoke broken English, was feeling lucky. So he goes all in. Of course, I had been winning. Of course, I could read him like a book. My gift has no language barrier." Butcher snorted. "I called his last hand. He had two pairs – threes and jacks. The guy puffs out his chest," Butcher mimicked it, "and says, 'You, amigo, are full of bullshit!' and

Chapter 8.

then he reaches behind him and pulls out this bottle of wine. 'I am so confident of my cards, I will wager this!' It was a bottle of Pingus.*"*
Rhonda, Leslie and John simply stared.
Butcher explained. "It's one of the most expensive bottles from Spain."
"Aaah," the other three said simultaneously.
"Anyway," Butcher said slowly, "I had three kings. When the Spaniard saw that he'd lost, he stood up quickly and put up his fists as if wanting to fight me." Butcher smiled at the memory. "He hadn't seen how big I was, so I pushed back my chair and stood up. The guy was about a foot shorter and a lot less muscular. He takes a look at me, salutes me and says, 'Salud, hijo de puta.' I know enough Spanish to translate, 'Congratulations, son of a…" he snuck a look at Rhonda, who was frowning deeply, and finished the sentence, "Son of a butcher." Rhonda's frown unraveled slightly.
"So I took his Pingus, *uncorked it right then and there, and in front of him, I poured the whole bottle of wine over my head. From head to toe I was one big wine stain. It looked like I was bleeding out. The guy's face turns white with fury, and just when I think he's about to break, I wring out my shirt in a small cup and hand it to him and said, 'I saved a little for you, puta.'"*
They roared with laughter. By the time they regained their composure, John had repeated the punchline three times.
After the last repetition, Leslie made it clear to her husband that it was time to go home. John, thrusting out his chin, grabbed Butcher by the arm and pulled him close. Raising the glass above their heads, he tipped out the last bits of red wine over Butcher and him. Laughing hysterically, the two men then stood unsteadily and hugged.
John peered at his wife through wine-dripping eyebrows and smirked. "I'll be a son of a butcher, baby."

"I'll be a son of a butcher, baby," John mumbled to himself.

"What did you say?"

Startled, John turned to find Leslie and the girls behind him. So absorbed in the memory that he hadn't heard them enter.

"Nothing. Nothing. Just thinking."

Leslie placed a brown paper bag of groceries on the table, checked her phone and moved towards her husband. "Hi," she said softly and kissed him on the lips. "How was your day?"

His half-hearted smile hung to one side. "Interesting."

Leslie turned her head to listen, but busied herself by putting the groceries away. John helped. "What happened?"

"J.T. and Murgatroyd stopped by this afternoon so that I could go up to Peterson's with them."

"The shop? Why?"

"J.T. has it in his mind that the new butcher is some kind of guardian angel."

"That's weird." Leslie opened the fridge and placed a gallon of milk in the door.

"Well, you know how kids are." He handed her a bag of carrots and a container of butter. "Anyway, we walked up there and for about ten minutes, J.T. and Murgatroyd, and I'm not kidding, interrogated the poor guy about his past. Like he's going to say, 'The Lord sent me to watch over you.'"

"Doesn't he have a bunch of scars or something?" She received the bacon and frozen pizzas and stuffed them in the upper freezer.

"I'm not sure that's the determining factor of guardian angelhood, but yes, he does. And yes, that question came up."

"And...?"

John handed her the last package of sliced Velveeta. "He got flustered and a little upset. He even removed his sunglasses. He's only got one eye and the other one is really scarred. I can't even imagine what happened to him."

Leslie shut the fridge and moved past her husband to put the bags in the recycling. "It seems like everyone else in town knows."

"We all love the rumor mill, don't we?" he said sarcastically.

"Did he say what happened to him?"

"No, and he made it quite clear to the kids that prying into his business was not particularly welcomed. Murgatroyd, she..."

"She what?"

"She's a real spitfire. It's hard to explain her, but she's like a bucket of sizzling fireworks and you just don't know when she's going to go off."

"I like her. She's a breath of fresh air."

Chapter 8.

He held up his hands. "I know, I know, I do too. I'm just saying she's very different."

"Different is a good thing. We have far too many 'sames' in Amicable again. Everyone is trying to circle the wagons. Can you feel it?"

Shrugging, John turned towards his daughters who were both preoccupied with their phones. Although only ten years old, John and Leslie had tried not to capitulate to their daughters' desires for the devices, but the constant badgering was an unwinnable battle. Leslie justified it to John by telling him that it was safer for them to have phones, but he was unconvinced. It seems like there were so many things that could come through the phone that were far worse than what could happen 'just in case.'

"I get what you're saying. It's just fear. We're all frightened."

Leslie circled his waist with her arms. "But we don't have to be afraid of the new butcher, even if he has some scars. Right?"

John's eyes alit on the outdoor scenery. Only a few birds braved the blustery November winds. And what scarce leafage remained fluttered wildly, clinging desperately to a past already gone.

"I hope not," he said softly.

* * * * *

Gustav lay on his floor stretching. His mind replayed the events of the afternoon when the brats gave him the third degree. The little girl – who did she think she was asking him all those questions? – was the more dangerous of the two. Females tended to be like that.

Stretching his legs out in front of him, Gustav grunted as his marched his fingers towards his toes. Each inch was torture, but the pain drove him deeper into the reserves of his anger. As his hamstrings and back screamed out, Gustav imagined the pain which Rhonda would feel. But now there was also another face, a young girl, who needed a little comeuppance also.

Rolling onto his front, Gustav began to do pushups. His quivering muscles told him to stop, but the vision for the future encouraged him to continue. When he thought he couldn't do any more, he forced himself to do one more. Each pushup was a symbolic reminder of the perseverance it would take to finish the job.

Once finished, Gustav gulped air and headed to the cupboard for a glass. Filling it with water, he drank deeply and then refilled it before moving to his computer. Moments later, while Gustav was checking and rechecking his calculations, he was happily surprised when an email popped up. When he opened it, he smiled.

He had passed his driver's test. After fifteen grueling years, Gustav Keller was legally able to operate a vehicle again.

Things were looking up for Gustav. The part of him that was Barnaby wanted to celebrate, but there was no room for him in this moment. Swallowing this good feeling, Gustav touched his eye patch and focused on the task ahead. Tomorrow, he would purchase a car from the dealership in Clancy. Something innocuous; a second-hand pickup, maybe. Once he had the pickup, Danny would take a backseat in the upcoming days. Less of Danny meant less chance of Danny talking. That was a good thing.

Gustav checked his timeline. Just a few weeks until Thanksgiving, then the countdown would begin.

All good things to those who wait.

Chapter 9.

Thanksgiving was a time of wonderment for Amicableans. Typically, they would wonder how much they could eat in one day, how long their nap was going to be, which shops they would drive to on Black Friday and when the snow would begin to set in again. When times were devoid of stress, the citizens, just like in every other city, would pull back into their individual homes and be grateful. But peace was never a foregone conclusion even if there was no present conflict. On that particular Thanksgiving, Amicableans could not have known the coming firestorm. Just like those New Yorkers who went to sleep on September 10, 2001, only to have their world shredded above and below them, so did the Amicableans casually believe that this irenic point in their history would continue.

It was not to be.

Glory and Murgatroyd piled into their car and drove past the reconstructed elevator, beyond the school to the Jensen house where J.T. and Georgie were waiting with Gabi and Michelle for Murgatroyd to arrive.

Although Gabi and Michelle were not quite as enamored of Murgatroyd as J.T. was, they were young enough to put aside their petty differences for some good-natured play. J.T. and Murgatroyd had constructed the treehouse to a point where it had a floor. As of yet, the treehouse was bereft of walls, but there was enough room for them to squeeze onto the boards. The ladder was enticing for the children. Even though Rhonda worried that one (or possibly all) might fall from the burgeoning treehouse, she hoped the ground was still soft enough that they'd bounce rather than break.

Murgatroyd bounced in her seat excitedly. "Mum, our very first Thanksgiving! All the food! People everywhere!"

"Yes, it should be fun," Glory said.

"You don't sound as excited as me."

Glory glanced at her daughter as she drove. "Well, I just don't know the others as well. I know Rhonda. The pastor and his wife seem cold, I guess."

"I like them."

"I'm sure I will also." *Eventually*, she added inwardly.

As they pulled up in front of the Jensen house, the girls raced to the car while J.T. watched from the porch. By the time they were rolling to a stop, Murgatroyd had already unbuckled her seatbelt and thrown the door open. Glory chastised her on the way out, but the kids were already on their way to the backyard leaving Glory to carry in her homemade meat pie. The process of making it had brought back many memories of her time in England, some positive, some less so. As the scent wafted up from the backseat, her mouth watered. Reaching down to the seat, she picked up the tray and carried the pie to the front porch. After ringing the doorbell with her elbow, she waited. She could hear the children's laughter over the house. Glory was happy for her daughter.

The door swung open, and Rhonda greeted her with a smile and a hug. "Happy Thanksgiving!"

"Likewise," Glory responded barely holding on to the baked goods in front of her.

"Can I take those for you?"

Glory handed them over.

"You've made a pie! How wonderful! I'll put it with the other ones."

Glory followed Rhonda into the house where Leslie and John were standing in the kitchen holding cups of apple cider. Looking slightly uncomfortable, John and Leslie greeted Glory with their smiles. Rhonda wanted them to like Glory. She had moved into a prominent place in her life. Leslie was still her best friend, but Glory had filled a need for moving on.

"How are you?" Glory asked as she watched Rhonda place the meat pie near the other sweet ones on the counter.

"Fine, thank you."

Eyes wandering around the house, they rested on Leslie who was watching her intently. "I'll show you around," Leslie said as she moved toward the Englishwoman.

"Marvelous," Glory said as Leslie pulled her into the living room.

"It's good that you could come," Leslie said.

Chapter 9.

"I'm so nervous. I've never been to a Thanksgiving party before."

"What are you nervous about?"

Glory scanned the room unwilling to look at the woman to her side. "The customs, the things we say. Do you shout out, 'Happy Thanksgiving,' like 'Happy Christmas?' or are we formal, bowing, you know, scraping our foreheads on the floor in reverence. I mean, your husband's a priest for God's sake." She reddened. "Jesus, sorry about that." Now, smacking her head she held her hand there. "Bollocks, I'm such a tosser."

Leslie laughed. "Relax, Glory. He's a pastor, not the pope."

"Thank Christ for that."

"Sure," Leslie smirked. Leading her farther into the living room, Glory saw more photos. Generally, when she came over to Rhonda's house, they stayed in the kitchen. Now that she saw the family photos, she could begin to understand a little bit more of Rhonda's life.

"Chri... miny, he's a big sucker." Glory had stopped to stare at a photo of Rhonda, Butcher and the kids on the shore of Ikmakota.

"He was. And he had an enormous heart, too." Leslie's eyes lingered on Butcher who was smiling widely. He appeared to be the proudest man in the world.

"Rhonda hasn't said much about him."

Leslie nodded and released Glory's arm. "She wants to talk about him and then again, she doesn't. It hurts a lot. They were kind of a perfect match."

"They're both pretty tall."

Leslie smirked. "It wasn't just that. Rhonda is stubborn and Butcher was flexible. Rhonda understood things whereas Butcher could see them. When Rhonda couldn't laugh, Butcher couldn't stop. They were amazing together."

"So he died?"

Turning away from Glory, Leslie paused in front of another photo of Butcher with the Peterson twins in the shop. "About three years ago. Lou Gehrig's."

"I'm sorry, I don't know who that is."

Son of a Butcher

"It's a what. ALS. Motor Neuron. It affects the nerves. You know, the disease that Stephen Hawking had?"

"Oh, God. That's awful."

Once again nodding, Leslie's lips pressed tight before she spoke. "Other than dementia, there aren't many worse diseases. He just kind of melted away from us. But he always kept his mind. Always the same Butcher."

"Is that why his headstone is made out of wax?"

"Yes. It's quite powerful, isn't it?"

"As far as headstones go."

Leslie smiled. "It's probably best if you don't bring it up too much."

"I wouldn't think of it." She already had quite a bit.

Rhonda poked her head in from the kitchen. "Are you ready to eat?"

Less than a minute later, five young bodies bounded through the back door and down the hallway towards the kitchen. After a noisy handwashing, they perched themselves around the table. Georgie and the twins on one end with J.T. and Murgatroyd on the other. The adults' table, because there were fewer of them, was a green card table with metal legs. Although shaky, the table had withstood many Thanksgivings and knee knocks.

"Now," John started as they settled in, "who would like to say 'grace?'"

The children looked around at each other. Surprisingly, it was Murgatroyd who volunteered. "Let us bow our heads," she said dramatically. "Oh, Lord, thank thee today for thou friends and thine goodness. Givest us thine mercy and supplication and benevolence." She opened an eye to look towards John who was grinning. "And," she included loudly, "forgive us our sins as we return the favor. Now that we're about to swalloweth the food, guide it into our bellies where it will be turned into…"

"Murg!" Glory's eyes widened.

"What? I was about to say 'energy.' Jeesh." Murgatroyd bowed her head again. "In thine holiest of thy names, Amen."

The kids all clapped which made Murgatroyd beam.

Chapter 9.

"That was wonderful," John said. "Where did you learn to pray like that?"

She shrugged. "Me mum dropped me off at the Anglican church a couple of times while she went shopping on Sunday mornings. I listened."

John smiled. "You're very good at remembering things."

"I know." Murgatroyd had already reached for the mashed potatoes and was heaping them on her plate.

With saucer-sized eyes, the children loaded up their plates with turkey and stuffing (which was also a new experience for Murgatroyd), cranberry sauce, green bean casserole with French fried onions on top, mashed yams with melted marshmallows (which was decidedly *not* Georgie's favorite, but she was required to take a small spoonful anyway) and the strangest of jiggly sweet salads – lime Jell-O with pears suspended in the middle. As the dishes went by Glory, she glanced around to see the correct portion size and way to situate both sweets and savories on the same plate. It didn't seem to matter much as John heaped everything on his plate and dug in with relish.

Glory was disappointed to see that her own offering had not been set out, but perhaps her meat pie was not considered appropriate for Thanksgiving. Oh well, she shrugged and dug in. If nobody ate it, she'd be able to take it back home with her.

Conversations ranged from what kinds of things 'would you definitely not eat,' (Georgie drew the limit at grasshoppers) to Christmas traditions. While the discussions meandered, Rhonda's thoughts flitted back to Butcher and his mother's tradition of moving house around Christmas. Glad that they weren't relocating, yet somewhat stirred to *move*, Rhonda smiled as she perused her friends. Maybe she was beginning to recover. Maybe this year would be better than the last.

Near the end of the first mounded plate of food, Glory swallowed and motioned with her fork. "Have any of you had an interaction with the new butcher? What's his name, Murg? Barry?"

"Barnaby."

The pressure in the room increased and silence followed.

"Why do you ask?" John's voice broke it.

Son of a Butcher

"Murg and I were chatting the other day. She said that J.T. and her had talked to him. I was wondering if you knew who he was. His background?"

"He's an interesting one. He keeps to himself. Lives in Clancy, or so the twins tell us." Gabi and Michelle turned to listen to their mother. "Not you two. The Petersons." They went back to eating. "No one seems to know where the scars came from."

J.T. shifted uncomfortably in his seat. He didn't know how the butcher came to have them, but he did know what was underneath. He had seen it.

Leslie continued. "I've only seen him once, but that was just in passing. He doesn't come out from the back that much."

"On the day we were there, he seemed quite... agitated." John wiped his mouth with a paper napkin imprinted with a cornucopia and gourds. "It's to be expected, I guess. I feel bad for him. It must be hard to make friends." He grunted. "We know that outsiders can struggle in Amicable." Suddenly, he realized his faux pas when he looked at Glory. "Maybe you've encountered that already, Glory."

She shook her head. "Not really. People have been very friendly. The ladies in the exercise group have taken me under their wing and showed me the ropes. Very nice ladies, those."

"Yes," John said under his breath, "just don't believe everything that they tell you. They can bend the truth slightly for a good story."

"Oh, I know that." Glory insisted. "It's just great to see how people are the same wherever you go, whether Chigwell or Amicable."

During the discussion, Rhonda remained quiet. She had not met the new butcher, nor would she go out of her way to do so. Others were helpful and picked up her meat for her, but one of these days, she would have to go. Even if it was just to take the next step of recovery. The hardest thing for her had been to sell Butcher's office, the Chop Shop. Cleaning out the memories, the photos and the books, the furniture – she had donated most of it to Goodwill.

"Maybe I'll get to know him a little bit." Glory sounded as if she was asking permission.

"That would be a great idea," John said.

"I could let you know anything that I find out."

Chapter 9.

"No, no, that's fine," Leslie responded, but her voice meant *Yes, yes, that would be great.*

Conversation stilled uncomfortably until John clapped his hands together. "Now, I have just this much room," he indicated with his thumb and forefinger, "for dessert."

The kids voiced their enthusiasm for this idea. Glory glanced over at Murgatroyd's plate. She had finished everything except the odd Jell-O concoction and a few green beans pushed under the side of her plate. Glory had chided her about the practice of food deceit, but she had not broken her yet.

Rhonda stood with Leslie, moved to the counter and began to slice the pies. "What does everyone want?" Leslie asked.

The kids agreed on a variety of pies, pecan being the most popular. Glory had always wondered what pumpkin pie would taste like. For her, the thought of mashing up a pumpkin and baking it in pastry seemed revolting, but as it was her first Thanksgiving, it was worth trying.

"I'll have a piece of Glory's pie," John said.

Glory frowned. She thought this strange as the savory course was already done, but maybe this was how they did it in Amicable.

"Who wants ice cream on theirs?"

All the children raised their hands.

So did John.

Now Glory was very confused. It was one thing to serve a meat pie with the other desserts, but to top it with ice cream? That seemed downright disgusting. But, they were Americans.

As the small Corelle plates were placed in front of each person, they licked their lips with anticipation. When the pie was placed in front of John, the ice cream had melted over the pie hiding the meat. Glory grimaced, but she didn't want to offend her hosts.

"All right everyone, dig in," Leslie encouraged.

With great relish, the children shovelled the pecan pie into their mouths. Glory tasted her pumpkin pie and was surprised by its sweetness. Whatever Rhonda had done to the pumpkin had magically transformed it from an object of scorn into one of enjoyment. She nodded and watched John cut the tip off his piece of pie and run it through the melted ice cream. Then, with a smile he toasted her with his fork and stuck it in his mouth.

The effect of meat pie and ice cream was instantaneous.

Suddenly, the smile froze on his face and he stopped chewing. The corners of his mouth turned down and his nostrils widened.

He gagged. It wasn't a quick, silent throat reflex, but a full *Aaaaawkgh*. He covered his mouth with his hand, but that brought on another gag.

"John!" Leslie exclaimed. "What is it? Are you okay?"

With great effort, John Deakins swallowed the large piece of meat pie that he had swirled in ice cream and chewed. The mixed flavors of beef, mushroom, gravy and vanilla ice cream were almost too much for his stomach.

One last gag forced its way from his throat and his face reddened as he turned towards Glory whose own face had widened in horror.

"Oh, God. Is it that bad?"

"No, no," John held up his hands, "I just wasn't ready for it. What... er... what is it?"

"Beef and mushroom pie. It's a traditional autumn meal in England. I thought it would be a nice tradition to include with yours." A tear formed in the corner of her eye.

Rhonda looked over at Leslie who was struggling to control the laughter that was about to erupt. "Oh, Glory," Rhonda came around to her and hugged her, "you've just made our entire Thanksgiving." She broke into a small chuckle. Leslie caught it then passed on to John and the children. Soon, the entire room was filled with cackling laughter. Taking deep breaths, John waved his napkin in front of his face. The cornucopia was stained with the remainder of mushroom and gravy.

"I haven't done something wrong?"

"No, absolutely not," Rhonda answered once her laughter was under control. "I don't think John has ever had a meat pie before, let alone topped with ice cream?" Her face contorted again and suddenly the laughter re-emerged.

Glory felt a sudden glow, not that she was being teased, but that she had been part of something bigger and better than she had ever

Chapter 9.

known. These people, mostly strangers, had invited and accepted her into their home. Now, their Thanksgiving happiness had soldered them together. Wiping the tear from her eye, she smiled

"Would anyone like some more?" she asked.

The kids pushed themselves back from the table and rushed for the door. Rhonda brought them back. "Put your dishes in the dishwasher, kids, and then you can go out and play."

Retreating back to their table, they hurriedly packed the dishwasher and ran out of the house before the parents could change their minds and make them do more work.

Once outside, the kids continued their construction efforts. The floor of the treehouse had begun to take shape. Discarded 2 x 4's (J.T. and Murgatroyd had begged the lumber yard for castoff pieces which Jeff Davids had reluctantly donated) had been hammered together across two lower branches roughly six feet in the air. There were small gaps between the boards which couldn't be helped, but by the end of Thanksgiving, J.T. and Murgatroyd hoped to have the floor covered with castoff carpet, and the sides raised with holes for windows. At first, they talked about making it two stories, but then reality set in. Gabi and Michelle were not that much help, and Georgie proved more of a distraction than anything else.

"Now," Murgatroyd stood with her hands on her hips, a diminutive forewoman barking out orders, "J.T. is going to climb the ladder and stand on the base. He'll haul on the rope while we steady it going up. Then, we'll pass the nails and hammer and he'll put it together."

"Why does J.T. get to do all the fun stuff?" Georgie complained.

"Because he's the boy."

Georgie snorted. "That's stupid."

"I don't make the rules."

"Obviously, you do," Gabi responded.

"Only some of them." Murgatroyd moved closer to Gabi who backed up. Michelle inched closer to protect her sister.

"This is crazy," J.T. stepped in as he towered over all the girls. "If everyone wants to take a turn, by all means."

"Sounds good to me." Georgie brushed her hands and smiled up at her big brother.

J.T. climbed the rickety steps which were both nailed to the trunk and held together with rope. Once, he almost lost his balance, but he steadied and finished climbing. Tossing the rope over a limb using it like a pulley, he lowered it to the girls where they corded the plywood board and stood it up. J.T., using his strength, hoisted the side up. He then tied the board off and began to nail it into place. When he had hammered the ends in, he invited the girls to come up. Georgie was the first one up the ladder. As she stood beside her big brother, he held the board in place. Without any stretch of the imagination, Georgie was a hopeless hammerer. Holding it near its head, she barely produced enough force to set the nail. J.T., though, accustomed to his sister's weakness, waited patiently for her to give up. Handing the hammer back with a smile, she climbed down the ladder and jumped the last few steps.

Gabi and Michelle arose in succession but soon gave up also. Murgatroyd watched with amusement. She'd done some 'construction' work with her mother before and knew how to wield a hammer.

Grabbing the hammer, she hefted it and began to nail in the rest of the row at the base. While she pounded, J.T. looked up. His eyes caught movement between the two houses, past the school, beyond the church and next to the bowling alley. Focussing his eyes like no one else, he was surprised to see Barnaby Koppel limping up the street. He had something in his hands, a few packages, it looked like. Brown paper tied up with string. J.T. waited for Barnaby to reappear, but he was interrupted by Murgatroyd.

"Hey, Boyo. Haul up the next piece."

J.T. untied the back half of the house and made sure that it would remain standing before tossing the rope back down. Up came a wall and J.T. positioned it. Once again, Murgatroyd went to work hammering. While this was happening, the bystanders below grew bored and soon, Georgie was leading the twins back into the house to play with dolls.

"Looks like it's just you and me, Boyo."

"I guess so." His eyes shifted back to the bowling alley where Barnaby came back out. He was one package lighter.

Chapter 9.

* * * * *

Gustav made his way out of the bowling alley with difficulty. Walking had grown easier for him, but steps were still hard. And because his hands were full, his balance was off also. Wincing as he found the ground, he paused and leaned against the siding. The remaining two packages were heavy, but he was able to keep moving.

Gustav thought about the packages in his arms. Tiny bundles of joy. The idea had been fertilized the year before after he watched the community miraculously recover from the elevator explosion. The elevator's demise, in and of itself, obviously had not been enough. Something else would have to rip its heart out.

And these packages were just the way to do it.

Walking across the street, Gustav leaned his head back and pondered the church's steeple. Testing the door, he was pleased to note that even in today's climate of theft and destruction, the church leaders had left them open.

After entering the foyer, he climbed the stairs with difficulty to the sanctuary and made his way down the aisle. As he looked to the east, the stained glass visage of St. Clement stared beatifically down at the empty seats.

Shaking his head, Gustav unwaveringly marched up the aisle on his way to the altar. Uninterested in placing his offering, Gustav smiled malevolently.

* * * * *

J.T. leaned to his left and watched Barnaby enter the church.

"What are you looking at?" Murgatroyd asked as she finished a nail.

"Barnaby."

"What? Where?" She stood up next to him. In the diminishing light of the afternoon, she struggled to even see the street.

"He's going into the church."

"That's weird."

"I think so too."

It didn't even register anymore with Murgatroyd that J.T. could see from that distance. "I wonder what he's doing in there. Do you think he's going to pray?"

J.T. remembered what he had seen in Barnaby's face. "Maybe."

"Should we go check it out?"

He glanced down at her. "Do you want to?"

"Bloody right, I do." Her grin lit up her face. "We've got to keep an eye on your guardian angel."

"He's not my guardian angel." J.T.'s eyes were drawn back to church.

"I know that, but maybe he needs us."

J.T. snorted. "I doubt it."

Murgatroyd began to descend the ladder. "Come on, let's go."

A moment later, J.T. jumped to the ground.

Looking behind him at the unfinished treehouse, two walls and no roof, J.T. grabbed Murgatroyd's hand and opened the back door of the house. "We're going for a short walk!" he yelled out and shut the door without waiting for a response.

They crept stealthily along the side of the school and past the playground and parked themselves in Peter and Ginny Olson's pine tree. From there, they had a birds-eye view of the church.

"Do you think he's come out yet?"

"No, I haven't seen him."

"Maybe he's fast," Murgatroyd countered.

J.T. shook his head and frowned. "He's a half-blind, limping butcher. He won't be breaking any speed records."

"I suppose you're right."

Rubbing their hands, the two tried to keep warm. For fifteen minutes they waited in the branches of the tree. After each minute, Murgatroyd was certain that he had already left the premises and let J.T. know. He told her to practice patience, which she replied with a certain hand gesture of two fingers which J.T. did not understand, but assumed it meant the same as the American one finger.

Finally, Barnaby emerged from the church and shut the door behind him. He still had one package with him. After leaving the church,

Chapter 9.

Barnaby looked both ways and then made his way to the school.
"What the bloody hell is he doing?"
"I'm not sure," J.T. said, "but I want to know what's in those packages."

Chapter 10.

Although it was not Gustav's intention to be so public in the distribution of his packages, he felt an air of rebellious indifference while doing it. If the commoners caught him, so be it. Sooner or later, everything would be out in the open anyway. While he placed his brown paper packages, tied up with string, he truly realized that they represented his favorite thing – to reset the Fates.

Though he had no idea he was being watched as he crossed the street from the bowling alley to the church to the school, he felt a spring in his step. Glorious things were about to change, things which would create a different set of circumstances. Maybe he'd be able to move on, move away from Amicable and the soon-to-be-despised Rhonda Jensen, nee Redman.

When Barnaby opened the door to Peterson's Butchery that morning, he had no idea that his life was about to shift even more than it already had.

Because, on the other end of Main Street…

Carley opened the X-Er-Size studio. Those who came regularly felt that after the Thanksgiving feeding frenzy, some calorie-burning would be highly necessary. Carley dropped the keys once, then stooped to pick them up from the ground. Frost gilded the front entry. She briefly wondered how soon before the snows would accumulate and she'd be shoveling snow from her stoop.

Letting the door shut behind her, Carley moved into the studio and flicked on the overhead fluorescent lights. Humming, flickering, buzzing, finally they caught like an old engine and came to life.

Whistling non-melodically, Carley dropped her keys into the wicker basket at the front of the room and flipped on the disco ball. The scintillating, reflected lights moved around the walls flashing over photos of famous workout artists, Jane Fonda and Richard Simmons among them. Carley had a signed sweat band from Richard, one of her most prized possessions, that read, *Work it, girlfriend.*

Chapter 10.

As she loaded her MP3 player with Christmas music, the front door opened and the women started entering.

"All right everyone, settle down." Carley switched the music to Christmas dance and soon they were bopping back and forth, three-pound weights in their hands. The exercise was anything but strenuous, but the good-natured laughter seemed as health-improving as the side-to-side stepping. For the next fifteen minutes, they continued their movements until Carley grabbed a towel and wiped her face.

"Let's take a break, ladies."

Leona took a swig. "Has anyone heard any more about the new butcher?"

Donna shook her head and adjusted her dry sweatbands. "I heard he's got a new car."

"What kind of car?"

"A Ford, I think." Donna didn't really know, but it was a safe bet.

"Why don't Carley and Glory go and talk to him today," said Penny.

"Me?" Glory held a hand to her chest. "Why me? I've only been here for a little while."

"Because you can *empathize* with him," Donna tapped her temple. "You know what it's like. You said so yourself."

"Just because I can *empathize* with his situation doesn't mean I want to be the first to interrogate."

"I'd love to be part of that." Carley's face lit up.

"It's settled then." Donna nodded confidently. Their faces all turned towards Glory whose mouth had dropped open. "I don't know about this."

"Come on, it will be fun," Carley caught her elbow and linked it.

"And we'll be waiting just outside," Leona said, "minding our own business." They packed up their bags and excitedly meandered southwards on Main Street, past the grocery store and hardware to Peterson's Butchery.

Barnaby Koppel checked his watch at 10:47.

Son of a Butcher

"Hey, Hoot," Derek mimed with his hands, "you've got some visitors."

Frowning, Barnaby wiped his hands on his apron and then washed them in the sink. Every time he had visitors, a bad conversation occurred. He took out his earplugs before journeying into the front of the shop. He was surprised to see two women waiting for him. He'd never met either one of them personally, but he'd seen them around. Especially the bigger one.

"Hello."

"Oh, hi, Mister Barnaby. I'm Carley from the X-Er-Size studio, you know the one on the end of the street across from Human Beans, the coffee shop. That's a really great place. Good coffee and good prices. We usually go there..."

"Excuse me, Carley, but..." he interrupted her monologue by raising his hand as if wondering what the point of their visit was.

The other woman interjected. "I'm Glory MacDonald. Nice to meetcha." She shook his hand and noticed it was rough and clammy. When she retracted it, she tried to not make it too obvious that she was wiping her hands on her blue jeans.

Barnaby looked Glory up and down. She was smallish, with fidgety movements – twitchy, as if she was nervous about something. She had a nice figure and an alluring accent.

"Hello, Glory. I'm Barnaby Koppel."

"We've come to introduce ourselves. Thought it would be the nice thing to do."

He shrugged. "I've been here for two months now."

"Ah, yes," Carley leaned into him, "we can be a bit, how shall we say, slow in our welcome."

Barnaby didn't respond, signifying agreement.

"Would you care to sit down?" Carley pointed to the small coffee area. "Derek, would you please pour us some coffee?"

"Mine with milk, please." Glory pinched her fingers indicating the amount.

"What do I look like? A secretary?" Derek's indignation was good-humored, but it was apparent that fixing coffee was not on his list of priorities.

Chapter 10.

"What if I said 'yes?'" Carley answered.
"Then I'd say get your own dang coffee."
"Tut, tut, Nash. Poor customer service leads to poor sales."
Grumbling, Derek moved towards the coffee machine. "I'm Derek, by the way."
Carley giggled. "Now, Mr. Koppel, tell us about yourself."
Barnaby felt Gustav begin to surface, so he took a deep breath. "Why does everyone start a conversation with me in exactly the same way?"
Embarrassed, Carley blinked rapidly and looked to Glory to take over, but she refused. "What do you mean?" Carley asked.
"It's like everybody wants to know some information about me, but I have no idea who you are or why you want to know. If I tell you about myself, you'll probably traipse outside and blab to those ladies over there."
Their eyes swiveled to glance towards the exercise group women who were standing on the opposite side of the street, in the cold, drinking coffee.
"Guilty as charged, your honor," Glory said as Carley's eyes widened. Derek came back with three Styrofoam cups filled with coffee, two black and one with creamer in it.
Barnaby's eyes fell on Glory. "Finally, someone who speaks the truth."
"I'm new around here too," she said with lowered voice.
"Gee, I couldn't have guessed that."
"They wanted to know all sorts of things about me, also."
Motioning towards the group across the street, he pointed. "Who? Those ladies?" Linda caught the movement and his finger. She overtly turned and pretended to point at the sky. Jeannie followed her and pointed also.
"Yes, them, but others too."
"Did you find it insulting?" Barnaby asked.
"At first, but then I got to know them. They're great." Carley watched the dialogue and suddenly felt out of place.
"Why do they want to know stuff about me?"

Glory fingered the rim of her cup and then took a sip of the coffee. Cringing, she set it back on the table. "What the bloody hell is that?"

"You asked for coffee and milk," Carley said.

"That's not milk."

"It's creamer. It's just like milk."

"Look, I don't even know what 'creamer' is. Just because 'cream' is written on the label doesn't mean that it has anything to do with milk. Just because a carton reads orange juice doesn't mean any oranges have been squeezed. Ever heard of Tang?"

Carley's face lit up. "Ooooh! I love that stuff! So squeezy good."

"I rest my case."

Barnaby watched the interruption with interest. The Englishwoman was fascinating. Her accent was beautiful and she had a nice face. "I've got an idea," he said. "How about we go tit for tat."

Glory almost spilled her creamed coffee. "Pardon. Is it polite to mention that..." she motioned to her chest.

Carley snorted. "It's tit for tat, silly. It means that you each give something, like information. Boy," she sipped, "I'm glad I'm here to help translate."

"Speaking of which," Barnaby said, "I'd feel more comfortable if Glory and I could get to know each other alone, so would you mind crossing the street to the rest of your friends?" Carley glanced at them. Jeannie waved and Linda play-swatted her arm.

"You want me to go?" Carley looked crestfallen.

"Yes."

"Well, okay then." She pushed back her chair and stood. Moping, she carried her coffee past the counter and out the door. The other women waited impatiently for her to cross the street before they circled around her. After Carley had finished speaking, they returned their collective gaze to the butcher's shop window.

"How did you get mixed up with them?" Barnaby asked.

"I was lonely."

"And they're your kind of people?" he chewed on the Styrofoam cup. It squeaked.

Chapter 10.

"I don't really have a 'kind' of people," she responded, eyes lowered. "I'm just looking for kind people."

"That's a nice turn of phrase."

She smiled. "They are kind, you know?"

His mouth pursed. "Not yet."

"I'm sorry."

"It's your turn," he said.

"It's my turn, what?"

"To ask me a question."

Glory blurted out the first question that came to mind. "What happened to your eye?"

Barnaby Koppel was used to the question. He'd made up many stories over the years. He had been in a car accident. A diving mishap. He even convinced a few men in Clancy that a classmate had thrown a fork at him. People were gullible.

For some reason, though, Barnaby felt a strange connection with this woman. Outsider's intuition, or something like that. A lie felt somehow profane, more painful than the truth. "I was in jail." His face registered the shock that he felt in speaking the truth and he wanted to cover it up quickly, but he was unable.

"You're just saying that, aren't you Mr. Koppel."

"What do you think?"

She attempted to read his face, but his sunglasses hid most of the damage. "I'd like to think you were yanking my chain."

"Why?" he prodded.

"Because you're mysterious. A man waltzes into a small town like Amicable, no one can open the locked box that's his history, and it seems a bit perplexing that you'd spill the beans to a total stranger who has a gaggle of gossipers across the street."

"Mysterious. I like that." He put his arms behind his head and noticed Derek and Nash smirking at him. "Well, I suppose I should get back to work."

"Wait…" Glory stopped him. "Wait. Perhaps we could have a cup of coffee together, sometime after you're done working. I work at Human Beans, the one that…"

Son of a Butcher

"I have a better idea. How about we have dinner together? Tomorrow night. Sunday night. Come to Clancy. There's a restaurant there. The Creek Restaurant. We could get to know each other better."

She studied him. It was dangerous to do this thing, but she was tired of playing it safe already. She'd changed her hair color and her clothing style. What about a little more spice in her life? Rhonda would babysit Murgatroyd for the night.

"I… well…"

Barnaby's heart fell. "Of course, don't worry about it. I was being too forward."

"No, that's not it at all. I simply have to find someone to mind my daughter, Murgatroyd."

Suddenly, things clicked quite neatly into place. A new avenue opened for him. His inner Gustav sat up at attention. So, this woman was the mother of that brat. He should have known. With that accent! How could he have not put two and two together?

He leaned to the table across from her. "I hope that you can find someone. We might have a night to remember."

Glory felt a sudden chill. What is excitement or danger? Both?

Chapter 11.

For the third time, Murgatroyd exasperatedly repeated that Glory looked very nice. Each time she came out from her closet wearing a new outfit, the first a sinuous dress, much too thin for the cold weather, Murgatroyd nodded and smiled politely.

"I can't wear this," Glory said as she stripped it off and headed back into the bedroom. Five minutes later, blue jeans and a sweater.

"Too casual?" she asked.

Murgatroyd gave her the thumbs up, but Glory shook her head again. "No, you're right. I still want to be mysterious."

Finally, the white pantsuit came out with a woolen turtleneck to match. Pulling her hair back behind her ears, she revealed a face that hadn't been so nervous and excited in a long time. Murgatroyd raised her eyebrows and smiled hesitantly.

"Yes?" Glory asked.

"Yes!"

Glory kissed the top of Murgatroyd's head.

As Glory nervously drove to Clancy, she whistled happily to the radio. As the time passed, she thought about her daughter and how excited Murgatroyd was about spending the night at the Jensen house. It was her first sleep over in America. Even though she always assumed it would be at another little girl's house, Murgatroyd was quite happy that it was with J.T. At first, Rhonda expressed concern that boys and girls should not do sleepovers but at nine years of age, Glory convinced her that the children would be okay.

While Glory turned right to approach Clancy, Rhonda pondered how quickly J.T. was growing. Too fast, in Rhonda's opinion. But he was also opening up in a way that she had always hoped. Because most of his first formative years were overshadowed by Butcher's sickness and death, J.T. had built walls behind which he hid his amazing, beautiful, strange personality (and gift). Now that he was coming out from behind the wall, Rhonda was grateful for the MacDonalds – both of them – who had helped new life start to bloom.

Son of a Butcher

  Rhonda went to the back door of the house and peered through the dirt-streaked window at the two kids putting the roof on the treehouse. J.T. was grinning as he nailed the boards from the top. Eventually, he said, they'd get some shingles from the lumberyard and tack those on also. Rhonda was impressed by the largess of the treehouse, but even more by their stick-to-itiveness. She never really thought they'd be able to do it, but she was grateful that they had a place of their own.

  J.T. and Murgatroyd did not notice her standing in the window watching them.

  "What did you think about church today?" Murgatroyd asked.

  "Same as always. Long."

  "Unca John is pretty good though, right?"

  J.T. swung the hammer. *Smack. Smack. Smack.* "Sure."

  "Is he really your uncle?"

  He gave her a look. *Smack.* "Of course not, but my mom doesn't have any brothers or sisters, so I've got lots of substitute uncles and aunts instead."

  "He seems to really like those stories out of the Bible. Do you think they're real?"

  J.T. shrugged. "I like stories. When you like stories, they're real."

  Murgatroyd handed him another board which he positioned and began to pound. *Smack. Smack.*

  "Did you see Barnaby at church?"

  Stopping, J.T. looked down at her through the shell of the treehouse. She was sitting cross-legged. "Of course."

  "It's weird that he was there, don't you think?" Murgatroyd picked at her fingers.

  "Why?"

  "It doesn't seem like it… fits him. I don't know how to explain it," she spoke towards her hands. "But it's like he was there in spite of church, you know. And worse yet, he was talking to me mum."

  J.T. rested his head on his forearm which was positioned on the roof. He had seen that also, but he didn't want to say anything. "What did he say?"

Chapter 11.

"I couldn't hear, but she was kind of giggly. But then, she got taken away by the rest of the ladies. I don't know where he went after that."

"He went away," J.T. stated simply.

"Where? Did you watch?"

J.T. shook his head. "I didn't follow him, but I wanted to." He reached down for another board when Murgatroyd handed to him. "I did notice that he was very interested in Jesus, though."

Murgatroyd pulled herself up from the floor. "How could you know that?"

"Because his eyes were always up front. Always watching."

* * * * *

When Glory pulled into the parking lot of the Creek Restaurant, she clicked on the dome light above her head which did little to reveal her face but illuminated her billowing hair in the rearview mirror. Sighing at the wilfulness of her hairdo, she snapped off the light and walked across the cold asphalt to the front door. Taking another deep breath, she smoothed her pants and stepped inside.

The Creek Restaurant, a quaint dining/drinking establishment situated on the banks of the Kisahani River, had not changed much over the years. Apart from Kelvin Murra's table dancing escapade and subsequent broken chandelier, the interior decorations were much the same as they were in the 1980's: it was a dimly lit room with square tables and black, fake leather chairs which wiped down easily. As the Creek served a menu of beef, chicken and a smattering of pork, the furniture was continuously covered in grease. A buffet table was centered in the room separating customers like bulkheads on an ocean liner. First class diners sat near the windows overlooking the river; second class sat on the opposite side of the buffet with a view of the front door. Steerage had the bonus scenery of drunk patrons stumbling to the bathroom.

A young woman, whose name tag read CHELSEA, took Glory to the table where Barnaby was waiting for her. He attempted to stand but lost his balance. Chelsea reached out to help. This embarrassed him. Instead, he fell back into his chair, and motioned to the seat across from him. Glory thanked the waitress and primly sat down. It had been a long time since she had acted primly.

"Hello, Barnaby," she said lightly and reached out her hand awkwardly which he shook.

"Glory."

"It's nice to see you." She gazed into his sunglasses seeing only a dulled reflection of herself. It was disconcerting to not be able to see his eyes (or in his case, the singular), but she was determined to look past it.

"I've got my eye on you," he said with a smirk.

Blushing, she looked down and away from his face.

"I'm sorry," he started and leaned forward, "when people meet me the first time, I try to put them at ease. A joke at my expense, if you will. My appearance is not easy for some."

"I think you look right well."

He stared until she felt uncomfortable.

"Okay, well, have you eaten at this establishment before? What's delish?" Grabbing a menu from the metal stand in the middle, she began to peruse the offerings.

"I've only been here once before. I had the steak."

"Red meat," she waggled a finger at him, "no vegephile you are." Her awkward laughter sounded strange in the near-empty room. Only one other couple dined morosely in second class, a pile of used plates listing dangerously on their table.

"I eat vegetables," Barnaby responded, "but a man's got to feed."

"I would have thought that someone who works as a butcher would get tired of meat."

"Does a librarian ever stop reading? A mechanic stop driving cars?"

She smiled shyly. "I've never thought of it that way before."

"Tell me about yourself, Glory."

"I see what you did there. It's the question I asked you yesterday in the butchery." He nodded. As she pondered the menu, she spoke. "My name is Glory MacDonald. MacDonald is my maiden name, never married. I've almost murdered two of my boyfriends, but…" Suddenly, she stopped. "Oh, bollocks, I hope I haven't offended you."

Chapter 11.

A smile played at the corners of his mouth. "Murder was not my crime. Continue."

"Well, that's a relief. I'd probably have to run out of here screaming." Her laughter was again forced and too loud. The second-class couple poked their heads up like prairie dogs to see what was so funny.

"Not yet," he said enigmatically. "Keep going."

"My daughter, Murgatroyd, and I come from a place called Chigwell, in England."

"Tell me about it."

"Not much to tell. A suburb, really. Boring streets, boring people, boring life..." Why was she not telling him the entire truth? Too early? Would *he* want to run out screaming?

"How did you end up not being boring?"

She snorted. "Anyone with two eyes could see that I'm boring, why..." she stopped again and slapped her head with her menu. "Damnit! I'm so sorry. I'm nervous."

Sighing, he leaned forward and rested his arms on the table. Taking off his sunglasses, he let her see him. His dilated pupil made him squint, but he was glad she didn't recoil. That was the usual response. "I have one working eye, Glory. I cannot change it, just as I cannot change the story that goes with it. Thus, we either decide to live with our stories, relax about saying something silly, or we part ways and that will be that." His voice was not angry, but tense, as if expecting the worst.

Glory held his gaze. "I choose the first one," she said quietly.

"Good," he put his glasses back on, "we'll get to my story in a little bit, but let's keep going with yours."

He was not what she'd ever thought of as her 'type.' Generally, she fell for good looking, well-dressed men, with nice haircuts and thin waists. Those men, self-confident, assured, with an air of 'the world cannot harm me' were always looking for someone like her. Yet tonight, sitting across from her was a slightly overweight man with a large beard, shaggy head of salt and pepper hair dressed in blue jeans and a polo shirt. He seemed ill at ease in the restaurant setting, no doubt from his scarring and cane. Her eyes wandered over the scars at his temple which led down to the top of his facial hair.

Son of a Butcher

Taking a nervous sip of water, Glory set the menu down. "My parents lived on the back side of a slag heap in Devon."

"Is Devon a town?"

"A county. It's on the pointy tip at the base of England." She smiled at him. "My mother and stepfather were tenant farmers barely making enough money to live on much less provide for the family. My mother was an insufferable nag. She would pick, pick, pick, like an obsessive hen, finding flaws in everything. I had the misfortune of being born first. My stepsister, Delilah, barely felt the pain of my mother's dulled beak. She had worn it away on me."

In the middle of her story, the waitress came by to take their orders. Barnaby did not look at her when he ordered his steak medium rare, while Glory thanked the woman for the chicken pasta that was to come. He ordered a beer and she a gin and tonic, also.

"Keep going," Barnaby urged.

"I'm not used to doing this."

"You're doing fine."

She smiled at him, conscious of his sunglassed gaze. "We never really take time to tell our stories, do we? We kind of gad about through life, flapping around in a tiz from here to there; things get busy and anxious and we move on to the next thing to avoid the last thing."

He didn't say anything.

"Well, where was I?"

"Delilah."

"Yes, my little sister. We were not great friends; she was four years younger. My father doted on us, perhaps her a little more than me, but such will be life." She spread her hands. "But my mother's constant nit-picking drove me insane. So, I gave her lots of nits to pick. I was smart enough to do well in school, but stubborn enough not to do it. I was sporty enough to succeed, but wilful enough to ride the pine, as you Americans say." She snorted, embarrassed. Thankfully, their drinks arrived. Glory received it with both hands and immediately took a drink.

"Why did you not want to stand out?"

"It's called the Tall Poppy Syndrome." He scrunched up his face, not understanding.

"In a field of poppies, which one is cut down first?"

Chapter 11.

"Aah," he said in recognition.

"For my mother, to stand out was to be brought down. To her, I was always an opponent. She was jealous of my abilities, my intelligence – she never made it past year 10 – and my athletic prowess."

"Not to mention your beauty."

She blushed again. "Flattery will get you almost everywhere."

He leaned forward to sip his beer. "It's not flattery. Truth. You're a very attractive woman."

The crimson shade deepened. "Yes, thank you, I suppose. But when the attentions of the boys rested upon me, my mother told me to 'Act like a lady!' 'Sit properly!' 'Stand up straight!' 'Get your hair out of your eyes!' It was infuriating, so I did the opposite. I didn't cross my legs, I slouched, I grew my hair long and dyed it blue. It was the last straw for my mother. When I was eighteen, she kicked me out of the house. Left to me own devices, I found my own vices." Glory swirled the lime around in the glass. "Sex, drugs and rock and roll, baby," she said quietly. "I'm not sure why I'm telling you all this…"

"Maybe you find me trustworthy?" Barnaby said.

"I hope so."

Barnaby felt a stab of conscience as he watched the Englishwoman opposite him. This date now seemed like a mistake. He was supposed to be finding ways to destroy, not create relationships. It had been such a long time since he'd thought about anyone else's feelings. The last thing he needed was to be turned aside by matters of the heart. At that moment, Gustav rose to the challenge and reminded him what the ultimate purpose was. Barnaby gritted his teeth.

"Now, you can tell me about you," Glory grinned. She had a lovely, wide smile with white teeth and full lips. Her nose, long, beakish, pointed between hazel eyes, deep set and expressive. She was an open book, a story worth retelling.

"Not much to tell, really."

She crossed her arms and legs simultaneously. "Okay, here's what I know so far and you fill in the blanks, okay?"

He spread his hands in tacit approval.

"You're not from Iowa. You've been injured in some kind of prison episode. I've conjured up this Shawshank Redemption vision, but

I'm sure that's not right." She tried to read his impassive face but was unrewarded. "You live in Clancy and you're a butcher. There you go. That's what I know."

"You've got it all," he said evasively.

"Oh, don't be such a knob. Come on," she encouraged, "give it to me. Even if it ain't pretty."

He laughed. To tell the truth or not? "I'm from Wisconsin."

"Is Wisconsin a town?"

"It's a state north and east of Iowa. Very cold in the winter."

"Bloody hell, it can't be colder than it is here in bloody Amicable already. England is cold, but this is a witch's tit."

"Be that as it may," he continued, "Wisconsin is a state of extremes: political, meteorological, social. I'm from just north of Milwaukee – a city on Lake Michigan."

"I've heard of that. Power tools."

"Something like that."

Their meals arrived. Barnaby's steak seemed to be bleeding into the black serving plate below. Pooled in its juices, the steak smelled delicious. Glory's pasta paled in comparison, both literally and figuratively. "I should have gotten one of those."

"You can change your mind, if you like?"

"No, no," she said. "I've got to watch my figure. No one else will." *Except you, Barnaby*, she hoped.

"I'll leave you some of mine," he suggested.

"Like an old married couple, we are." She poked a pasta tube and stuffed in her mouth with a smile.

Without comment, he cut into his steak. Deftly, he sliced through the perfectly cooked beef and set down his knife to transfer the fork to his right hand.

"What is it?" he asked noticing her smirk.

"Americans. They're not good with a knife and fork."

He frowned, unsure of what she meant. "I'm a butcher. I'm pretty good with a knife."

"We English only use the fork in the left hand. Properly."

"So you're judging me for my utensil aptitude?" he asked.

Chapter 11.

"I'm not judging you. I just think it's a waste of motion to switch hands, that's all." Her pulse quickened at his defensiveness.

He shrugged and stubbornly committed to eating the way he always had. They were quiet while eating a few more bites. Then, Glory took her napkin and wiped her mouth. "You said you're from Wisconsin."

He paused, nodding, then copied her mouth-wiping. "My parents owned a restaurant. They made Reubens."

"I don't know what that is."

"Corned beef and sauerkraut on rye bread. Lots of mayo."

Glory cringed. "Sounds revolting."

"Of course," he tried to mimic her English accent, "for someone used to eating truffles with a knife and fork."

She frowned, hurt. "I'm sorry. I didn't mean to offend you," she said softly.

Barnaby shook his head. "It's my fault. I should apologize. I'm not used to civil conversation anymore. This is the longest I've spoken to anyone in years. We never really get past my appearance before people move on."

Eating again, Glory accepted his apology with her eyes. "Please, continue."

He pushed his sunglasses up on his nose and recalled the past.

"Gus!" his mother cried out. "We need more sauerkraut!"

Frowning, Gus trudged to the basement. Now that he was seventeen, he had grown to loathe both restaurant and the obtrusive smell of sauerkraut. It pervaded his whole life – before school, after school, weekends. It wasn't just the amount of time, but the odor. Keller's Cellar was famous among locals and outsiders alike, but Gus was done with it. In one year, he would be moving on to the University of Wisconsin in Madison, far enough away from the Cellar that he wouldn't have to work on weekends, but close enough that if he really needed something, he could quickly drive back home.

Gus doubted that he'd drive home very often.

"Gus!" his mother's repeated shout broke his reverie of the future. "Sauerkraut!"

Son of a Butcher

In the basement, Gus grabbed three glass Ball jars of homemade fermented cabbage and trundled back towards the stairs. Reaching up, he pulled the yankchain from the naked overhead light. Consumed by the darkness, Gus felt the instantaneous stab of fear. From his early childhood, he had been afraid of the dark, afraid of the things that go twitch-twitch when he couldn't see. One time, a blind woman had come to the restaurant. She had accidentally knocked her glasses off revealing milky, dead and unfocused eyes. Gus had shrunk back in fright. There could be no greater curse than to be blind.

Hurrying up the steps, Gus closed the cellar door behind him and brought the Ball jars to his mother who was standing in the kitchen with her hands resting upside down on her substantial hips. With her hair up in curled braids, she wore her apron like a German frau cooking in her kitchen. Grabbing the jars, she looked up at her tall, handsome son.

"Thank you, Gus. Now," she said as she began to scoop out the sauerkraut onto the corned beef, "what are you up to?"

It was a Saturday afternoon. Late lunch diners sat alongside the windows at the front of the restaurant enjoying the view of Lake Michigan across the road. A few walkers were taking in the unseasonably warm fall weather. They'd already had a few nights of frost (not rare for September, but unwelcome nonetheless), but they were thankful for the warm days to keep the winter at bay, just for a while longer.

"I'm going to go out with Jeff and Chad," he responded with a cringe, hoping that he could have one Saturday night to himself.

"We're expecting a big night tonight..."

"Yes, but it's my last year of high school. I won't get to see all my friends next year."

His mother studied him, her boy, her only child. Smiling and nodding, she waved a hand to him. "Off you go. Have your fun. Tomorrow, there will be plenty to do."

Relief washed over him. Freedom. The Cellar was a prison to him at times. Gus and the boys were going down to the lake for a party. He hadn't told his mother that. Some things were better that she didn't know.

Another thing he hadn't told her was that Fern Schnebly was going to be at the party. Fern was in his Calculus class – a brilliant young woman and very pretty. They'd been working together for the last few weeks. Gus felt like things were progressing pretty well and he was hoping to make the next move tonight. A walk

Chapter 11.

down by the water. Hands grasping for each other. Faces turned. Those beautiful lips…

"Gus," his mother interrupted his daydream. "I know I've said you can go, but can you slice up some corned beef quick before you leave?"

Gus sighed and nodded. His mother was too hard to refuse.

The party was fun. Gus, not much of a drinker, drank two beers and was feeling free and lightheaded. Most of that had to do with Fern, who stood beside him, holding her red plastic cup with a wine cooler in it. He hadn't seen her drink any of it. It was more of an accessory.

"Are you having fun?" Gus asked.

She smiled coyly at him. "It's a beautiful night."

"That's not what I asked." He swallowed hard.

"I think we should take a walk," Fern said. Gus glanced at Jeff and Chad who saw him leaving. They gave him a thumbs up.

As they walked, the moon reflected in shimmering sparkles across the water. A light breeze had picked up and Fern shivered. Past the sand, cars were parked along the walkway. It was a busy night on the beach. "Do you want to go back to the fire?"

"No, you can keep me warm."

Gus's heart raced. Nearing her side, he put his arm around her. This was what he had dreamed of. Here they were, strolling along Lake Michigan, his arm around her. Now they only needed to stop and turn towards…

"Go get her!" a voice yelled out from the road. Laughter and the sound of a car driving away.

Gus swore silently inside his head and he glanced at Fern. "Sorry about that."

"It's not your fault."

"I know, it's just…"

"Just what?"

"I wanted this to be perfect." Gus turned towards her. Over his head, the lake was mesmerizing.

"What is 'this?'" she asked.

If the sun were shining, it would have reflected his rapidly reddening face. He stumbled for words. What was 'this?' What was he feeling?

"I don't know. I was kind of hoping that you would want to…"

Coquettishly, she batted her eyes at him. "Want to what?"

Taking a deep breath, he reached out to kiss her. Awkwardly, yet not uncomfortably, their lips met. For Gus, this was electric. The feeling of her soft mouth, his hands on her neck. Then, she put her hand behind his back and pulled him closer. Their kissing became more intense. Fern was the one in charge. Fern wanted him! Suddenly, it felt as if Gus couldn't breathe, but he didn't want to stop. Everything inside him was like a bull charging a red flag. He knew that she liked him, but even more, she wanted him! Now, madly mashing, tongues engaged, Fern pulled back. Gus sensed a change in her, but he didn't want to stop. Not at all. Reaching for her face again, he pulled her to him. They kissed again, but now she was resisting.

"Gus…"

"What?" He couldn't stop kissing her.

"Stop. We have to stop."

"No. We don't. This feels so good."

She grabbed his hands. "I know. I like it, but I'm not ready."

"But I am…" he smiled.

"Gus, please."

Suddenly, he heard in his head the pleading. Like water thrown onto a fire, Gus knew that the moment had passed. The midnight stroll, the arm around her, the kissing – it was all over. Frustrated, he dropped his hands.

"I see," he said. He wanted her to feel guilty for leading him on. He had been so sure she had wanted to go further.

"I like you, Gus. But we really don't know each other that well."

He turned away from her and took a step back towards the party.

"Don't go like that, Gus. Come on, let's start out as friends and then we'll see where it goes."

She ran up to him and slipped her hand in his. It was smooth and cold, but gentle. Even though his needs had been aroused, he was thankful that she hadn't run away from him.

"Thank you," she said quietly. "You're a real gentleman."

Sighing deeply, they made their way back to the bonfire.

Fern dumped him a week after graduation.

"So you worked in a restaurant growing up?"

Barnaby finished his steak and washed it down with a mouthful of beer. Feeling some meat in his teeth, he bared his fangs and sucked.

Chapter 11.

The effect was strange and frightening. Glory looked away. "Yes, until I went to college. I majored in business. Got a great job and then ran into some trouble."

"What was it?" she whispered, unable to control herself.

He paused. This was the moment of truth (or lies, in this case). Of course, he was not going to tell her about Rhonda or detail the things that happened in jail. Instead, he shifted the conversation back to her. "If I asked you to reveal your darkest secret to me, would *you* do it?"

She frowned. "No."

"Why not?"

"Because I barely know you."

He spread his hands. "There you go. I barely know you. How could I tell you what led to my prison sentence? Why, you could run back to Amicable and meet with your gossipy ladies revealing that secret and destroying me."

"I wouldn't do that."

He pondered her. "But if I tell you, you will have control over me."

"I won't tell anyone," she whispered.

The silence escalated the tension. "I think maybe I'll wait until next time."

"Next time what?"

"Our next time out. Another date."

A pleading look came into Glory's eyes. "But I'll be undone with mystery."

"Consider yourself undone."

"Oh, you," she said disappointedly. "And I thought this was going to turn out differently tonight."

"Really?" his eyebrows raised. "What were you expecting?"

"That we would get to know each other, have a few laughs, drive home and…" she left the words unsaid.

"And what?"

"I don't know," she laughed explosively. "I really don't know. It's been such a long time since I've been on a date with someone so… deep. When I was in England, the last men were so shallow – no life experience, no hopes for the future, no… secrets. And now I've met you;

you're mysterious and, how shall we say, dangerous, if that's the right word. And you've piqued my interest only to yank the tablecloth out from under me."

"But that's a good thing, right? To keep wanting for more?"

Glory tilted her head back and the ceiling and groaned. "Yes, I suppose. But how long will I have to wait?"

"How can I know you're trustworthy?" he asked.

"What if you told me to do something, within reason, and I did it and I didn't tell anyone else? Would that do it?"

Suddenly, a thought came into his mind, a very Gustavian thought. "All right. I've got an idea."

She clapped her hands lightly. "Lay it on me."

"You know Rhonda Redman, right?"

Frowning, she tilted her head to the side. "I know Rhonda Jensen?"

Chiding himself at his mistake, Barnaby nodded. "Yes, sorry. Rhonda Jensen."

"What about her?"

"Do you know her well?" he asked.

"Not well, I suppose. Our children are best friends and I like her very much. Why? Do you have a thing for her?"

Barnaby's foot jerked out and he kicked the table. Glory jumped. "No. But the Peterson twins have been talking about her, you know, with regards to her late husband."

"Butcher?"

He nodded. "I never met him, but I hear he could do some interesting things. Tell the future, or something stupid like that."

"I've heard that too," Glory responded conspiratorially. "Bollocks, probably."

"Here's what I want you to do. I want you to get a picture of Rhonda and this Butcher and bring it to me."

"Why?" she responded distrustfully.

Barnaby shrugged. "That's the price of my story. Perhaps I'll weave it in there somehow."

"You know Rhonda personally?" Glory asked.

Chapter 11.

"Like I said, no. But this would prove to me that you're not pulling the wool over my eyes."

"Pardon?"

"Yanking my chain. Lying to me. Got it?" Barnaby's voice lowered.

"I'm not sure I like the idea of that." She saw her reflection in the mirror and then glanced back at him. "But I'll do it."

Gustav whispered inside Barnaby's head. *You do that, Glory. You do that.*

Chapter 12.

They finished the treehouse the week before Christmas vacation. The walls and roof went up quickly, but the other decorations had been debated with gusto. Murgatroyd wanted a retro look – something from the 80's, an Andy Warhol thing with cowskin rug and weird collections of art on the walls. J.T. argued that there wasn't enough room in a treehouse for anything but a small rug, a few camping chairs and a little table to play cards on. They negotiated and finally settled on a small rug made out of old blue jeans that Grandma Connie had made and two beanbags with a wooden board in between them for games.

J.T. had hung a dangling light from the ceiling (for Murgatroyd's sake, not his) and strung an electric cord from the roof, down the tree and to the side of the house where an outlet connected the outdoor Christmas lights across the bushes. J.T. loved Christmas lights. There was something beautiful about the unnatural glow of Christmas lights on faces. Something pure and unadulterated. As J.T. and Murgatroyd sat across from each other in their small beanbags, cross-legged, winter coats covering their cold bodies, playing cards in their hands, J.T. was suddenly overwhelmed with thankfulness for his newest (and only) friend.

A few classmates and Amicableans snickered at the physical mismatch, the giant and the dwarf, the Yank and the Pom, the quiet and the noisy, but it didn't bother the two of them at all. J.T. and Murgatroyd began to share mannerisms. J.T. was, without acknowledgement, using the word 'bloody' in front of things while Murgatroyd was learning to stand with her hands on her hips.

Every day after school, the two would wander across Amicable stopping here and there, sometimes at a shop, other times at Winslow Park. They would pick up pieces of this and that; they would find humorous bits of information and stash them in a journal they kept in the treehouse. When the weather warmed up, they were going to ask Liam Wilson if he would allow them to build a twin treehouse in the backyard of the rental, that way J.T. could go to her house too.

Chapter 12.

"What are you getting for Christmas?" J.T. asked Murgatroyd as he laid down a card on the board between them.

"A set of tools." Her eyes followed his hand back to his cards and then at her own.

"Why would you want that?"

"If we're going to build my treehouse, we can't very well be carrying all your stuff over. Too heavy."

"Are you sure you don't want a Barbie or something?" he laughed. His breath misted in the air.

"Are you sure you don't want a punch in the face?" Murgatroyd's mouth was set firmly.

"That's not what I want for Christmas." He played another card and watched her reaction.

"Bloody hell, J.T. Are you sure you can't read me? You win this bloody game every time."

"Maybe you're just bad at it."

"Don't be a wanker," she said.

"Don't be a bloody sore loser."

Murgatroyd flopped her cards down, leaned back in her beanbag and covered herself with a blanket. "I'm not a sore loser. I just want to win."

"Same thing."

Mouthing the words back to him, she glanced up at the ceiling where the Christmas lights gleamed brightly. "What do you want, J.T.?"

"A video game," he responded without hesitation.

"Which one?"

"The Last Starfighter."

She sat up. "Is that actually a video game? I thought it was just a movie."

"Yeah, Atari made it. I've got an Atari."

"What's an Atari."

"Video console from the 1980's. It was my mom's. Grandma Connie kept it in a box for a lot of years until my dad found it one time. We started playing it together. Or, I would play and he would laugh. He couldn't move much then."

"Was that when you watched Starman, too?"

"Yup."

"Do they even make the video game anymore?"

He shrugged. "You don't always ask for things that are possible. It just tells people what you're thinking about."

"I've never thought about it that way before."

"Haven't you ever asked for anything that you knew you weren't going to get?" J.T.'s eyes poked over the edges of the blanket while his feet stuck out the other end.

"Well, I suppose," she said and thought about it. "I guess there was the time I asked for a cow for my birthday."

"Why a cow?"

"It seemed like a perfectly acceptable request. I like milk. Milk likes me. Why not get a cow and I can have all the free milk I want."

"Fair enough. But have you ever had fresh milk before? Like straight out of the..." he pantomimed milking a teat.

"No."

"It's disgusting," J.T. said. "There's a farmer outside of town who has Jersey cows and one time, my class went over there, and he..." more pantomiming, "into a glass. He took a sip and then said we all could if we wanted to. Nobody else did, but I was curious."

"What did it taste like?" Murgatroyd asked.

"Like the inside of a shower."

Murgatroyd began to snort with laughter. "You've licked the inside of the shower?"

"No, but it tastes like it smells, all..." he wrinkled up his face with distaste and made a smacking sound with the roof of his mouth.

"You're bloody funny," Murgatroyd kicked his foot.

"And you're a bloody nose."

They settled into comfortable silence. Staring up at the ceiling, the Christmas lights appeared as a rainbow of stars illuminating the rafters of heavens. The cold, now reaching the oppressive stage, began to bite at their ears and noses. Soon, they would have to go inside.

"Do you think there are stars in heaven?" Murgatroyd asked.

"I don't know."

"I hope heaven is not all dark and spacey. People keep saying when you go to heaven you go up there," she pointed to the ceiling, "but

Chapter 12.

I want to stay right here in the sunshine and the grass. It's all right if it snows, but I don't want to wear a spacesuit."

"I would highly doubt that God would forget human's need for oxygen."

"Don't forget the lack of pressure," she raised a finger. "I've seen *Total Recall*. That's pretty gross when Arnie's face explodes."

J.T. nodded, but he'd never seen it. He'd have to put it on his mother's Netflix list.

"Naw, I think heaven's gonna be a lot like this, just better."

"How so?" Murgatroyd asked.

"Because my dad will be there. As long as he's there, it will be heaven."

"I think the stars remind us that dead people are still alive somewhere."

"What, like the Lion King?" J.T. asked.

"No, eejit, like… hmmm… I don't know how to explain it. It's like their lives still burn even while their bodies don't. It's like God lights a candle and says, 'See, I told you so! We're waitin' for ya!'"

"I like that."

Murgatroyd stared up at the ceiling for a moment longer. "I'm getting cold. Let's go inside."

"Okay."

Murgatroyd climbed down the ladder and ran to the house. J.T. remained fastened to his beanbag mesmerized by the lights. Which star was his dad?

* * * * *

Glory watched Barnaby limp towards his car.

The night had been full of sexual tension and excitement. They were not yet at the point of exploring anything deeper. Glory still did not know if he would be interested in her that way, but as he started to leave, she had pulled him closer to kiss him. It was a peck, not lingering, but he recoiled, surprised.

"What's wrong?" she asked.

Son of a Butcher

"Nothing," his voice was husky, "It's just that it's been a long time since that's happened to me."
"What? A kiss?"
He nodded. "Any of it. The last time I kissed a woman..." He left off. That had been Rhonda Redman.
"Sounds like a song."
"Very funny."
"Do you want to kiss some more?" Glory asked coyly.
"I think it's best if I go home now."
She couldn't see behind his sunglasses. Was he upset or worried?
After returning home from the Creek Restaurant, Barnaby shut the door quietly behind him. Something was happening to him. It felt as if he was being ripped apart, shredded by something he hadn't felt in so long. But this feeling, acceptance, (love?), genuine hope, was unwelcome. The task ahead required absolute focus.

Barnaby yanked the black book out from the bookshelf and dropped it on the table. Shrugging out of his coat, he blew on his hands and sat at the table. Grabbing a pen, he began to write down exactly what he was thinking.

```
It's almost Christmas. It's cold outside.
People are happy, or near enough to it. That
emotion feels so foreign as it tries to infect me.
I've repelled it for so long, that I wouldn't know
how to open the gate if I could.
    I drove my car to Clancy, to the Creek
Restaurant, to go on a date with Glory MacDonald.
Yes, I've written about her already, but I never
expected to…
```

He chewed on the plastic pen. What didn't he expect? Did he assume that all of life would remain terrible as long as he held onto the hope of his vengeance? But now this. Now Glory.

```
    To care.
```

Chapter 12.

It's one thing to establish a working relationship with the Peterson twins, but it's an entirely different thing to reveal what I have already to Glory. Instead of passing on information, I'm making a connection, and I can't do that. I just can't. I'll have to find a way to keep her handily close, but I can't let my emotions get carried away. There is too much at stake.
I saw Rhonda in church this morning and I almost couldn't contain myself. I've never felt rage like that before. It flooded me, and as I stared at the ceiling, for the entire hour of boredom, I wrestled with the need to destroy her. When we were finally released, I ran from there. I can't go back. It would wreck me.

Barnaby sighed as he reveled in hope and despair. Just as he was about to close the book and return the rubber band to its place, a thought came to his mind and he wrote it down.

Be smart, Barnaby. No attachments. None.

But when Barnaby Koppel fell asleep that night, there was only one face haunting his dreams. Frankly, he was quite happy she was there with him.

* * * * *

Over the next week, they didn't see each other. Barnaby didn't want other Amicableans to know about their relationship, or at least not yet. The constant harassment he would take from the Peterson twins would be more than enough to grate on his nerves, or at least that's what he told Glory. For her part, Glory worried about his strange fascination with Rhonda Jensen.

Son of a Butcher

The next time they met for dinner at her house, he mentioned her name again. Furtively, he glanced up from his applesauce smeared pork chop. Glory tried to smile, but it was hard to be compared to Rhonda. She was tall and beautiful and very Midwestern. It really was no surprise that Barnaby might be interested in her, but she had so hoped that they might move to the next step.

After dinner, though, Glory was both proud and ashamed to produce the picture that Barnaby had asked for, one of Rhonda and her husband. She couldn't tell what was going on behind his sunglasses. He glanced at it and then gave it back to her.

"Thank you," he said simply.

"There, I did as you asked. You can trust me."

"It appears that way," he said.

"Now will you tell me the rest of your story?"

They settled into her sofa. Once again, Murgatroyd was at the Jensen house so that she could have some 'time to herself.' This was how she approached it with Rhonda who was more than happy to have Murgatroyd.

Glory pulled her knee up next to him. He sat staring straight ahead, his hands on his legs.

"About ten years ago," he started, his voice a deep monotone, "I made a mistake. I was in the wrong place at the wrong time. While the tired cliché of 'I'm innocent' rang on deaf ears, it wasn't I who did the thieving, I was the victim."

"Can you tell me about it?" Glory asked.

"I met a woman. I didn't know her well and even though we'd only just met, we became romantically involved. We went to a secluded spot and things got steamy. When she told me to stop, I did. But I was angry. What gives a woman the right to lead a guy on like that and suddenly she flips the switch. 'Oh, sorry, did you think we were going to go that far?'" he mimicked a voice.

"I didn't hit her, but she fell to the floor. It must have scared her because she ran from the house. When she did, one of the neighbors found her and put two and two together and came up with five. Either way, the cops came and arrested me. During the trial, my parents sat in the front row torn to shreds by 'what I'd done.' My mother cried and my

Chapter 12.

father ground his teeth. After the jury pronounced me guilty, the judge sentenced me to ten years in prison for something I didn't do."

"I'm so sorry," Glory said as she reached out her hand to touch his shoulder. It surprised him and he flinched, so she withdrew it.

"They sent me to a maximum-security prison for the 'worst of the worst,' the murderers, the pedophiles, the rapists, copkillers, you know. I didn't fit the bill in any way. I was a young man wrongly accused and the other inmates could smell it. I won't scare you with details, but I ended up disfigured and mostly blind from one specific incident. I spent almost a month in the hospital. I lost one eye, my face was mangled and I couldn't walk very well."

"Are you still angry?"

His mouth tightened and he tried to relax. "How would you feel?"

"I would still be angry. Actually, I might try to get revenge." Glory covered her mouth as if she'd said something wrong.

Barnaby had to tread softly. "I had to give that dream up or it would have eaten me alive. So, I moved to Amicable. The middle of nowhere in the middle of nobody but you, Glory, and a bunch of Iowans." He now turned to her and tentatively reached out for her hand. "If you speak of this to anyone, especially Rhonda Jensen, I'll be fired. My life will be ruined again." He tried to smile but it came out as a grimace. "You're the only friend I have now."

"Okay, but…"

"But what?"

"What is it with you and Rhonda?"

His jaw twitched. "Let's just say Rhonda Jensen carries eerie similarities with the woman who put me in jail."

"Oh, dear," she said. "I won't tell a soul, Barnaby."

She had sealed her promise with a kiss. It was light and crisp, almost businesslike. Certainly, she did not want to dredge up any negative memories. But once they stepped out onto the porch, in the biting December air, she kissed him again, stronger, a different kind of promise. Glory wanted to be with him as he recovered from the trauma of that horrible situation.

Now at the car, he waved behind him without looking at her.

Son of a Butcher

Glory's phone buzzed from a text message. It was Murg. She was on her way home from the Jensen house.

It seemed like the Jensen house was the nexus of everything here in Amicable.

Twenty minutes later, in the bone-biting cold, Murgatroyd bounded through the backyard of the house. She had been staring up into a maple tree measuring with her eyes how much wood they would need for her own treehouse.

"Hi, Mum." Murgatroyd bustled in through the front door into the living room where she dropped her coat and boots in the middle. Then, she tromped into the kitchen where her mother was standing at the window.

"How was your day?"

"Good. The treehouse is finished and we played cards." Murgatroyd poured herself a glass of water.

"How is Rhonda?"

Murgatroyd turned to her mother while she drank, spilling water over her chin and down onto her shirt. She sighed and burped. "Fine."

"I can't imagine what Christmases are like for her. She must be lonely."

"I suppose."

"She doesn't talk about it?"

Shrugging, Murgatroyd set the glass on the counter and walked past her mother again into the living room. "No, not much. She does look at photos on her computer often. I heard her mumbling something the other day that didn't make sense, but I didn't ask her about it."

"What was it?"

Murgatroyd eyed Glory. "Why do you want to know?"

"She's my friend. Was it something we can do for them at Christmas? Do they need company? Does she need someone to talk to?"

Weighing this thought, the little girl sighed. "She mumbled, 'If I'd never done that, I wouldn't be punished now.'"

"What do you think she meant by that?"

"I'm only nine, Mum."

Glory laughed. "Of course. I'm sorry." Moving across the living room, Glory gazed through the front window into the darkness. The

Chapter 12.

lights from the house illuminated the glistening flakes of snow that covered the grass. They sparkled like tiny stars, each so different, yet all the same. Glory thought about Barnaby and the difficulties that he'd encountered throughout his life. She wondered if she could somehow be a catalyst for his continued healing. Certainly, she hadn't felt attracted to a man in a long time; the attraction wasn't beauty, certainly, but a magnetic dangerousness that made her shiver. She'd be cautious, but something good would definitely come of it. She was sure.

Now, she just had to decide what he'd like for a Christmas gift.

And no one could know anything about it.

Glory's eyes unfocussed as she thought about a specific, formative, Christmas past.

"What do you want for Christmas?" Glory asked Eddie.

"What?"

She repeated the question, but he was distracted by the telly. Eddie was a local lowlife, beautiful in his own way – lost, but she enjoyed being useful to him. He had moved in a few months before. There were many things that she did find distasteful about him: his open dislike of her three-year-old daughter was certainly foremost in the list, but at least she had company. When Glory returned home from work after a long day, she was quite happy to talk through her day as he drank beer and watched soccer.

"I don't know," he said. "Maybe you could get a new telly. This one's crap."

"I'll think about it," she said.

She wanted him to ask her the question. What would she like for Christmas? It had been a few years since there had been anyone to actually buy her something. Her mother and stepfather had backed out of her life, even more since Murgatroyd's birth. So, Glory bought a few gifts for Murgatroyd and then they usually went for a drive on Christmas Eve.

"Can you get me a pint, Luv?"

"I'm preparing the meal, Eddie. Can you get it yourself?"

"I'll wait."

It used to be that this kind of reaction would have frustrated Glory, but now she was numb to the inconsistencies of men in her life. Perhaps if her father would have taken her with him. Maybe then she wouldn't be in this predicament.

Son of a Butcher

Turning back towards the stove, she began to boil water for their traditional night of pasta. It was as much as they could afford. Though Eddie provided some support, his work as a janitor at a local train station did not bring in enough income. Especially when he stopped off most afternoons at the pub after work.

As the water began to simmer, the doorbell rang.

"Someone's at the door, Glor," Eddie shouted from his chair.

"Can you get it?"

"Somefin's wrong wif me leg. Asleep. I'll get the next one."

Grinding her teeth, Glory turned off the burner and headed to the door. When she reached door, she was startled to see her mother and her stepfather, Nigel. What were they doing here? How long had it been?

"Mum. Nigel!" she exclaimed after opening the door. "What…? What brings…?"

"We're here to check up on our granddaughter."

"But… why now?"

"Don't start, Glory." Her mother pushed past her and into the house. Nigel shrugged and followed his wife. "Now, where is Murga…" Pause. "Oh, hello. Who are you?"

Glory cringed. She knew what was coming. Firstly, there would be fake niceties; her mother would inquire of his name and background, then she would pick him apart. Finally, after he had had enough, he would roust himself from the chair, grab his coat and wander out into the darkness to have the pint of beer she had not provided.

"I'm Eddie."

Glory rounded the corner to see her boyfriend reaching up from his recliner. He had decided not to stand up. Perhaps it was something with his leg.

"Delaney Adams and this is my husband, Nigel."

"Howdee Doo," Eddie responded as he grunted from the effort of turning in the chair.

At that moment, Glory wished that she could meet a nice guy with a nice job who could provide for her and Murgatroyd. She wished that Eddie was that nice guy with a nice job so she wouldn't have to put up with what was about to happen.

"Where are you from, Eddie?" Delaney asked.

"Here and there. Mostly here."

"You live here?" Delaney's voice rose at the end of the question, not simply questioning where he lived, but his mere existence in the world.

Chapter 12.

"You bet!" he said with a smile. His stubbled, bearded cheeks stuck out angularly from his face.

Delaney turned towards her daughter. "Interesting that you have a roommate."

"Don't start mother," Glory said exasperatedly.

"I just don't want you to ruin your life any further, dear," she said testily.

"What do you mean by that?" Eddie asked.

Delaney looked down her nose at the young man. "My daughter Glory has had an interesting life, as I'm sure you would know." Delaney's sarcasm expressed her true convictions that she did not believe at all Eddie would know much about Glory. "Now that you've entered her life, she must be thrilled by her Prince Charming who has arrived to rescue her from her struggles."

Glory angrily turned from the rapidly approaching dispute in the living room and went back to the kitchen. She slammed a spoon into the pot.

Although Glory couldn't hear everything that was going on in the living room, it was only minutes later when Eddie's face peeked through the kitchen door. "Heading off to the pub, Luv. Really wish I could stay but..." he motioned with his head at her mother and stepfather, "I'm not sure my ears could handle that kind of stabbing." He grabbed his coat nearly running from the house.

Shortly after the door slammed behind him, her mother appeared in the kitchen holding Murgatroyd in her arms.

"She doesn't smell very good."

Murgatroyd was watching her grandmother with something akin to distaste.

"Maybe you'd like to give her a bath."

"Me?" Delaney placed a hand on her chest. "That's a mother's role."

"Would you like to make dinner for us then?"

Delaney sighed dramatically. "If there's any way that I can help, I will." She set Murgatroyd on the floor who ran quickly from the room. Glory was envious.

Taking the spoon from Glory, Delaney slowly stirred the pasta. "How are you, Glory?"

"Exhausted," Glory said as she leaned against the wall.

"I suppose that's what happens when you have a child out of wedlock."

"Spare me, Mum."

"You've always wanted your own way, dear, and now you have it. I guess it hasn't turned out as wonderful as you would have imagined. No husband, a low-paying job, a toddler, and Saturday night pasta."

Son of a Butcher

"Did you come here to fight, mother, or did you have a better reason for showing up unannounced?"

"I wanted to see my granddaughter."

Glory rolled her eyes. Her mother hated that.

"I can see how much you wanted to see her. You told her she smells and then stepped in to do something you could control."

"What's that supposed to mean?"

Glory took the spoon from her mother. "Why are you *really* here?"

"It's about your sister."

"What about her?"

"She's dying."

Glory almost dropped the spoon. "What?"

"Yes, she has Multiple Sclerosis."

The news struck Glory hard. Even though she and Delilah had not communicated in years, to have multiple sclerosis at such a young age. That was horrible.

"Where is she?"

"At home. With us."

"I... don't know what to say, Mum. We'll come right over." Glory put a hand to her forehead. "I... this is incredible." Glory searched her mother's eyes and was shocked to see neither tear nor emotion.

"We'll expect you for lunch tomorrow."

"O... Okay," Glory stammered.

The reconnection the next day had not gone well. Delilah, incapacitated and in bed, stared dolefully up at her stepsister. As she lay in the bed, legs and torso covered by a star encrusted quilt, Delaney dominated conversation. During the time given them (Glory's mother had allotted only half an hour due to Delilah's weakness), Glory had no chance to say what she *really* wanted. By the time the half hour was up, Delaney tapped her watch and declared that 'time was up.' Glory leaned in to hug her sister's frail and emaciated body.

The next time she saw her was the week before Christmas at the Anglican church in a casket.

* * * * *

Chapter 12.

Rhonda drove to the MacDonalds' house to pick them up for church. Although Glory had not really warmed to the idea of church after the trauma of seeing Delilah's casket, she went for the social aspects. The service itself was not new, not at all. In fact, in the months that she'd lived in Amicable, Glory found that the predictability was numbing, but in a much more pleasing way than a funeral, obviously. When one knew the routine, one could observe and participate with one eye and one ear. It was like watching a soap opera. If you skipped a couple of weeks, you knew you hadn't missed anything because it was exactly the same as it was before you skipped.

Rhonda showed up ten minutes before the service started. Glory had dragged Murgatroyd from bed with a whimper and a complaint.

When Rhonda's car appeared, Glory and Murgatroyd stepped out of the house and Glory closed the door behind her. The biting north wind swirled around the house and nipped at her ears. This kind of cold was not really Glory's thing and she wished for a summer beach house, somewhere far, far away where she could sip umbrella covered drinks flavored with coconut and rum and forget the difficulties of her past.

Murgatroyd sailed past her towards the Jensen car. J.T. and Georgie were in the back seat. He slid over when she opened the door.

"Hey, Purgatroyd."

"Boyo."

Glory sat down in the car and it shook. "Good morning."

"How are ya?"

"Bloody cold."

"Just wait," Rhonda said with a smirk as she put the car in drive.

They were greeted by shivering ushers who stood by the front door distributing bulletins. Greeted with a friendly 'hello' and hearty handshake, the ushers smiled and urged them up the stairs into the sanctuary. Rhonda, as Amicablean royalty, and the MacDonalds, as Amicablean novelty, were welcomed by various other churchgoers. Already, Merry Christmas, was the greeting du jour, even though the holiday was still two weeks away.

The sanctuary's fifteen-foot-tall Christmas trees, one on each side of the altar, were decorated with sparkling tinsel and religiously themed baubles. White lights twinkled between the branches. Large white stars adorned the peaks of the trees. Warmly dressed parishioners were interspersed throughout the spacious room. Although no one sat directly next to each other (there were social norms that couldn't be overcome no matter the season), conversations took place diagonally across pews. People were in high spirits. Truly, it was the most wonderful time of the year for Amicableans to let their collective hair down.

Some of Glory's exercising friends waved delightedly to her. She waved back, but followed Rhonda to the front, to 'her' pew where they scooched in close to Leslie Deakins and her children.

"Merry Christmas," Leslie said as she patted the seat next to her.

"And to you," Rhonda responded. She organized her kids with their children's bulletins and then fixed her attention back on Leslie. "How is everything going at your house?"

"It's Christmas. It's the most stressful time of the year," she sang.

"Do you have all your Christmas presents?"

"Yes, thankfully, but it's organizing schedules, visiting people, making sure church stuff is in order that's the hard part. We're having a hard time relaxing."

Rhonda wished she had the same problem.

"I think this is just beautiful," Glory leaned across the kids to the other women. "All the pageantry, the lights and sounds – no wonder people believe in God."

"You seem very lively today," Leslie said.

Glory touched the side of her nose. "I've got a bit of a secret."

Leslie and Rhonda both raised their eyebrows simultaneously.

"I need some advice, though."

"What is it?" Rhonda asked.

Murgatroyd nudged her mother. She needed help deciphering the Christmas clues in the children's bulletin. Also, Murgatroyd wanted to point out the weirdness of the coloring-picture, the serene manger scene replete with an Eeyore-ish donkey and bored camels. Joseph looked like he was about to fall asleep, while Mary seemed like she'd given birth to a peanut, rather than a baby. The shepherds who had run away from their flocks to mindlessly stand watch over a somewhat anachronistic barn,

Chapter 12.

looked nervous, edgy, as if waiting for a phone call from their boss remanding them back to their fields.

Georgie also took that moment to point out the discrepancies between two Christmas pictures. Spot Christmas trees with four differences. She loved those things, whereas J.T. was completely bored with them. He could pick out the differences within seconds.

Suddenly, the room was filled with song. Jim the Organist/Mailman launched into *O Come, All Ye Faithful*, which delighted Murgatroyd. Unlike so many other hymns they'd heard in church the last months, she'd at least heard this one before. Humming and bouncing her head with the organ, she looked up at Glory and smiled.

After the song finished with a flourish, John Deakins stepped out from the side room. Dressed in his seasonal regalia (he ditched his civvies during Lent and Advent for tradition's sake), he strode to the center aisle and spread his arms. "Good morning, everyone."

Murmurs and returned greetings resounded.

"As the cold wind blows in and the darkness settles, we are reminded of the light that has come into the world. Just as the star sat over Bethlehem focusing its light on the baby Jesus, so does the light still settle on us today."

Murgatroyd's eyes glowed with happiness, and she elbowed J.T. "Did you hear that?"

Unwilling to look up from his coloring, he shook his head. "Hear what?"

"Jesus was the original Starman."

J.T. snickered and imagined Jesus as the twitching alien unknowledgeable of human customs, but ready to ride around in a 1977 Mustang.

"As we go through the service today, kids, make sure you pay attention to all of the references to light."

Murgatroyd glanced around the room to see what the other kids in the room were doing. She hopped up on her knees and noticed that not one single child was listening to what Unca John was saying. They all were too busy browning up the shepherds' faces in their bulletins. Glory patted her butt to settle her back into her seat.

"Now," John continued, "Let's sing."

Son of a Butcher

For most people, the service dragged, but not for Murgatroyd. As a newbie to church, every part of the show was different and intoxicating. From the weird sound of an organ to the colored glass in the windows; from the strange intonation of John's voice (sometimes he sounded like a robot, especially when he was praying), to the smell of the scented candles. Each week, Murgatroyd found something different.

After the service, they traipsed down the stairs to the basement where the delicious smells of coffee and doughnuts greeted them. The kids hurried past the adults to line up for the first fruits from the doughnut trays. Delighting their eyes were not only green and red encrusted doughnuts, but daintily sprinkled sugar cookies in the shapes of reindeer, camels and Christmas trees. J.T. grabbed three cookies and two doughnuts before one of the old ladies behind the counter snapped at him to save some for the rest. With joy, J.T. bit the head off a particularly well-decorated shepherd.

The adults were more moderate in their choices and tended to select carefully from the tray and then motion for their cup of coffee. Glory asked for a cup of tea which brought a quizzical look from Gladys Thompson's face. She looked around at the other ladies who shrugged. People didn't normally ask for tea. Glory's frowned deepened. She did not want weak, percolated coffee brewed three hours beforehand. No, she very much wanted a warm cup of tea. Glory made a mental note to bring her own tea bags.

The ladies took their coffees and sweets and moved to the far end of the basement, past the shuffleboard court, very near the covered stage. Once seated, they warmed up the conversation by asking about any juicy tidbits of information in the community. After the first round of gossip, Glory smiled and leaned towards the center of the table.

"I've got something to share."

Leona's eyes lit up. "Do tell."

"I think I'm falling for someone."

Carley almost burst with excitement. "Who is it? Who is it?"

"You don't know him," she said, not untruthfully. "I recently met him online."

"Everybody does that nowadays," Jeannie stated with absolutely no knowledge. "It's like the new disco."

Chapter 12.

"Tell me one person you know *personally* who met their spouse online," Linda said to Jeannie.

"Connie. Connie did, right Rhonda?"

"She's right," Rhonda agreed.

Jeannie crossed her arms with smug satisfaction. "There, see?"

"One person," Linda grumped.

"But an important one," Rhonda smiled. "Now, this is not about my mother. Tell us a little bit about him, Glory."

"Tall, dark and handsome, baby," she grinned broadly and took a bite of an elf cookie.

"How do you know if he's tall?" Linda asked.

"Because," Jeannie winked at Glory, "it says so on the website. Right, Glory?"

"Absolutely."

Leslie read something else in her reply but remained silent. Something wasn't adding up. "How long have you been chatting?"

"About three weeks."

The ladies cackled at this little bit of information.

"And what advice do you need?"

"Is it of the..." Carley looked around and lowered her voice, "... carnal nature?"

Glory waved her hands at her. "Of course not. It's been three weeks."

"I know when I met my husband," Leona said, "I was hot and bothered in the first few days. But that was just because it was summer and we'd had a storm."

Leslie rolled her eyes. "Focus, people. Glory's asking for serious advice."

"I want to know if there, uh... is something, uh... different about American men that I should know about as we, uh... move forward with the relationship."

"So he's American. That's good," Angela said as she nodded to the others. "Nothing like a Captain America."

"Oh, he's a hunky morsel," Carley said, "with his little shield and his big shoulders, and tight little..." she glanced around her eyes widened, "... suit."

"Glory," Leslie interrupted, "American men can be strange, and it's dependent on where they're from."

"Yeah," Penny interjected, "if they live in Nebraska, kinda stiff; and stay away from the boys from Missouri. They haven't included a dental plan in their insurance."

"And, and..." Jeannie reached her hand out, "... the boys from Illinois, big city guys with their fancy cars and their gold chains. Hairy chests." She grimaced and stuck her tongue out a few times.

"What about Wisconsin men?" Glory asked with a smile. She caught Rhonda's small gasp.

"Ooooh," Carley clapped her hands, "He's a cheesehead. Isn't that exciting? A boy from Wisconsin!" She pronounced it 'Wis*can*sin.'

"I didn't say *that*," Glory said, but meant otherwise. "I've just been working on my Iowan geography. I suppose Minnesota boys are cold."

"No," Linda said, "but all the trees lean north towards Minnesota, did you know that?"

"Why is that?" Glory asked, intrigued.

"Because Minnesota sucks," Linda slapped her hand on the table.

Another roar of laughter. Other church tables filled with other casually conversing people stopped to stare at the women.

"What about Iowa boys?" Glory asked.

"Oh, good for you," Jeannie fanned a hand at her. "Iowa boys are the best – considerate, well-mannered, easily tamed...'

"Thank you for the rundown, ladies, but I was wondering if you could tell me what kinds of things these American men like to do. Do they like to be outside? Do they like to drink tea? Wine? Do they dance?"

"Ha ha," Leona laughed derisively. "The only time they dance is at their own wedding, and only then with great hesitancy."

"You've come to the right place," Jeannie interrupted. "How old is he?"

"Late thirties."

A circle of nods.

"And general fitness?"

"Quite good. Robust, as it were."

Chapter 12.

Nods and 'oohs.' Linda elbowed Carley who was a little too exuberant.

"Rich?"

"I haven't asked that question," Glory admitted.

"Probably not, then," Angela said. "Usually if they're rich, they're quick to tell you about it, or show you. Pinkie rings, you know?"

"That means they're from Illinois." Jeannie said.

"Glory," Rhonda asked quietly, "isn't all this stuff on the website profile?"

Glory stammered. "Yes, but, erm, you are all old hands at this."

"Who are you calling old?" Linda laughed.

"That's not what I meant. It's just that your experience with American men could prove invaluable."

Leona shook her head. "I can see how you might think that – most of us have vast experience with American men," Glory caught Rhonda rolling her eyes, "but to be honest, the last time I was out on a date was ten years ago, and that was for a niece's wedding."

Rhonda leaned back in her chair. "I would suggest going someplace where none of us are. Maybe Clancy, or if you're really adventurous, Council Bluffs. Get something to eat, go for a walk along the river…"

"In December?" Leona questioned. "Nothing like first-date frostbite."

"Okay, I didn't think about that. Maybe just stick to dinner."

"Oh, oh," Jeannie bounced in her seat. "Be mysterious. Pretend like you've got some secrets. Don't reveal anything too fast. American men like that."

"I don't know…" Glory was suddenly regretting asking for advice.

"And wear something casual," Penny included, "like light blue jeans and a button-down sweater. Something feminine."

"I don't have a sweater."

"What?" All the women responded at the same time.

"I don't have a…"

"We heard you," Linda said. "It's just hard to believe that any self-respecting Iowan woman does not own a herd of sweaters. They are so flexible for different occasions. Why, I've got at least a dozen myself." The others nodded.

"So you think I need to get some sweaters?"

"No doubt," Jeannie responded. "Then, let him pick you up for dinner and take you out to a restaurant. When you're done, a hug will be enough for a first date."

"And," Carley added, "if you need any advice of the carnal nature…"

The women groaned. Rhonda watched Glory's eyes. Glory held hers.

As the women continued to prattle on, J.T. and Murgatroyd sat next to each other on the stage at the front of the room. Not wanting to be stationary, all the kids huddled together at the front eating cookies and doughnuts then running back to the kitchen window to load up for more.

"J.T.," Murgatroyd broke a piece off of a green doughnut and stuffed it in her mouth, "what do you think they're talking about?" She pointed at the table of ladies.

"Carnal nature."

"What? What is that?"

"I don't know." He refocused on his own doughnut, savoring the sweet doughy taste and crunchy sprinkles.

"Then how do you know that's what they're talking about?"

"Because I'm good at reading lips."

Murgatroyd made a lap around the top of her doughnut with her tongue and then dropped the breading part of it into her napkin. After balling it up, she set it beside her. "What about the men's table over there?"

"Corn prices."

"The old ladies in the kitchen?"

"Grandchildren."

"How do you see all of that so quickly?"

He shrugged and popped a sugar cookie in the shape of a star into his mouth. "I never really thought about it. It just happens."

"Do you ever get tired of seeing everything? Remembering everything?"

Chapter 12.

He looked down at her. She was wearing a striped shirt with Rudolph's nose and antlers sticking out from it. Her red hair seemed dull compared to the redness of her shirt. "No, not really. But once again, I don't know any different."

They sat in silence again until Murgatroyd slapped her hands together scattering cookie crumbs onto the floor. "Do you want to explore?"

J.T. sniffed. "What for?"

"So we can get away from everyone here. No carnations, no corn prices and no grandkids. Just adventure."

"Okay."

"Is there any place that's out of bounds?" Murg asked.

"Not that I know of. Although I'm pretty sure we're not supposed to go into the bell tower, but…" He smiled.

"What they don't know can't hurt them, right?"

"Bingo."

Surreptitiously, the duo rose from the carpet. J.T. scanned the room and noticed no one watching them. Escaping out the side door, they ascended the back steps. During their retreat, the sounds of the basement faded behind them until all that was left was a hum from underneath their feet. J.T. led Murgatroyd through the sanctuary, past the Sunday School rooms and up the next flights of stairs which would take them to the crawl space of the bell tower. Unca John had showed it to him a while ago, but he made J.T. promise not to go in there without him.

Feeling guilty, J.T. turned to see if anyone was following them, then pushed on the door. At first it wouldn't budge. He feared it locked until he pushed harder and almost fell through when it opened.

Moving his large boy's body into the crawl space, he made way for Murgatroyd to come behind him. "Don't shut the door too tight. We don't want to get locked up here."

"Ya think I'm a dimwit?" Murgatroyd responded sarcastically as she eased the door closed.

The short light of the belltower revealed dust floating in the rays. It was cold. The wind whistled between the spaces in the boards creating an eerie effect.

Son of a Butcher

"Are you scared?" J.T. asked with trembling voice.

"Are you?"

"Bloody hell, no," he said hesitantly.

They crawled across 1x8 boards lying side by side to the center of the tower. The boards groaned under their weight, but held. They could see between the cracks in the boards. It was a long way to the bottom. Approaching the bell, J.T. was startled by a mouse darting across the boards in front of him. Almost losing his balance, Murgatroyd steadied him by grabbing onto his butt. She giggled. "Sorry about that, Boyo. Better your bum than seeing you splattered on the ground."

"Shut up, Purg." He continued crawling.

Finally, on the far side of the belltower, a circular window with slats appeared. Standing up, J.T. could just see through the lowest slat. Amicable was stretched out below him. At this height, he could see on top of the school. There were a couple of plastic balls on top. Bird droppings dotted the flat roof and leaves eddied in the corners.

"Lift me up so I can see."

J.T. remained as he was for a moment, but then turned to her. "Crawl up on my back."

He bent down and he lifted her. Shakily, he stood, still on the thin, boarded path. With her face near his, Murgatroyd, too, saw Amicable's school and further northwards. It was fresh and clean, sparklingly white. Cars were parked in the street. Very few people were out and about at this time of day, but some were leaving the basement to drive home.

"It's pretty," she said.

"It's home."

"Do you ever think about what it will be like to move away?"

"Maybe I'll think about it once I get to high school. We'll be pretty old, then." J.T.'s eyes noticed movement near the east side of the school. He frowned.

Barnaby Koppel.

What in the wide world of sports is Barnaby doing at the school? It's a Sunday.

J.T. followed the limping man with his eyes. He seemed to be trying all the doors on the east side of the school. Suddenly, Murgatroyd

Chapter 12.

started to slip off his back. Reaching back, he caught her under her butt, which made her giggle, but the laughter quickly turned into a scream as she tumbled backwards. Landing awkwardly on the planks, her leg fell off the side. Then the lower half of her body.

"J.T.!" she screamed in terror. Her voice stirred the mice in the belfry. One ran dangerously close to her arms as she held on for dear life. Half on and half off, she dangled over the chasm below that dropped almost thirty feet to the ground.

"Hold on!" J.T. dove for her, but when he came further off the plank, it tilted dangerously up. Losing her hold, Murgatroyd's eyes were round with terror.

Grabbing onto her forearms, J.T. held on. Another mouse skittered towards them. J.T. kicked it over the ledge where it squeaked its way to the bottom of the abyss. "I don't want to die like this, J.T."

"You won't. I promise." The young boy summoned the power of his oversized body and exerted a force almost beyond nature. Pulling her up, inch by inch, he breathed a sigh of relief as her leg came over the plank. "I told you we'd be all…"

Unfortunately, the weight of both children was too much for the plank and it began to crack. "Bloody hell!" Murgatroyd shouted and scrabbled up and back towards the round window. J.T., left in the middle of the cracking board, looked on hopelessly as it creaked under his motionless weight.

"Get over here!" she yelled at him. With a quick lunge, he made for her, but the board broke under him. Just as he was about to fall, his fingers found the ledge just under her. Now, it was her turn to pull him up. With intense effort, she edged him up and over. With one last tug, his knee found security on the ledge and he stood up.

"Whew, that was a close one."

"You can say that again."

They looked out over the belfry. The bell hanging from the middle of the tower dangled ominously silent. As they pondered their situation, J.T. wondered how they would get back across without the planks. They could try hand over hand on the 2x4's above, but how strong were they?

"What are we going to do?" Murgatroyd asked.

"I don't know. I suppose we could yell and someone could come up here and get us."

She shook her head. "I don't want to get in trouble."

"I guess that leaves us just one choice. We have to make our way along the narrow beams over the drop."

She gulped. "I guess so."

"You and your adventure," he muttered under his breath.

"We didn't have to come up here," she countered.

"It doesn't matter now." J.T. tested the beam above their heads. It seemed strong. They'd have to hold on above their heads while they tightroped over the darkness. "Whatever you do, don't look down."

"You nitwit. Why did you say that? I just looked down."

J.T.'s face was ashen. "Me too."

"Well, we'd better get going. Pretty soon they're going to start looking for us." Murgatroyd could barely reach the 2x4 above her head.

"Be careful," J.T. said.

"Shut up!" She took a few tentative steps. When she slipped once, J.T. sucked in his breath. Twenty seconds later she reached the middle joist and hugged it. "All right, now your turn."

"You have to go one more. We can't hang on to the same one."

"I didn't think about that." Taking a deep breath, she completed the next part of the course. There was only one after that.

"Good job," he called out into cold, crisp air.

"Get over here."

Because of his height, J.T. was able to complete the task easier than Murgatroyd. Less than a minute later, he joined her at the far end of the belltower near the entry door. She hugged him. "That was fun."

Aware that they had crossed the next stream of their relationship, J.T. hugged her back. As he did, he glanced down and noticed for the first time, that there was a package to the right of the door. Someone had hidden a present in the belltower. Wrapped in brown paper and twine, there was a note on it that read:

Merry Christmas, Amicable. Do not open until Christmas!

"Look at that," J.T. pointed into the darkness.

"What is it?"

"It's a package for the people of Amicable."

Chapter 12.

"Who do you think it's from?" she asked.

"Probably Unca John for Christmas Eve service. He's always doing stuff like that."

"Should we open it?"

J.T. shook his head. "We'd be in bigger trouble if we did that. No, let's leave it and get out of here."

They pushed out the small door from the belltower and into the hallway. J.T. could hear his mother yelling out for him below. He grabbed Murgatroyd's hand and they rushed down the stairs.

Rhonda looked angry as they approached.

"Where have you two been?"

"We just went exploring?"

"Where? It looks like you crawled through a rat's nest." She brushed off his hair, clothes and smacked him on the butt. "Get downstairs to the car. We're going to drive the MacDonalds home."

J.T. looked at Murgatroyd who was grinning. She had cobwebs in her hair and one of her hands was bleeding. She looked very happy, though.

Chapter 13.

The Bowling Ball Ball was an event the entire community looked forward to. When an enterprising group of high school students wanted to celebrate Christmas in a new way, they began the Ball as a foil to Halloween. Where Halloween was about fear and candy, the Ball centered around happy celebration and noise. Instead of dressing up in scary costumes, Ball debutantes were invited to clothe themselves in the most creative, festive ways. Not only had the costumes grown more original and extravagant over the years, so had the prizes. The bowling alley was the annual sponsor, but other Amicablean businesses provided door prizes. Human Beans offered ten free cups of coffee. Peterson Butchery contributed a gift certificate for a hog roast or a rack of venison (your choice!). The elevator donated a free tour of the facilities (this didn't enthrall many) and Casey's gifted a one-week supply of gas AND two large pizzas. All in all, December 20 was a date that every Amicablean yearly marked on their calendar.

When Rhonda invited Glory and Murgatroyd to the Bowling Ball Ball, Glory was agog with excitement. Although Halloween had been eye-opening, the Ball would be full of happiness.

Glory had chosen her costume carefully. Rhonda had given her hints of what not to wear: no snowmen or women, no reindeer (too cliché), no Mrs. Claus or any kind of elf. No sirree, you had to prepare in advance by thinking on different planes. Glory had already figured out the best way to become the 'Belle of the Ball,' but the process had been difficult.

Murgatroyd was equally excited. J.T. would be there in his costume, which was a five-pointed star, selected for comfort rather than extravagance. Wanting to fit in with his lead, Murgatroyd decided to dress up as Jeff Bridge's character in Starman. No one would understand the reference, but the two of them would be able to bowl a little easier than if they were in long outfits.

Rhonda wore the same thing every year – a stunning blue dress made of shimmering fabric. She was the snow queen, Elsa herself.

Chapter 13.

Georgie dreamed of living up to her mother's beauty, but she contented herself at the age of seven to be Anna, Elsa's sister.

By the time Glory and Murgatroyd stepped through the doors, the bowling alley was crackling with excitement. Moving into the lanes area, many people turned to stare. Accompanying Scott Hayden (Jeff Bridges' Starman character) was the most exotic and beautiful angel most Amicableans had ever seen. From fabric she'd found at a shop in Clancy, Glory had intricately sewn reflecting bits of silver and gold into it. As she walked, she appeared to be a heavenly disco ball.

Jeannie and Leona approached her with broad smiles. Jeannie, an unimaginative Elf on a Shelf, and her compatriot Leona, a very disconcerted candy cane, blocked Glory from entering any further before they interviewed her.

"Oh, Glory, you look glorious!" Jeannie exclaimed.

"Very funny," she responded with a radiant smile.

"You are going to love this night." Jeannie clapped her hands with each word. "There is a bowling tournament beginning soon – you can be on our team, if you'd like – and then there's dancing in the Greedy Pecker." She motioned towards the bar. "Some of the stick-in-the-muds play cards out here, if you're into that." A few men who decided that the best Christmas costume was the one they wore every night, sat with beer on the table in front of them, playing cards held at the ready, carefully shielded from the other players.

"I think I'll stick to the dancing."

Leona smirked. "I just love how you say that 'dahncing.' It's so sexy. I'm going to try that out on my husband tonight also."

"Well, how can he turn down dancing with an Elf on the Shelf."

Leona snickered.

"Some of the others are here already." Jeannie began to point them all out. Finally, she leaned in close. "He's here."

"Who?"

"The butcher, Barnaby."

Glory's heart raced. He told her he wasn't coming. The night had suddenly turned more interesting. They had agreed not to announce their relationship until they were ready, but it would be hard. This would be a perfect opportunity for others to see them.

Son of a Butcher

"Where is he?"

Jeannie pointed to the video games where Barnaby was leaning against the wall standing by himself. He was not playing, only watching.

"He looks lonely," Glory said.

"Are you going to talk to him?" Leona's eyes widened.

"Why shouldn't I?"

"Because he's..." Jeannie's mouth pinched.

"He's what?"

"Scary."

Glory crossed her arms. "How can you see anything scary about a lonely man standing in a corner? Honestly, ladies, you should be ashamed of yourselves."

Shocked, Leona and Jeannie took a simultaneous step backwards.

"Now, I'm going to have a chat with him."

Leona and Jeannie watched the angel as she floated towards the man dressed as nobody but himself.

Meanwhile, Murgatroyd scoured the bowling alley for J.T. It was not hard to find him. Giant stars stuck out in the midst of reindeer, Santas and people too self-conscious to dress up.

"Hey, J.T.!"

The star turned. His face, already aglow, stuck out from a hole in the middle. "Purg!"

It was impossible to hug each other so they uncoordinatedly did a high-five and called it good. "This is so cool," Murgatroyd said.

"It's one of the funnest nights of the year. Come on. I'll show you the dance floor."

Winding their way through the crowd, J.T. turning sideways to avoid spilling drinks and knocking into people, they found their way to the shimmering entrance of the Greedy Pecker. Silver, white and blue streamers shielded the door. Pushing them aside, J.T. allowed Murgatroyd to enter the winter wonderland that awaited them.

Murgatroyd's eyes shimmered with amazement. The decorating committee had strung hundreds of snowflakes from the ceiling. A disco ball in the middle of the room lit and shaded the snowflakes creating an eerie, chilling effect. It was as if the bar had been transformed into the

Chapter 13.

North Pole. At the bar, three Santas sat on stools pulling their beards down to drink beer. Above the conversation, Christmas music played. A dance floor had been constructed in the middle of the room where dining tables and chairs used to be. A handful of children swayed to the dulcet tones of Frank Sinatra crooning about how cold it was outside.

"This is like a fairy tale." Murgatroyd's voice was reverent.

"I know. Or even Narnia."

"Does everyone from the town come to this?"

He shrugged. "I don't know. I guess most of them. Don't tell anyone I said this, but it's almost better than Christmas."

"What do you mean?"

"It seems like most people get stressed out about getting the right presents, going to everybody's houses, pretending to have fun. But here, at the Ball, everyone relaxes. They can talk to whoever they want. They can stay as long as they want. They can leave. And there's bowling and dancing and video games."

"Did you see who was standing by the video games?"

"Yeah. It's him."

"What's he doing here?"

"Unca Nash said they brought him. They didn't want him to feel left out."

Murgatroyd nodded. "That was nice of them."

"I suppose."

"You don't think he should be here?"

Shrugging, J.T. pulled her out of the Greedy Pecker and into the chaotic noise of the bowling area.

More people had arrived and a few had started bowling. The thump of the ball, the grumbling rolling sound and crash of pins, followed by screams of exultation or faux despair, were familiar sounds, even happier, now that it was Christmas.

As newcomers continued to roll in, the noise increased. Soon, the bowling tournament started; people of different generations paired off by drawing numbers from a Santa hat. There were also special rules for each adult. Some had to throw with their non-dominant hand; some had to bowl with both hands; others had to roll without stepping up to the line; some had to sing their favorite Christmas carol while they rolled the ball.

At this point, Murgatroyd and J.T. were split up. They were positioned lanes apart with people they didn't know very well, but their mothers still kept eyes on them (and Georgie). J.T. noticed that Barnaby had chosen not to take part in the bowling. No, he stood stock still by the pinball machines, one leg pushed up behind him against the wall, the other a peg under him. His arms were folded and his sunglasses gave no indication of the direction in which he looked. If J.T. concentrated really hard he could see through the lens to his one eye. Surprisingly, it always seemed to be in the same direction.

Towards his mother.

With a shiver, J.T. thought back to the night in the cemetery watching Barnaby apparently scratch his mother's stone effigy.

He turned his attention to his mother who, in her Elsa dress, was required to sit on the ground and roll her ball. He watched her smile and laugh. It had been a long time since she had let loose. Maybe this would be the night that changed everything.

A loud bray of laughter erupted behind him. It was Glory the Christmas Angel. Her rule was that she had to roll the ball between her legs first. This, of course, was almost impossible due to her floor length dress. The first time she rolled the ball it got caught up in the folds and almost ripped it.

Murg stared down the lane intensely. With her tongue stuck out the corner of her mouth, she dropped the ball and it rolled slowly down to the other end. After picking up a little bit of speed, the marbled-blue ball careened into two pins and then dropped unceremoniously into the gutter. She raised her arms triumphantly above her, nodding and smiling, while her teammates clapped loudly.

J.T. was ready for the game to finish. For him, certain things should carry more gravity, bowling being one of them. His dad had taught him that goofing around was acceptable on the playground and in the backyard, but when in competition, winning was fulfilling. Taking five quick steps J.T. tossed the ball towards the pins shattering the set up. Eight fell, leaving only two. As his ball returned, he picked it up and happened to glance back to where Barnaby was supposed to be standing.

Chapter 13.

He wasn't there.

Searching, J.T. caught sight of Barnaby sneaking behind the front desk and peeking into one of the lockers.

J.T. frowned. What was in there? Why was the new butcher back there?

Taking his second shot, J.T. completely missed the pins. His teammates consoled him, slapping him on the back; he apologized and made his way up the stairs, past the tables to the front desk.

No one was there.

Glancing around, J.T. saw that he was not being watched so he took a step back.

"Hey," a voice said behind him, "what are you doing, J.T.?"

It was Phoebe, a slight, teenage girl, shorter than J.T. with long, straight hair and severe looking braces. It looked like she could chew a wire cable in half.

"Uh, nothing. I was just checking my, uh..."

Phoebe waited with her hands on her hips. J.T. imagined her teeth chewing through his star arm or even his star thigh. What if she gnawed on his skull? Could she do that?

"Do you have a locker?"

He looked behind him. "Uh, my mom does."

"What number is it?"

"Thirteen."

"Lucky number thirteen," Phoebe smiled and approached him. Her teeth terrified J.T. and he backed towards the wall of lockers. "Don't worry, I won't bite."

It was the wrong thing to say. J.T. tripped over his own star feet and fell to the floor.

"J.T.!"

The boy saw Murgatroyd appear on the other side of the desk. Phoebe turned at the same time. Seeing the little girl, Phoebe opened a pathway for Murgatroyd to get to the sprawled out boy. She reached down for J.T. who thankfully took her arm and pulled himself up. Quickly, they edged past Phoebe who shook her head and turned back to her duties of handing out bowling shoes and taking money.

"She freaks me out," J.T. said.

Son of a Butcher

"Me too," Murgatroyd said, "her pimples."

"What? Not her braces?"

"She has braces?"

"Jeez, Purg, you really got to start paying attention."

They made their way back to lanes area when suddenly a voice came over the loudspeaker. "Attention Amicableans! The Bowling Ball Ball will begin in five short minutes in the Greedy Pecker. First order of the night, the Belle and Beast of the Ball! Best costume with least convincing Christmas costume!"

A roar of excitement went up from the crowd as the bowlers finished their last frames quickly. Shedding their handicaps, an amazing display of skill suddenly showed up. Strikes, spares, the crash of pins. As the noise ramped up, J.T. saw that people were beginning to part the streamers and move into the bar. Music, now louder, modern music with a beat, pumped. Here and there a reindeer and a Mrs. Claus were spinning towards the room. Laughter, jubilation, all mixed until it was just one emotion of happiness.

J.T. saw Leslie and John Deakins enter together. Leslie was dressed as a snowwoman and John as Buddy the Elf. Behind them, Nash and Derek walked. Nash was wearing a three-piece suit and sporting a darkened beard. Derek was wearing a sweaty tank top with a button-down shirt opened wide. His face was full of dirt and he had a police badge draped around his neck.

Murgatroyd and J.T. walked in behind them. Murgatroyd stopped Nash. "Who are you supposed to be?"

"He's John McClane and I'm Hans Gruber."

Frowning Murgatroyd looked up at J.T. who explained. "From Die Hard."

"I've never seen that. Are you sure that's a Christmas movie?"

They nodded at the same time. "Of course it is," Derek said. "It's one of the best Christmas movies of all time."

"Sounds like a real heart-tugger." Murgatroyd grabbed J.T.'s star hand and moved to the edge of the dance floor where an emcee, an older gentleman in a Grinch costume stood with a microphone.

"Okay, okay, settle down, everyone." It took a while for the talking to die down. He waited and then raised his hands again. "Now,

Chapter 13.

the jury has voted," he pointed at Shania, the bartender, and two of the town's most prominent locals, the mayor, Tracey Peterson and the newest manager of the elevator, Larry Borstrud. The locals raucously clapped for the 'jury' who were standing behind the bar with their clipboards.

"For the Belle of the Ball, we have Amicable's newest citizen and Human Beans employee, Glory MacDonald!"

Shouts of exultation and laughter exploded through the room. Glory was pushed forward by many of her exercise compatriots. As she entered the middle of the dance floor, her gown shimmered with iridescent beauty. She looked the part of an angel. "Now, as you all know, but Glory might not, the Belle must dance with the Beast for the first dance of the night. All of you men who did your best to dress up, you're off the hook, but if you thought you'd be safe by ignoring the customs, you might be in trouble." More boos.

"That being said, Glory's partner for the opening dance of the Bowling Ball Ball is…" Duane, the emcee, paused for dramatic effect, "none other than our newest butcher, Barnaby Koppel, who dressed as himself!"

The crowd went wild. Nash and Derek turned to each other and gave high fives. They had been the ones to single out their newest laborer to the jury. As a practical joke, the twins had told Barnaby that he didn't need to dress up for the dance, but now that he had been chosen for the 'honor' of the first dance, a few citizens pushed him forward. He looked decidedly uncomfortable and edging closer to angry. Derek and Nash yelled out 'Hoot! Hoot! Come on, Hoot!"

Unable to control the pressure from the audience, Barnaby found himself standing in the middle of the dance floor next to Glory. His sunglasses sparkled with furious light as the disco ball strobed above him.

"Let's give it up for the Belle and Beast of the Ball!" Everyone clapped wildly as the music kicked in.

Standing opposite each other, Glory beamed with excitement while Barnaby glanced wildly around him for an avenue of escape. Then, the music started. Bing Crosby's voice issued from the speaker and the crowd whistled. At the center of attention, Glory and Barnaby found that they were trapped. She held out her hands to him, encouraging, but he was reticent. His jaw jumped. He wanted nothing to do with this escapade, but if he refused her, he would draw even more attention to himself, and possibly to the plans he had made. Taking a deep breath, he took one step towards her.

Barnaby was roughly three inches taller than the angel in the high heels. Although they had shared this closeness before, the familiar feeling of her hand, the smell of her hair, the warmth of her cheek, it had never been in public.

"How are you doing?" she whispered in his ear.

His mouth was twisted into a fake smile. "This is not what I wanted."

"You didn't want to dance with me?"

"You don't understand," he said. "I don't like the spotlight."

She squeezed his hand. "Just live for the moment. Enjoy it."

They swayed back and forth, Barnaby holding on to her back, she onto his shoulder. For both, it had been a long time since they had danced with anyone else. Glory had, of course, in the X-Er-Size studio, but to be intimately close was excitingly different.

As the song continued, Gustav felt something he hadn't felt in a long time, a swirling of desire. Not lust, per se, but a desire for a normal life. To be with a woman, to hear her voice in the morning, to laugh and argue with her, these were the things of his prison dreams. As he and Glory moved back and forth in the dim lighting of the Amicable bowling alley, Gustav felt himself retreating from the cliff of his vengeance. Maybe it would be all right for him to set aside the past. They could move away, perhaps to the mountains or the coast, far away from Rhonda Redman.

Here was Glory MacDonald, a fine woman, who could overlook his physical deformities and his chronic ill-temper. She was begging to hold on to him, a deformed and almost-blind butcher. Why couldn't he settle for that?

As the dance finished, the emcee sidled next to them. Barnaby felt Glory squeeze his hand. Her reticence to pull away was nice, but he was ready to move. Breaking away from her, he turned to melt back into the crowd.

Chapter 13.

"Hold on, Barnaby. We have a special prize for you tonight. The judges have decided that Glory was not the only angel in the building tonight. There is one other who is worthy of a first dance." Duane turned to the crowd who cheered. "Barnaby Koppel, this is your lucky night! Two Belles! Rhonda Jensen, come on down!"

Gustav Keller felt the blood drain from his face. To be singled out and, if worse came to worse, if she recognized him, everything he had planned would come crashing down around him.

Rhonda, the snow princess, disengaged herself from Georgie and embarrassedly moved towards Barnaby. He stood rigidly, side by side with Glory who seemed particularly perturbed that Rhonda was going to interrupt their moment. Rhonda, taller than Glory by at least four inches (and an inch or so taller than Barnaby), took Glory's place. Glory backed up a few steps to watch enviously as Rhonda held her hands out to the new butcher.

Gustav was held in place by his fear. To see her this close, the object of every ounce of his hatred, was difficult in and of itself, but to dance with her? How could he possibly do it?

"Come on, Barnaby," Duane encouraged, "every other guy in the building would love to have danced with two angels tonight."

"I'm Elsa the Snow Princess," Rhonda corrected with a laugh.

He couldn't move and yet she closed in. Suddenly, she was touching his hand. An electric jolt of recognition hit him as their finger touched.

"Don't be afraid," she said.

The irony of the moment, she telling him the words that he had spoken to her long ago, resonated deeply within him. He felt his body tremble as Rhonda began to twirl him around the floor. As she looked into his sunglasses, she saw herself. His remaining eye, widened with horror, fixed on her excruciatingly beautiful face.

"I'm sorry that I haven't met you earlier," Rhonda said as she spun him on the floor, "but the timing never seemed right. I'm sure that you've heard about my husband." She ducked under his hand. "I wish you could have met him. He was wonderful."

Speechless, Gustav hyperventilated, desperately wanting the dance to be over so that he could run outside and get some fresh air.

"Thank you for dancing with Glory," Rhonda said, "she's a good woman and new to town, just like you."

They reconnected in the middle, his hand on her waist and hers on his shoulder. "I hope that you enjoy Amicable. It's a good place to live. It has a lot to offer."

Gustav couldn't look away from her eyes. Such beauty, so rare. He had forgotten. Quickly, he focussed his anger on something else. He couldn't be confused by her. He had a task to finish.

"Maybe you'd like to come over for a meal sometime. Perhaps we could have a get together and you could meet some more people."

As the song ended, Rhonda frowned and smiled at the same time. "You know, Barnaby, I have the weirdest feeling that we've met before. It's like déjà vu, do you know what I mean? It's like you're someone who's come to life that I didn't expect." She shook her head. "That's silly. I'm so sorry."

The music finished and the crowd whistled. Derek and Nash started the shouts of 'Hoot!' while others clapped him on the back. Rhonda stopped to talk to Glory, but she was not happy. Glory had seen the way that Barnaby was looking at Rhonda. It was obvious that he was smitten with her. She was gorgeous and tall and curvy, much different than the Englishwoman. For the first time, Glory didn't like Rhonda.

As the next rocking Christmas song started, Glory turned back to find Barnaby, but he had already disappeared. Like Cinderella drifting into the night, Glory fled from the crowd to find him, but the only people she saw were J.T. and Murgatroyd.

J.T. stared at the bowling alley door which was swinging shut.

Chapter 14.

Danny Thul was worried.

Since Barnaby got his driver's license, he'd seen almost nothing of him. A few times, Danny waved at him as he drove down the street. Once, Barnaby had appeared wraith-like in the Supervalu grocery store. Other than that, it was as if he had disappeared into thin air.

So, Danny decided to visit him at his home. It seemed like a right, neighborly thing to do. Danny believed it was his duty to bring over a frozen pizza and a six pack of beer. It was almost Christmas, for Pete's sake.

As he turned his car down Barnaby' street, Danny was surprised to see Barnaby getting out of his vehicle. Danny glanced at the clock on the dashboard display. Only 10:10, not late. Danny was happy to see that Koppel's limp was less pronounced. He must have been doing more walking – getting stronger. That was a good thing.

Danny slowed his car as Barnaby trudged towards the front door of his house. As he stepped into the house, he slammed the door behind him so hard that the windows rattled.

Danny hesitated before pulling his immense bulk from the car. Would Barnaby be pleased by his intrusion? Would he take offense as if Danny was patronizing him?

Hoping for the best, he grabbed the pizza and six pack and exited the car.

Breathing heavily, Danny crunched through the thin layer of snow which had fallen during the last week. He was careful not to slip. Pausing at the stairs, Danny caught his breath and peered through the front window. Even though the shades were drawn, Danny could see Barnaby's silhouette. Barnaby was on the phone because the tone of his voice was audible through the walls. He sounded very angry.

"What the hell was I thinking!" Barnaby screamed across the room. As he approached the doorway to the kitchen, he kicked out at the wood. It hurt his foot, but the pain felt good.

Son of a Butcher

The night was a disaster. Not only had he been publicly humiliated, his grand plan teetered on the edge of failure. If Rhonda put two and two together, it would not be long before he ended up in prison again.

Barnaby's face burned with shame. She had spoken to him pityingly. How dare she! Barnaby felt the intensity of rage electrify his senses and solder his resolve. Moving to the shelf, he grabbed one of the journals, jerked the rubber band off and opened it fiercely.

The entry was from the week after he got out of intensive care in the prison hospital. His handwriting was shaky from both pain and learning to see in only two dimensions.

Dear future me,

When you read this, I hope that you'll hold on to this very moment, the time in your life when you've fallen so low that the light has finally been extinguished and you have faded into oblivion. To the rest of the world – hell, to yourself – you are dead. Your life is gone and the empty shell of who you were is filled with nothingness and no one.

Hold onto this moment because if you don't, you'll kill yourself. The pain is too much for any one person.

Hold the fire in your fist. Feel the burn. Let it set you ablaze, because someday when you are resurrected, you'll remember this moment and how it shaped you as an angel of vengeance.

What happened to you was unfair and unkind. None of this was your fault, but now it is your life.

Jacob will be out there, smiling, pointing – he took from you many things, your sight and your ability to walk, he might even think he took your dignity. But he did not take your revenge.

She will pay.
An eye for an eye.
A tooth for a tooth.
A year for a year.
A life for a life.

Build on this day, Gustav Keller. From now on, you must bury Gustav until he is necessary again to ride the pale horse.

From now on, you will be Barnaby Koppel.

Chapter 14.

Barnaby felt along the faded page, the words staining his fingertips. These words gave him hope and purpose. An eye for an eye.

As he replaced the rubber band around the red and black book, the doorbell rang. Only one person would dare disturb him at this time of night, but he was not in the mood for Danny Thul and his small-town good nature.

No, Barnaby Koppel wanted to stew in his resentment and ire.

Holding on to the railing, Danny rang the doorbell. Barnaby did not answer so he pushed the button again.

"Barnaby!" he yelled out. "I know you're home. Open the door so we can talk." He rang the doorbell a third time.

It did the trick. The door behind the screen opened slowly. It was dark in the front alcove so Danny couldn't see his face.

"Go away, Danny. I'm not in the mood."

"I wanted to see you."

"I'm fine. Merry Christmas." He began to close the door.

"Barnaby, what's going on? What's wrong?"

"Nothing. I'm just tired."

"Can I come in?" He lifted up the beer and pizza.

Gustav sighed and looked behind him. "Just a minute." He closed the door and a moment later, after some reshuffling in the background, it cracked open again. "All right, but it's late."

"Do you have anywhere else to go?" Danny joked as he stepped sideways through the door.

"No."

Danny Thul had never been allowed into the house before. He had tried, certainly, but each time, Barnaby made it clear that he was not welcome. Now, though, it looked as if the house had been cleaned thoroughly. It smelled of lemon disinfectants and lavender air fresheners.

"You've been doing some cleaning?"

"Did you come to check up on my hygiene?"

"No, sorry." Danny shuffled over to a dining room chair. It groaned as he sat down. Taking two cans of beer from the plastic rings, he popped the top on one and handed the other to Barnaby. Gustav's beer spurted froth and he covered the opening with his mouth. Barnaby watched disdainfully as the beer erupted from the sides of his mouth, like a foamy volcano, and onto his carpet.

"Drink up," Danny said and gulped down half in one swig.

Gustav set his drink on the table but did not sit down. "What would you like to know, Danny?"

"Jeez, can't a guy sit and have a beer with his friend?"

"Are we friends, Danny?"

Danny frowned. "I thought so. I mean, we go to the bar together, have a few laughs. I got you some things from the store. Say, where's all your computer equipment? What about the…?"

"I've packed it all away for another day," Gustav replied.

"So you're not working anymore?"

"Would it make a difference?"

"No, not really," Danny replied, "but sometimes when guys give up their hobbies it's a sign of depression."

"You think I'm depressed?"

"Well, I'm no psychologist, but you looked pretty angry when you walked through the door, and now you don't have your computer? I don't want to come over here sometime and find a dead body." He meant it as a joke, but his pinched laughter said otherwise.

"You've been following me. Don't do that. I'm not suicidal. Can't a guy be angry?"

"What are you angry about?"

"*That* is none of your business."

Danny was quiet, but then spoke after taking another drink. "It might help you to talk about it."

"I can guarantee you that it will not help me feel better. Nothing will. Only…" Gustav pinched his lips together.

"Only what."

"Only if you leave."

"That's not what you were going to say. There's something else. Something big is going on with you. That's why I haven't seen you around. Not even at the bar. When you bought all those cleaning supplies, I thought you'd gotten a new job and I thought to myself,

Chapter 14.

'That's good. Barnaby is starting to move on, get better.' But then I didn't see you and I started researching why you would need all that stuff."

Gustav stared at him behind his sunglasses. Danny was dancing too close to the edge of the truth. "What do you think, Danny?"

"Nothing. Nothing. It's just, never mind."

"I've got a job as a butcher now, Danny. We've talked about that. I'm in charge of cleaning up at the end of the day."

Danny breathed a sigh of relief. He truly had wondered why Barnaby would need so much hydrogen peroxide. And the acetone? Blending the two would be... well, not such a good idea, but for cleaning, that certainly made some sense.

"Okay, okay. I just wanted to make sure that there was nothing untoward going on with you. I consider you a friend even if it sounds like it might be one-sided."

"I'm sorry about that. I'm just not a very social person. I'm not used to conversation. People generally don't want to talk to me."

"I'll talk to you any time you want." Danny smiled and pulled off another beer.

"Maybe after Christmas?" Gus tried to smile, but it appeared like a grimace, which made Danny raise his eyebrows.

"Okay, so anyway, I can take a hint."

Fifteen awkward minutes later, Danny Thul left the Koppel house even more confused than when he'd entered.

It wasn't until it was too late that Danny put two and two together.

* * * * *

Rhonda and Leslie sat in the bowling area with their feet up sipping drinks with umbrellas. Leslie rubbed her feet while Rhonda leaned back in her chair and stared at the ceiling.

"It was a pretty interesting night, wasn't it?" Leslie asked as she winced from the pain.

"Yes, different." To her left, Rhonda saw J.T. and Murgatroyd picking up bowling balls and replacing them in the racks for bowlers who had left for home. It was almost one o'clock in the morning. J.T.'s eyes were red-rimmed and Georgie had already fallen asleep on the chair beside Rhonda.

"Barnaby looked very uncomfortable, didn't he?"

"I felt bad for him."

"One of these days the Peterson twins are going to get themselves into trouble. They never should have nominated Barnaby for Beast of the Ball. He looked like he was about to explode."

"Glory seemed to enjoy it," Rhonda said. "She doesn't seem to have a problem with him."

Leslie raised an eyebrow. "But he seems to have a thing for you…"

"Are you kidding? He was rigid, like a corpse. Rigor mortis, you know."

"I thought he did pretty well with you. It must be hard to have those deformities and be the center of attention."

"It felt kind of creepy to be dancing with him, like I was dancing with a ghost."

"Well, when you can't see their eyes, you don't know what they're thinking." Leslie yawned into her hand.

"It was weird, though. I felt like… oh, it's crazy. I must be tired."

"What were you going to say?"

"It's nothing. Really."

"Come on, tell me," Leslie insisted.

Rhonda took a deep breath and exhaled. "Okay. It was like déjà vu. I felt like I'd known him from somewhere else."

"Maybe you've met him on your travels with Butcher."

"Yeah, maybe," she sounded unconvinced. Rhonda tried to place where she'd seen him before, but with those scars, she should have remembered.

As the last of the Bowling Ball Ballers were picking up their belongings, donning their coats and wishing the stragglers good night (many of them would be taking a sick day from church in the morning), Glory emerged from the Greedy Pecker. Her face was bright red and her angelic hairdo had fallen out into a tangled halo at her shoulders. After the dance, she had consumed quite a few drinks. Rhonda would have to get her into the car soon.

Chapter 14.

Glory noticed the two sitting at the table and frowned. She caught Rhonda's eye and looked away quickly.

"Glory," Leslie called out, "come and sit with us."

Wiping her forehead, Glory's shoulders sagged and she took steps toward them. In her slightly inebriated state, she stumbled on a plastic chair and almost fell. She kept her footing but spilled the drink on her angel's clothing.

"Hello," she said when she finally reached them, "I hope you had a good night."

"I hope you did too," Leslie responded as she moved over to let Glory sit down.

"It was okay."

Rhonda reached out to touch her hand but she recoiled. "What happened? Are you alright?"

"Fine."

Rhonda was taken aback by her shortness. "Do you want to talk about it?"

"I'd rather not."

"Maybe we could help you," Leslie said. "Did someone say something to you?"

"No."

"Was it… dancing with Barnaby?" Rhonda asked.

Glory's eyes narrowed. "Perhaps."

"He didn't touch you… inappropriately, did he?"

"No, not at all."

"Is it his looks?"

Her ire raised, Glory crossed her arms. "What's that supposed to mean?"

"There is something disconcerting about his dark glasses and his scars." Rhonda responded.

"Just because you're drop dead gorgeous doesn't mean you should pick on the looks of other people."

"That's not what I meant."

"What did you mean? Somehow Barnaby isn't worthy to dance with someone like you? A real princess."

"Okay…" Rhonda said slowly. "Maybe it's time I take you home."

"Of course, your highness. Time to take Cinderella home so that she can turn back into the maid."

"Whoa, I don't know what happened tonight, Glory, but have I done something wrong?"

Glory attempted to stand, but fell back into her seat. "I'm going home now. Murgatroyd and I are going to walk."

Leslie reached out part way to her. "I don't know if that's such a good idea, Glory."

"What, you too? Protecting your best friend as she moves in on the new butcher."

Rhonda and Leslie gasped simultaneously. "Glory," Leslie said quietly, "I think you should apologize."

"For what? I'm just telling it like I see it. Bloody hell. You looked as if you were falling in love with him. You should have seen the stars in your eyes."

Rhonda could feel herself getting angry. "Let's get one thing straight. There is no one who will ever replace my Leo. No one. Ever." Tears sprang to her eyes. "And Barnaby, he couldn't hold a candle to *my* Butcher." Standing quickly, Rhonda called to J.T. to get his things.

"Aren't we driving Murgatroyd home?" he asked.

"No, they've decided they're going to walk."

"But Mom…"

"NOW, J.T.!" Rhonda scooped up Georgie who complained briefly about the manhandling but dropped her head back onto her mother's shoulder.

J.T. moved quickly. It had been a long time since he'd seen his mother like this. J.T. attempted to give Murgatroyd a high five as he left, but his star arms weren't working very well after lifting all the bowling balls. The three of them strode quickly to the door. J.T. opened it and saw that his mother was crying openly. Then, glancing back at Glory, she seemed perturbed. Aunt Leslie just looked sad.

They exited into the night and made their way home.

J.T. hoped that his mother wouldn't be unhappy for too long.

Chapter 14.

* * * * *

Rage. Unfiltered, undiluted rage.

For Gustav, this feeling was powerful and electric. Every part of his body thrummed with potency. The disaster at the bowling alley was exactly what he needed to snap him back to his task and thrust forward his plans for Rhonda and the town.

Oh, how close he had been to tipping. Surely, their niceness had almost trapped him and caused him to give up the chance at his reckoning. To feel her hand on him, her breath near his cheek causing him to shiver, the smell of her perfume and the beauty of her eyes; it was horrific. The object of his anger suffused him with glorious fury.

To be put in that situation, to be a public spectacle, first with Glory and then with her – it was like being swallowed by a nightmare. The Barnaby side of him felt bad for Glory, but she had done it to herself. She should have stayed away; she should have ignored him like every other person had done for many years.

The twins had fooled him. He felt ashamed because he had fallen for their buffoonery, their callous jokes, their 'nickname.' Yes, to his shame, he had enjoyed the attention. To feel part of a community, to have a new name, baptized into a new life – yes, this had felt good – but it was only a veneer of what simmered beneath Amicable. It was like every other place and every other time. The people might make you feel welcome, but you'd never fit in.

Never.

Gustav slammed the lid down on a box containing the bits and pieces of his revenge. Stalking to the dining table, he dropped the box on it. He felt a delicious sense of the table's pain as the wooden box scratched the surface, marring its polished reflection. Now the table was scarred like he was. And those scars couldn't be buffed away with a coating of Pledge. No, no, no – this table was now doomed for a garage sale with a polite little sign that said *$10 or best offer.*

Gustav was unwanted, which galvanized his need to hasten the predestined pain for Amicable.

Going through his checklist, he realized with bemused certainty that he only had three days left before…

His phone rang.
Glory.
"Hello," he said gruffly.
"It's me." She had been crying
"What do you want?"
"Talk to me, Barnaby."
"That's not my name."
"Don't do this, please."
Her pleading irritated Gustav.
"Don't do what? Don't be angry? Don't run away?" He snorted. "You're all the same. By tomorrow, you'll have gone to the police and claimed that I've molested you somehow. You know, the scary, scarred butcher – he probably held a knife to your throat. That poor Englishwoman with the shady past."

"You're hurting me, Barnaby." Glory's voice was choked with emotion.

"Didn't I tell you I was good with knives? My words are scalpels. Soul-slashers."

"Why are you doing this? I thought we were…"

"We were what? That we were falling in love? That's a fairy tale for Disney Princesses."

The phone went silent and Gustav was about to hang up. Then, she spoke again. "Come to me tonight."

The sentence made Gustav leap to his feet and a wrestling match ensued with Barnaby. How long had it been since he'd heard a phrase like that from a woman? To feel her arms around his neck, her lips pressed against his, to *understand* her need and enjoy his own, that was excruciatingly tempting. Gustav's fury battled Barnaby's desire for love.

Through clenched teeth, Gustav said, "Don't be stupid, Glory. Nothing good would come of that. People in this town talk. Your own daughter is friends with that little weirdo."

"We could be very secretive. Just once. No one would ever know."

"I WOULD KNOW!" he shouted into the phone. "I would give you what you wanted and then you would cast me aside, make

Chapter 14.

accusations. I KNOW HOW THIS WORKS! It's happened before!"

"What are you talking about, Barnaby? I've never done this before."

After a struggle, Barnaby found his way to the top. "Glory," he said softly, "just forget me. It's for the best."

"Barnaby," she pleaded, "let's talk about this. Please."

He held the phone with both hands to his ear. "If I come over, what will we do?"

Breath shuddering, Glory inhaled. "We'd have a cup of coffee. We'd sit on the sofa. We could talk. You could hold my hand. We could watch the sun come up."

Barnaby imagined it in his mind as Gustav tried to erase the vision as quickly as it appeared. To watch the sun come up, to see it glistening in the snow, to feel the warmth of a woman's body next to his. To hear someone – anyone – breathing and to hear the thoughts of someone – anyone – other than his own caused his heart to race. Could it work?

Gustav wrestled back control. "You almost had me, Glory. I almost gave in."

"No," she whispered. "I need you."

"You need *them*," he said.

"How can I prove it to you? How can I make you see that I think there is a future for us?"

His eyes alit on the box in front of him. He still had one more gift to give.

"There is one way…"

"Anything," she promised.

"Let's meet tomorrow, at Winslow Park, 9:00."

"Okay. Then we can talk," she said.

"Yes, then we can talk."

The last gift-wrapped package would do all the talking they needed. Glory would be helpful after all.

As Gustav pushed the red button on his phone, he could hear Barnaby beginning to cry deep inside his head.

Shut up, you feckless fool. This is for our own good.

Chapter 15.

On December 22, a Monday, the last day of school before Amicable school children took a break from their bookish ways and trundled home to revel in the festivities of their own households, life changed.

At 2:30 in the afternoon, J.T. and Murgatroyd sat in the corner of their school room on top of the ancient heater feeling the warmth emanate through their wet blue jeans. As they peeked outside, the sun already dipping lower towards the horizon, the winter solstice one day in the rearview mirror, Murgatroyd gnawed the head off of a particularly large sugar cookie in the shape of a reindeer. J.T. worried himself with a caramel bar made of Rice Krispies and some secret marshmallow ingredient.

"When are you going to open your presents?" J.T. asked.

"Probably on Christmas morning."

"Is that what they do in England?"

She nodded and then bit off Rudolph's front right hoof.

"We're opening on Christmas Eve. That's how we do it in Amicable."

"I'd like to do that, but my mum says that would be cheating. Santa doesn't even get here until Christmas morning."

"Do you want to come over and play on Christmas Day or the day after?"

"You mean Boxing Day?"

J.T. frowned. "What's that? Is that an English thing? Everyone boxes after Christmas?"

"No, Boyo, it's the day after Christmas. I think it's called that because you go buy more stuff in boxes after Christmas."

"That's stupid."

She shrugged. "So are flying reindeer, but that doesn't mean a little lie can't be useful."

"So you go shopping the day after Christmas," he asked incredulously.

"Sometimes. Probably not this year."

"You can come over then."

Chapter 15.

"I don't know. My mum is still kind of grumpy with yours. They haven't talked all week."

"I didn't see you guys at church yesterday." J.T. licked some caramel off his fingers.

"Mum said that Jesus for adults is like Santa for kids. A nice story, but kind of unrealistic."

J.T. snorted. "That's silly. Jesus was a real person."

"Let's not talk religion, Boyo. Let's talk about something more fun, like sledding. Should we go sledding on Boxing Day?"

His eyes lit up. "Now you're talking. Did you see the sheds at the football field? The snowplows piled up the snow at least a million feet tall."

"A million?" she raised an eyebrow dubiously.

"It's high, that's all I'm saying."

"Okay. It's a deal." They shook hands exchanging sugar for marshmallow surprise.

J.T.'s eyes were suddenly caught by movement outside the classroom. His eyes focused far up the street, two blocks away by the bowling alley. It was Glory. He pointed. "There's your mom."

Murgatroyd whipped around. "Where?"

"By the bowling alley. She's crossing the street."

"I can't see that far." She scrunched up her nose.

"You need glasses."

"Shut up, fart box."

He giggled and watched Glory approach. Finally, Murgatroyd saw her as she was about to enter the school. "What's she carrying?"

"A package."

"I wonder what it is?"

J.T. readjusted his eyes. "It has the same handwriting as the one in the belltower."

"What does it say?"

"For Mrs. Brown and her class. Merry Christmas."

Murgatroyd studied his eyes which appeared very birdlike, jumpy. "That's pretty strange. I didn't think she even liked Mrs. B."

"Maybe she's trying to get on her good side."

Son of a Butcher

Minutes later, without fanfare, Glory MacDonald appeared in the doorway. Wearing a rust-colored fake fur coat, corduroy with wooden toggles for buttons, she stamped her feet on the small rug outside the door. Glory had recently had her hair tinted. It was now green on one side and red on the other. Her cheeks were flushed.

"She looks… off," Murgatroyd said.

"What do you mean?"

"Wild, you know? There's something about her face, and her hair? I wonder why she did that?"

"You mean she did that today?" he asked.

"It wasn't there last night. Duh."

Mrs. Brown waved for Glory to enter the room. As she welcomed her, Glory handed the butcher-paper-wrapped present to the teacher.

"What's this?" Mrs. Brown asked.

"A gift and a thank you for your work with Murgatroyd." Glory smiled and Mrs. Brown nodded.

"I appreciate that. Thank you. Merry Christmas to you."

Glory nodded without saying anything. Then, her eyes sought out Murgatroyd. She waved. Murgatroyd hesitantly lifted her hand.

"You were right, Murg," J.T. said. "There is something wrong."

"What is it?"

J.T. stared at Glory's face. "She's lying. And she's really scared."

Mrs. Brown turned with the gift and set it on her desk. "Would you like some hot chocolate or apple cider?" she asked Glory.

"No, thank you. But I will collect Murgatroyd if possible."

"Of course." Mrs. Brown turned and nodded.

Murgatroyd grabbed her belongings and faced J.T. "We need to talk some more. Call me this afternoon or tonight, okay?"

He nodded. For the first time, J.T. wished he had another gift. X-ray vision. What was in the package?

Over the last few weeks, J.T. had seen Barnaby carrying packages. He saw one in a bowling alley locker. He saw one in the church's belltower. Lastly, he saw Barnaby taking one into the high school. Understanding Barnaby's actions was hard for J.T. to process, because stitching together what he *saw* with what he *knew* about him, was

Chapter 15.

difficult. The transformation from guardian angel to a very angry man was incomprehensible. As his emotional intelligence reached its limitation, J.T. inwardly shrugged and moved on to something much better.

Christmas presents.

* * * * *

Officially, John Deakins would be on Christmas vacation starting at noon on Christmas Day. The Christmas Day worship service was generally quite small. Most Amicableans showed up for worship on the Eve, agog with evening excitement. Children's eyes would be alight with happiness as they stared open-mouthed at the Christmas tree lights. There was festive organ music and general goodwill-among-men kind of thing.

John was ready for a break. The emotional strain of caring for his congregation was taking its toll. More and more of his aging congregation were entering the final phases of their lives. The lucky ones died quickly. The unfortunates were those who were moved to 'A Home' which would never be their home. It was a place to exist, but not to live. As he visited them, wishing them a Merry Christmas, he saw the jealousy and their frustrated grimaces of being fed Christmas pap instead of ham or turkey. All their lives they'd been the organizers, the cooks, the entertainment directors, the Santa Clauses, the hubs of the families, but now that they'd outlived that role, they were disregarded – or discarded.

It wasn't just those in the nursing home; it was the tense, peeled faces of contemporary earth. People worried about the next virus, both biological and digital, which could lead to an oppressive, unrecognizable future. They might ask him, even without words, 'How can God do this?' or more theologically palatable, 'How can God allow this to happen?'

For the victim of age and the tragic 21st century worrier, these questions were appropriate yet unanswerable. John did the best he could. Various scriptures always pointed to hope, but on the grand scale of life, he couldn't tell them that there was a bigger picture being painted. The artist's design was not yet finished. Those suffering would hear this as a trite platitude, thank him for his time and then go back to Googling a panacea for all life's ills.

Son of a Butcher

John reflected on the Bowling Ball Ball. It had been a marvelous night full of laughter and hugs. Those that stayed for the dance enjoyed the rhythmic song of slowly moving life. Yet, the first dance still troubled him. John had chided the boys for putting Barnaby in that spot. Although it seemed that Barnaby took it well, John searched for the butcher afterwards, but was unable to find him. The Peterson twins told John to relax. It was just a joke.

Unfortunately, 'just' jokes had a way of always coming back to 'just' bite.

Dressing in his warm winter coat, he pulled the collar up around his ears and stepped out into the cold. The stinging north wind bit his cheeks and he shivered while he pulled the door shut behind him. Breathing shallowly, lest his lungs be burnt, he descended the steps. Across the street, Glory MacDonald walked resolutely with a package in her arms. He called out to her, but she couldn't hear him. Shrugging, John walked the short distance to Peterson's Butchery and opened the door.

Welcomed by a warm blast of air, he saw other patrons loitering in the shop waiting for their packages or enjoying coffee at the table. Derek raised a hand to John and then turned his attention back to an elderly woman, Janice Bajur, a kindly woman with dark hair who loved to laugh. Derek handed her a package of mystery meat. She turned and wished Pastor Deakins a Merry Christmas, then opened the door to leave.

"Pastor John," Derek beamed, "Merry Christmas. What can we do for you?"

"Christmas ham, Nash."

Because he was misidentified, Derek rolled his eyes. "One ham coming up." He busied himself in the glass case procuring a smoked ham from inside.

While Derek wrapped the ham, John caught sight of Barnaby running the saw in the back room. His dark beard hung long against his chest. John felt a surge of empathy for the lonely man.

"Derek, do you mind if I go back and talk to Barnaby?"

Derek scrunched up a cheek. "Not really supposed to do that. Can he come out? You can talk in the café area."

Chapter 15.

John turned around to see three other people there. "This is more of a private conversation. Do you mind?"

After pausing, Derek nodded. "Okay, but not too long."

"No problem."

John lifted the flip counter and made his way into the back room. The walls were immaculately clean, but the cutting tables were splotched with gore. Cold stainless steel and ceramic tiles made the sound reverberate loudly.

Entering his blind spot, John watched him work until the saw finished. "You're very talented," John said.

Startled, Barnaby jumped and turned his face towards the intruder, knife out. John could see his reflection in the bright light of the room in his sunglasses.

"Are you supposed to be back here?"

"No."

"Maybe you should leave, then." Barnaby turned away from him.

"I wanted to talk to you."

"Some other time."

John circled the stainless-steel cutting table to stand opposite Barnaby. "I wanted to apologize."

Barnaby stopped. "For what?"

"For the dance the other night."

The muscles in his cheeks bounced as he gritted his teeth.

"I know it's probably too late and won't help, but I thought I would say it anyway."

"I don't know what you're talking about."

"It wasn't fair that you had to be the center of attention."

Barnaby glanced around the room and saw Derek in the front talking to customers. "Look, not to be rude, but I'm trying to work here."

"I realize that Derek and Nash were trying to make you feel like part of the family, they do that with everyone, but I think they overstepped the line."

"Not to be rude..." he repeated through clenched teeth.

"Okay," John held up his hands in surrender, "I'm going, but would you consider having a drink with me after you're done with work?"

"What, like coffee?"

"I was thinking a beer, or wine. Your choice."

Moving back to the cuts of meat, Barnaby piled them on a tray. "Aren't you supposed to be a teetotaler or something?"

"We Methodists have a few vices, in moderation, of course." John smiled to diffuse the tension.

"Feel free to drink alone then."

"Come on, one drink."

Barnaby flipped the cuts on another table in preparation for wrapping. "What for? What are you going to get out of this? Just a nice story about helping the downtrodden? Something for the Sunday morning sermon?"

"No, Barnaby, that's not it at all. I just want to get to know you."

"Why?" He threw a stack of chops into a pan and wheeled on him.

"Because I can appreciate the difficulties of a butcher's life."

Barnaby paused. "You're talking about the other guy. The one everybody loved."

John shrugged. "Yes." Barnaby stared. "Okay, the truth is: I had a best friend named Leo Jensen. He was an incredible man who became a pillar of this town. He started as an outsider." John ran a hand through his hair. "We tried to push him away, and if we had succeeded, our lives would have been infinitely worse. I don't want to make that same mistake with you. What is it that makes you tick? How can we find *acceptable* ways of helping you to acclimate to Amicable?"

Barnaby felt his chest tighten. He didn't need this kindness. "Will you leave me alone then?"

"Absolutely."

Putting his head down and arms on the table, Barnaby sighed. He wasn't quite sure why he would even think about it.

"Where and what time?"

"Wherever you want."

Barnaby smirked. "All right, in the church at five o'clock."

Chapter 15.

"What? In the church? Why there?"

He shrugged. "Why not? Seems like a nice place. You're not squeamish, are you? God won't strike you down, will he?"

"Not that I know of." John's mind raced furiously trying to think of possible parishioners who would be wildly offended if the news got out that he drank beer in the church. But he might not have another chance with Barnaby Koppel. "Okay, Barnaby, five o'clock and St. Clements it is."

Barnaby turned away from John Deakins ignoring him.

Slowly, John bid him goodbye and left the room.

* * * * *

"Where are you going?" Leslie asked.

John checked his watch. 4:45. "To the church. I'm just finishing up a few things." He felt a little guilty not telling her about his meeting with Barnaby. It would not be pretty if she found out. *When* she found out.

"Okay, but make sure you're back by 6:00. It's supposed to be your day off, you know."

"Yeah, yeah." He grabbed his coat and headed next door.

At 5:05, he rechecked his watch. No sign of Barnaby. Disappointed, John felt certain that he would not show up. Turning back to the pigeonholes, John used the time to place Christmas cards in each one. That had been Carol Mentgen's idea, except that he was now the one doing all the work. At 5:12, there was a knock at the front door. Barnaby stood in the covered area brushing snow from his coat in the alcove light.

John waved and smiled, then opened the door for him. "Welcome. It's getting cold, isn't it?"

"It's winter," Barnaby said stiffly as he entered the narthex. Stomping his feet on the rug, Barnaby glanced around his surroundings, looking as if he'd never been in the church before. "The holy place."

John smiled. "It's home."

"How long have you been here?" Barnaby asked.

"A long time. Almost twenty years."

Son of a Butcher

"That's a long time for people of your sort, isn't it?"

John laughed. "Yes, I suppose so."

Studying the architecture, Barnaby looked up the stairs to the sanctuary. "That's where all the magic happens."

"That's the sanctuary, yes."

"I know the meaning of sanctuary," Barnaby walked closer to the stairs.

"Really? What do you know?"

Taking a few steps up, Barnaby peeked into the large dark room. The eerie light glinted through the stained glass windows and cast ghostly shadows over the pews.

"The ancients believed that there was always a place for those accused of crimes, a sanctuary, a holy place, where there was no violence," he motioned toward the room. "Supposedly anyone who entered the room, no matter their crime, would be considered safe from any retribution."

"That's right," John responded as he stood below Barnaby at the base of the stairs. "But there was a caveat."

"What was it?" Barnaby asked

"Those that claimed sanctuary had to stay in that sanctuary – for the ancient Christians, grasping the horns of the altar – until they were cleared of the charge."

"Hmm, that sounds a little excessive."

John shrugged. "Fortunately, it wasn't always a building. Sometimes it was a city or a town."

"You wanted to have a drink?" Barnaby asked changing the subject.

"How about we go down to the basement – the cellar."

"Okay."

As they descended the next set of stairs, John flipped switches for the humming fluorescent lights above. They ticked and flickered until catching. Tentatively, Barnaby held onto the handrail and limped downwards. As they entered the room, there was a bottle of red wine and two glasses on a round table. "Do you want some music?" John asked.

"I'm not into churchy stuff."

Chapter 15.

Shrugging, John motioned with his hand, indicating where they would sit.

Once seated, Barnaby reached into his coat pocket and retrieved a bottle of blue Mad Dog. "I bring my own."

Laughing, John pointed to the bottle. "MD 20/20. That's funny. I had some of that in college."

Barnaby looked at the bottle. "This? Come on, you only have Communion wine. The blood of Jesus stuff."

Leaning forward, John pointed to the label. "Guess what. This is made by the same people that make our Communion wine. Look," he underlined the words, "*Made by Mogan David.* MD. Mad Dog. It's fortified wine – port, just like what we have upstairs."

Frowning, Barnaby pointed at the bottle of wine in front of John. "You mean you don't have that stuff?"

John shook his head. "Nope. This stuff is far too expensive."

"This isn't," Barnaby grabbed the blue Mad Dog. "Now, let's start with mine and finish with yours."

Swallowing, John looked at his watch. Six o'clock was going to come around far too quickly if they had that much to drink.

Barnaby noticed him looking at his watch. "If you don't have time…"

"No, no, I'm looking forward to getting to know you." He moved his wine glass closer.

Smiling, Barnaby opened the bottle and poured the Windex-ish looking liquid into the glass. Bravely, John smiled and toasted Barnaby. "To you, Barnaby."

"To sanctuary," the butcher responded enigmatically.

John winced after he swallowed. Barnaby watched his expression and his mouth twisted into a wry smile. "You want to ask me questions?" he asked.

John glanced wistfully at his bottle of ten-year-old rioja. "That would be great."

"Okay, let's make this interesting. For every drink, you can ask me a question, and I get to ask you one, okay?"

"Sounds fair, but I don't know how many questions we'll get through."

"No problem. You go first."
"Where are you from, Barnaby?"
"Wisconsin. Tell me why you became a religious man."
John held up his hands. "Come on, you didn't add any other information. What was your family like? What did your parents do?"
"Tut tut. Quid pro quo, Pastor Deakins. You'll have to phrase the questions better. Now, answer my question."
John laughed. "I guess I didn't *become* a religious, I always have been. While in Amicable, though, I've learned a big difference between religion and faith."
"What is it?"
"Tut tut, Mr. Koppel."
Raising his glass, he toasted again.
"Tell me about your life growing up, your parents, siblings and life in general," John said.
"Now you're getting the hang of it." Barnaby smirked. "I grew up on the banks of Lake Michigan. My parents ran a restaurant famous for reuben sandwiches. When I graduated, I went away to college. I'd had enough." He paused and thought about his question. "Why did you come to Amicable?"
John felt a burp rising already, but he stifled it with his hand. "I certainly didn't choose it. Most of my seminary classmates wanted the 'exotic' places like the Rockies or New England. Let's just say I think my seminary professors thought I needed a challenge so they put me in Amicable to, how shall we say, take the sharp edges off."
"Has it worked?" Barnaby asked.
John shook his head. Mad Dog was 13 percent alcohol. He'd have to get some water or Leslie would be *very* unimpressed *very* quickly.
"How did you get your scars?" John asked without thinking.
Barnaby took his time with the drink and with the question. "Why do you want to know?"
John grinned, the warm feeling already spreading. "I'll let that go for free. I'm curious," he responded. "Most people avoid scars, but I find them fascinating. They're memories that make us who we are."

Chapter 15.

"Okay, but if you want me to answer that, you get a hard question from me, also." John spread his hands in acceptance. "Tell me about the guy they called Butcher."

John's sharp intake of breath echoed in the large room. "Why do you want to know that?"

Barnaby responded in the same way that John did. "That one is free, also. Let's just say I'm curious. Everybody in this town seems to have some kind of memory about the guy. He seems like a superhero. The way the twins talk, it's like he had X-ray vision."

"I'll go first." Instead of pouring more Mad Dog, John opened his rioja. Pouring himself half a glass, he smelled the wine, rolling it around in the glass. "Leo Jensen was my best friend. When I first met him, I tried to get rid of him. He was an outsider and when he tried to date Rhonda, we tried to protect her."

"From what?"

John smiled. "How about we forget about drinking after every question and just have a conversation."

"All right."

"Rhonda Redman was something of a local celebrity. During high school, she excelled in almost everything that she did – basketball, volleyball, academics. But she grew up in a dysfunctional family – Rhonda's father ran out on them when she was little." John shrugged. "Her mother didn't cope well. As she became harder to live with, clingier, almost clinically so, Rhonda moved away to college. While on vacation, she met a man. Things didn't go well."

With every fiber of his being, Barnaby Koppel attempted to restrain the raging beast of his inner personality. Gustav banged against the walls of his psychological cell. It was only by sheer force of will that Barnaby kept him at bay. Barnaby, as an alter ego, was the man he could have been without Rhonda Redman, but it was hard. Gustav's power was palpable. The bars holding him in were bending.

Barnaby's hand slipped from his drink and the blue drink spilled onto the floor. Staining the carpet, the drink looked strange, like alien blood. "Son of a…"

"Don't worry about it," John said quickly. "We'll get it later."

Son of a Butcher

Behind dark lenses, John couldn't see the battle raging, so he continued. "Rhonda was a wounded woman, and it was only when Leo Jensen showed up that she started to heal. Yes, he was different – he had a gift of seeing people for who they were. Butcher brought Amicable out of its isolated shell to feel like a sanctuary," he smiled ruefully. "And now we're somewhat of an anomaly in the Midwest again. Thriving, growing."

"This is thriving and growing?" Barnaby waved his hand towards the walls of the town.

"Maybe not metropolitan, but certainly an anomaly for rural communities."

"It seems kind of like a dump to me." Barnaby reached his hand out for John's wine.

"For many, yes. Now you. What about your scars?"

Barnaby Koppel wrestled with the truth, with Jacob Reinhold, with pain and isolation, with lost years and incarcerated dreams. With Gustav's desire to set things right. Yes, the painful truth was that the guards were responsible for his limp, but his rejection by the greater world was due to Jacob.

"Prison."

John's eyes widened. He hadn't expected that.

"I might be lying," Barnaby said with a smirk.

"I don't think you are," John responded as he took a drink. The wine erased any of the nightmarish flavors of the Mad Dog.

"Maybe you have some of your friend's superpowers."

"If only that were true."

"A particularly nasty fellow named Jacob Reinhold caught me unaware after dinner one night. Supposedly, he thought I'd taken some of his cigarettes and that was enough to demand payment of my eye." Reaching up, he touched the side of his face. "Screwdriver. He laughed the whole time while I screamed."

"Oh, God, I'm sorry."

It's not you who should be sorry, Barnaby thought.

"It's in the past and I can't get it back. But it's been a long time since anyone has taken an interest in me other than..." He almost spilled the beans. Glory.

Chapter 15.

"Than who?"

"An acquaintance. Someone I met in Clancy."

"What was your crime?" John asked quietly.

Barnaby rubbed his nose with his finger. It still smelled of meat. "Tell me, Reverend, what did you do when this Butcher died?"

The question evoked powerful memories: Butcher's face, his laughter, his spirit, everything. Surprisingly, he felt a tear appear in the corner of his eye. "I realized that a future I had wanted was folded up like an old newspaper and discarded." He wiped the tear away. "For months, I moped, walking around town in a daze. Everything about my life was monotonous, empty of meaning."

"Sounds like prison," Barnaby interrupted.

"It was. My personal prison. I couldn't really communicate with anyone; not my wife or my children, not congregation members, not even Rhonda. I let her down."

"Maybe this Butcher died because he did something wrong. Maybe your God punished him. Or," Barnaby's mouth twitched up into a sneer and relaxed again, "maybe his wife was the one who did something wrong."

John shook his head. "I don't believe that's why things happen. God doesn't punish people for mistakes. Of course, there are always consequences for decisions we make, but not necessarily heavenly vindication. Not anymore."

"What about lying, Reverend? Any punishments for lying?"

John frowned. "What are you asking, Barnaby?"

Gustav was beating against the door. The key was rattling. A few more twists... "What if one person suffers for the lies of another. Tragic suffering, not any of this run-of-the-mill pity party stuff that happens when someone gets a disease and drowns in a lake."

John's jaw dropped.

Gustav was coming quickly. He was out and hurrying forward. "What happens when a woman who, after making advances on a man, suddenly decides that she's had enough, and when push comes to shove, accuses the man of something he didn't do? What about that, your Holiness? Should the woman be punished?"

"Barnaby, I don't know what happened, but..."

Son of a Butcher

"Try spending over a decade of your life in prison for something that didn't happen. How would you feel? What would you do? Any thoughts of taking a little vengeance into your own hands?" Barnaby's voice lowered. "Should the shamed and maimed man suck it up and go on with his life, or should he seek retribution."

"Barnaby, maybe we should stop. Go home."

"Go home! That's rich. This is *not* my home. This is *not* my sanctuary. This is *not* a place to stay but only one to pass through. As soon as I've finished, I'll find those places somewhere else. Far, far away."

"Finished what, Barnaby?"

"Finished… hurting."

"I think maybe we've had a little too much…"

Gustav had arrived. "What's wrong, priest? Not used to some righteous anger? Do you need to splash some holy water on your head, or swallow a little more Savior juice?" He pointed at the wine. "Too much honesty? Yes, you're right. Time for more lies. More deceit. I'll play the dutiful butcher who kowtows to the first-class citizens of Amicable." He swallowed the last dregs of his wine.

"Do you need someone to drive you home?"

"No, I don't."

Unsteadily, Gustav stood up. "A toast to you, Pastor John. This has been enlightening, to say the least." Spittle flew with every word.

As Gustav turned towards the stairs, shadows led the way up. Strangely, when other faces appeared, Gustav's turned ashen. "You'll get your merry Christmas," he mumbled under his breath.

As Gustav stumbled up the stairs, he almost crashed into Leslie and Rhonda who had come to find out what was taking John so long. Righting himself, he turned the corner and slammed the door as he headed out into the darkness again.

"What was that about?" Leslie asked John concernedly.

He held their gazes and then took a sip of his wine. Disconsolately, he stuck his finger in the glass, pulled it out and drizzled the wine across his hair.

"Son of a butcher," he said.

Chapter 16.

As per their wishes and prayers, snow started to descend noiselessly to the earth, not on December 24, but the 23rd. While children began their Christmas holidays by dancing delightedly in the frosty flakes, their parents, or otherwise responsible adults, wrapped up last minute budget busters and stuffed them in various nooks and crannies around their homes.

December 23, a Tuesday, was a day of tormenting impatience. To occupy their thoughts and imaginations, anticipating the Eve, some children went to the school playground to run around.

J.T. had built a snow fort. It was not particularly imposing in size, but its reach was admirable. As of 3:00 in the afternoon, neither J.T. nor Murgatroyd had yet to fire a single snowball. For most of an hour, they sat with their backs to the ice wall tossing small snowballs back and forth between each other. Strangely, they did not speak much. Murgatroyd had been morose and short. Her mother's mood had infected them both. On the other hand, J.T. was as upbeat and talkative as he had ever been. With his legs stretched out in front of him, he moved his boots back and forth tapping them together.

"You haven't said much. That's something new."

"Oh, shut up. I'm grumpy."

"No kidding."

"Somethings going on with me mum and she's taking it out on me."

"What happened?"

"I don't know. It started at the Ball. She got cross with your mum and then we stomped out."

"Maybe she's got a crush on Barnaby?"

"What? Don't be stupid. He's a weirdo."

"You say 'stupid' funny. It's like 'stchewpid.'"

"That's how we say it in England, pal."

J.T. shook his head. "Well, you're not in England anymore, Purgatroyd."

"You ain't kiddin'."

Son of a Butcher

"Seriously, though, your mom might have a thing for Barnaby. I saw it in her eyes." He showed her what it looked like.

"You look like a moony cow." She copied his gesture. "There's no way she's falling for him. That's daft."

"I'm just telling you what I saw."

"Then why would me mum be cross with yours?"

"Maybe she was jealous."

Murgatroyd clopped her much smaller boots together. "Of your mum? Because he was dancing with her?"

"Maybe..."

She shook her head. "It's ridiculous to even imagine the two of them together. With those strange glasses and the scars."

"They do make it difficult to read him."

"What should we do about it?" Murgatroyd asked.

J.T. picked up a snowball and tossed it at the chain link fence. "We have to get them together to sort it out. They seemed like they really enjoyed each other's company."

"Yeah, well, mum was talking about packing up and moving on." Murgatroyd picked up another snowball and hurled it even harder at the fence.

"What?"

"Yup. She said she was almost fed up with this town. One more thing goes wrong and we're out on the road. Maybe to Oklahoma."

"What's in Oklahoma?" J.T. asked.

"How should I know? You're the Yank."

"I thought there might be a reason she chose Oklahoma over some other more popular state like, I don't know, North Dakota."

"I don't care. It's all so stupid. I finally fit in. I've got a friend. We built a fort. Bloody hell, I don't want to go."

J.T. stared at his diminutive, redhaired friend. It scared him to think that she might move away. Finally, he had found someone who didn't look at him like a freak.

While J.T. pondered the unfairness of *what if*, Rhonda and Leslie sat together in Human Beans at their regular seats by the window. Glory, sullen, in spite of the festive mood inside the café, stood behind the counter serving a few patrons who had stumbled in through the flurries.

Chapter 16.

"What are you thinking about?" Leslie asked Rhonda.

"Oh, I don't know. I just feel strange."

"About what we saw yesterday?"

"Yes," Rhonda nodded. "There was something so… I don't know… familiar about the scene."

"Familiar about my husband and Barnaby Koppel sitting in the basement of the church drinking cheap alcohol and telling stories? Maybe you need to take a little vacation because that's never happened before. It took us almost an hour to get that horrible, cheap blue liquor out of the carpet."

Rhonda's laugh was forced. "No, of course not that. It's just that Barnaby, the more I'm around him, it feels like we've met somewhere else."

"Like in another life?" Leslie rolled her eyes. "I think you'd remember if you'd met *him* before."

"I know. I know. He's not a person you would forget."

"So then let it go," Leslie insisted. "Be Elsa the Snow Princess."

Rhonda did laugh. "Okay. Now, what is the Deakins family doing post-Christmas?"

"Nothing. Nothing and nothing." She patted her belly. "This little gift will need some rest after this year."

Rhonda glanced at Leslie. "I'm so happy for you."

"I know. I'm glad you'll be here for me. I just wish Glory was in the same boat. Since the Ball, she's been so distant."

"I can't believe she thought there could be something between me and Barnaby. Gosh, it's been such a long time since I've thought about any other man than Butcher. It would have been…" Suddenly, Rhonda's eyes widened. Something tripped in her mind. The sound of his voice; the look of his hair.

Don't be ridiculous, Rhonda. He committed suicide. You got his letter. His name is Barnaby, not Gus.

"What were you about to say? Who was the last man you had your eyes on before Butcher? Dennis Campman?"

Rhonda smiled and waved her hand at Leslie. "No, Dennis was just a high school thing. It would have been in college."

"What was his name?"

"Gus."

"You've never told me about him before," Leslie pressed. "Was he attractive?"

Blushing, Rhonda took a sip of her coffee. "I don't want to talk about it," she said quietly.

At that moment, Glory began wiping down tables at the edges of the room. Noticeably, she ignored Rhonda and Leslie. Leslie motioned with her eyes to Glory; Rhonda shook her head. Leslie encouraged her with her hands. "Okay," Rhonda sighed.

"Glory," Rhonda called out. Glory did not respond. Rhonda pushed her chair back and walked to Glory.

"Can we talk?"

Glory continued to ignore her until Rhonda put a hand on her arm. Glory froze, and when she finally turned, she had tears in her eyes.

"Oh, Glory, I'm so sorry. I have no idea what I've done, but whatever it is, can we work through it?"

Glory sucked in a stuttering breath. "All my life," she said with lowered voice, "I've taken a back seat to people who needed things from me. My mother, my father, my stepfather, men. All of them. From high school to university, then with Murgatroyd. I thought once I came to Iowa, things would be different, and I wouldn't have to. I thought I could be in the driver's seat."

Rhonda remained silent.

"I know I should have told you this, but Barnaby and I have been seeing each other for a few weeks. When I met him, I thought, 'Here is a man who is not going to be targeted by anyone else.'" Glory let out a hiccupped sob. "But then, there is a gorgeous, tall, attractive, local woman who could have any man she wanted. And who does she choose? Barnaby Koppel."

"Glory…"

"Please, let me finish. When I saw you dancing with him, I saw the way he looked at you. He's in love with you."

"That's not true, Glory. You couldn't see his eyes. His glasses…"

"A woman knows, Rhonda. I know. You could see the emotion written all over his face and at that moment, I knew I'd lost again."

"But…"

Chapter 16.

Glory held up a finger. "You don't understand what's it's like to lose a man like that. He's..."

Leslie couldn't hold back any longer. "Glory, don't."

Suddenly, Glory realized what she'd said. Seeing Rhonda's face melt from concern, to anger, to hurt, all in the space of a few seconds, stabbed her in the heart by the words of a careless comment. Glory closed her mouth.

Without speaking, Rhonda turned away from Glory. A grief she thought passed, had suddenly U-turned and double-parked across her life. It was laughable that Glory believed Barnaby Koppel could hold a candle to Butcher. Sure, they had similarities, but Leo had been a pillar of strength and a beautiful man. Whereas Barnaby was... well, she didn't know what he was, only that his unattractiveness was not limited to his physical appearance.

Unable to vocalize these words, Rhonda watched Glory turn back to cleaning the table and wipe her tears with the other hand. Feeling torn, numb with concern for both women, Leslie wanted to go after Rhonda, but stayed with Glory instead.

"I'm sorry for what you are feeling, Glory."

"It's not your fault," she said shortly.

"I know, but I'm sad for your pain. It must be hard to live in another country, surrounded by people who all know the rules."

Glory stopped wiping and stood up. Although she didn't look at Leslie, she nodded. "Yes."

"Rhonda's husband was like that. Butcher. Maybe he wasn't from another country, but he sometimes seemed like he was from another planet. We didn't treat him well when he came."

Frowning, Glory turned. "It's hard to believe that. You? A preacher's wife?"

"My marital status has nothing to do with how I treat people," she replied softly. "Sometimes I'm as mean and callous as everyone else. Other times, like now, I really don't want to see people hurting."

It took a few moments for Glory to respond, but when she did, she turned. "Why is life so hard?"

"It's the oldest question in the book, isn't it? Sometimes we suffer the consequences of bad choices. Most times, we're just in the wrong place at the wrong time."

"Rhonda's husband, Butcher, did he feel the same way?"

Leslie's lips pursed in a wry smile and Butcher's face came to mind. "At the end, I suppose. It took him a while to get there. Pain and grief had a way of messing with perspective. In the last few months of his life, he saw things differently. I remember watching his face when he was able to do the smallest things: sit outside in the breeze, have one of his kids on his lap, feel Rhonda's hand on his face. Even though he couldn't smile, you could tell his body was smiling."

"I'm sorry for saying what I did," Glory said quietly.

Leslie approached Glory and put a hand on her arm. "That proves it then. You're human, just like the rest of us."

Glory covered Leslie's hand with her own. "Thank you."

Almost instantaneously, the day changed to dusk. Gentle blue-greys painted the white canvas of snow to match the closing day. Soon, a brisk evening would take over. The clouds would break sometime in the night. Over the streets, timed Christmas lights turned on and sparkled. Along Main Street, atop green light poles, large yellow stars were festooned to the peaks. If one were to walk along Main Street (humming Silver Bells, of course), one might feel a sense that they were walking through the Milky Way.

Amicableans mingled outside of stores pondering the freshly lit decorations, marveling at the beauty of the season and wondering if there was anything quite so beautiful as an Iowa winter. Kids would play, parents would revel, grandparents would remember, and the world would keep spinning forever.

Leslie was about to leave the café when suddenly, Rhonda rushed back in. Her face was flushed. Frantically, she ran to Leslie and Glory.

"The kids! The kids are gone!"

"What? Murgatroyd and J.T.?" Glory's face registered fear.

"Rhonda, Calm down. You're not making sense," Leslie said.

"They were supposed to be playing in the school yard, or even at one of our houses, but there's no sign of them!"

"Maybe they've gone for a walk," Leslie suggested.

Chapter 16.

"No! No! They haven't! Something bad has happened. They've been taken!"

Glory felt a cold wave of fear wash over her. "How do you know that?"

Face breaking into a tortured pain, Rhonda leaned into them both. "Because they left a note in the snow." She showed them her phone which held a picture that said.

"Starman is here."

Chapter 17.

Louise Nelson, the town police officer, arrived shortly after the phone call was made. Darkness had settled in. What had been a pristine night of hopefulness had made a profound detour into a nightmare. As they stood in Human Beans, Louise stood with hands on hips, a worried expression on her face.

"What does that mean, 'Starman is here?'"

Rhonda, pacing, faced Louise. "I don't know! I don't know! It was a stupid movie that J.T. and Butcher used to watch. It was J.T.'s favorite."

"Really?" Glory was incredulous. "That was Murgatroyd's favorite also."

Louise glanced back and forth between the two of them unsure where to begin. Kidnappings did not happen in Amicable. "Okay, let's go back to the beginning. Are we sure that the kids aren't out playing somewhere?"

"Yes. Before they go anywhere, Murgatroyd always texts me."

"Could her phone be dead?"

The word 'dead' sounded ominous. Rhonda and Glory stared at each other. "Yes," Leslie interjected, "there is always that possibility."

"Have you tried calling J.T.?" Louise asked Rhonda.

"He doesn't have a phone." When the other three women stared, she barked, "He's only nine, for heaven's sake. Why would he need a phone?"

"For times like this, of course," Glory said.

"Like what?"

"In case they've been kid…"

"All right, all right," Louise tried to calm the women down, "let's not jump to any hasty conclusions. I'm sure there's a reasonable explanation. Now, getting back to this message in the snow. It couldn't have been someone else, or they could have been playing?"

"It's J.T. – his handwriting, I'm sure of it. And it makes no sense that he was playing. I mean, if they were at our house, maybe, but not in the middle of the schoolyard."

Chapter 17.

"But what could this possibly mean? What is Starman about?"

"I don't remember much about the movie. It's been a long time since I've watched it, not since Butcher's passing. But what I remember was that a grieving young widow tried to get along after her husband's death, when suddenly her dead husband shows up alive again. He's been, jeez, I don't even know the right words, co-mingled? Is that right? Co-mingled with an alien who's used his DNA. Everything about his outward appearance looks the same, but everything on the inside is different. She tries to figure out if it's the physical man she loved, or the man inside the man."

"Could the movie have anything to do with where he is? Could they be watching the movie somewhere else? At your house, Glory?" Louise asked.

"I can't call. I don't have a landline."

"Could you go home quickly and check? Perhaps they just decided to walk to your house and lost track of time and phone battery." Louise smiled hopefully at the women. Glory nodded, shrugged her coat back on and raced out of the café. As it was now almost 5:30, Human Beans was closing for the holiday, and the owners were ready to go home.

"Now, Rhonda, take me to this snow message and we'll see if we can get some traction on where the kids are."

"Leslie, you might as well go home now. If we need you, we'll give you a call."

"Okay." Leslie turned to Rhonda. "We'll keep Georgie at our house until you come get her, okay?"

Rhonda hugged Leslie. "Thank you."

Leslie left. Rhonda and Louise buttoned up their coats and headed for the school playground again.

* * * * *

Murgatroyd MacDonald was scared out of her wits. So, too, was J.T., but for very different reasons. Murgatroyd's fear stemmed from the fact that the mysterious man had lured them to his car. Because Murgatroyd had seen her mother dancing with this man, the scruffy looking butcher with scars and sunglasses, she hadn't been afraid at first. But now that he had shown up inside the chain link fence of the school yard, she felt an ominous foreboding that she couldn't quite articulate. Something was wrong with the person who was supposed to be right.

J.T. recognized this fear as something malevolent. Over the time that Barnaby Koppel had been in Amicable, J.T. had struggled with his inability to read his eyes (or eye, in Barnaby's case). Barnaby stood intimidatingly over them, legs spread, arms crossed. J.T. wished he had his father's gift to *read*, not just to see. He saw the quickened pulse in Barnaby's throat as well as the tense jaw and threatening posture. But he couldn't *read* if Barnaby wanted to do them harm. Murgatroyd could feel it though. With a sixth sense far beyond her age, Murgatroyd intuited it.

"What do you want, Barnaby? We're playing." Murgatroyd crossed her arms as she stood behind the snow fort.

"Your mother is in trouble."

Murgatroyd frowned. "What kind of trouble?"

"She's at your house. She's hurt."

"Why are *you* telling me this?" Murgatroyd looked at her phone. "Why isn't *she* calling me?"

His jaw muscles pulsed. "She's asked me to come get you."

"Why would she ask you? Why not J.T.'s mum?"

"How would I know that? I'm only doing what she asked. Either you can come with me, or I'll go there on my own and take care of her."

There was something particularly sinister about the way he said 'take care of her' that caused Murgatroyd to pause. "What do you think?" she asked J.T.

Even if J.T. asked Barnaby to remove his glasses, J.T. knew the expressionless eyes were impossible to read.

"I can't see anything wrong, Murg."

"Do you think we should go with him?" she asked.

"It's your decision. It's your mom."

Murgatroyd crossed her arms. "I'll come with you, but J.T. has to come with me."

Barnaby breathed a sigh of relief.

As the children crossed outside the fence, past the jungle gym and snow-covered slide, beyond the frost-crusted front doors, through

Chapter 17.

the front gate to Barnaby Koppel's used vehicle, they couldn't have known they were making a grave mistake.

It was decidedly not.

As Gustav opened the back door to the car, he pushed a button on his phone which disabled the cell-phone reception for the children. He had bought this little piece of hardware from Danny Thul. Although his intention had never been to harm the children, it was the best way to get to Rhonda.

The naïve children climbed into the back seat and buckled their belts. Murgatroyd pulled out her phone and attempted to call her mother but grew frustrated when she couldn't get a signal. Gustav slid into the front seat and started the car. Driving southwards past the school, St. Clements, the bowling alley and library, he then turned west on Highway 10. Strangely, though, instead of turning left, just past the elevator, he accelerated down the highway.

"Hey," Murgatroyd said as her fear intensified, "where are we going?"

Gustav remained silent.

"This isn't the way to my house." She turned in her seat and pointed to the elevator. "It's back there! Turn around!"

J.T. stared into the rearview mirror trying to see past the dark sunglasses into the eye beneath.

"J.T." Murgatroyd's face was a mask of fear, "we're being kidnapped! WE'RE GOING TO DIE! HE'S GOING TO KILL US AND EAT OUR SPLEENS!"

Gustav turned in his seat. "Shut up, kid! You're not going to die and I'm not kidnapping you. I'm only trading you."

"Oh, well that makes me feel better. Watch the road, Cyclops!"

He turned back towards the front, his face unreadable.

"What are you trading us for? Drugs? Money? Sex? Popcorn?"

"Look, kid, this will go a lot easier if you just shut your mouth."

"WHY WOULD I WANT IT TO GO EASIER?" Her voice, now at shrieking level, filled the car and forced J.T. to cover his ears. At this stress level, J.T. could feel himself drawing inwards back to his sanctuary, to the time before Murgatroyd, when life was a simple, endless visual experience – no emotions, no pain, no joy, nothing but watching.

Son of a Butcher

J.T. felt the urge to curl up into the corner, to find comfort in a ball. He thought about his mother and his father, even his sister, and wondered what life would be like without them. He thought about Starman and wished he had the same abilities, metaphysical powers to blow up the man in the front seat. Even more, J.T. wished he could find the resolve to hate Barnaby Koppel so that he could do something. But he couldn't. J.T. had never hated anything or anyone in his entire life.

As Gustav drove, J.T. saw the tenseness in his shoulders and the throbbing scar on the side of his face. Looking out the windows of the car, J.T. saw miles of snow filled ditches. Telephone poles whizzed by the side of the car. Flakes of snow floated past the windshield like white butterflies. J.T. saw the twinkling stars. Strangely, he wondered if there was life on planets somewhere else in the universe. When he had written the note in the snow, he truly thought that Starman had come to be with him. Was Barnaby Starman, really? Maybe he was a copy of his father! What if that were true? What if his dad was just angry about being put in such a faulty body!

"HEY!" Gustav screamed. "If you don't shut up right now, I'm going to put you in the trunk!"

"You do that, mate, and I'll box your balls!" Murgatroyd had suddenly found a well of strength.

Gustav shook his head and kept driving.

"You know you're going to jail for this," Murgatroyd leaned forward. "I've heard what they do to people like you."

Gustav grinned evilly. "Where do you think I got this beautiful face?"

"You're a convict?"

"Not anymore."

"What were you in for?"

"Rape."

"Not children, I hope."

His eye focused on J.T. "Not children. And I didn't actually do it."

"That's what all convicts say. I saw Shawshank Redemption."

"A movie?"

208

Chapter 17.

She moved farther forward testing the limits of her seatbelt. "Movies are the best way of expressing truth."

He snorted. "Don't be delusional. Hollywood has a fundamental bias against truth." He muttered to himself. "Why are we talking about this?"

"Because you're kidnapping us," Murgatroyd responded.

"I'm not kidnapping you. I already told you that."

"Uh, yeah you are. You've stuffed two nine-year-olds in your car and driven them away from their parents. I think we can question your definition of kidnapping."

"Do you ever stop talking?"

"When I'm sleeping. And sometimes in class." Murgatroyd was beginning to feel a little bit better. Talking made her feel like she was in control. "So, you're a jailbird."

"I don't want to talk about it."

"Why not?"

"Because it's personal and it makes me angry."

"What happens when you get angry?"

"I snap. I turn into a different person."

J.T.'s eyes snapped towards Gustav. *Wait a minute... Is that what I saw? Is that what's underneath the scars? Is there another person trying to get out? Is there an alien under his skin?*

"That's weird."

"You can stop talking now."

"But it helps me. I like to know what's coming."

"If you just relax and do what I say, you'll be free in a couple of hours."

"What's this trade thing? Who are we being traded for?"

"You'll find out soon."

Murgatroyd cupped her chin in her hand. "I'd rather find out now."

"Get used to disappointment."

"Is your name really Barnaby?"

"It is now."

She rolled her eyes. "So in other words, 'no.'"

"No, my name is not Barnaby."

"What is it?"

"Gustav."

She snorted. "That's weird."

He shook his head. "You do realize that your name is Murgatroyd."

"I have a beautiful name. Right J.T.?"

J.T. did not respond. His retreat into himself was almost complete. Finding the place of sanctuary was necessary.

"Hey, Boyo! Wake up! I need you here."

Startled, a light came into J.T.'s eyes. He saw his friend, his diminutive red-haired friend, his one and only friend, calling out his name. From what seemed like a great distance, he began the long, arduous journey towards her. She deserved that.

"I'm here," he said at last.

"You like my name, don't you?"

Blinking his eyes rapidly, as if clearing an intense fog, he found her eyes, tense and starkly beautiful. "Yes, yes. I like everything about you. You're my best friend."

Without thinking, Murgatroyd began crying and fell sideways into J.T. She snuggled into his shoulder. At the touch of his body, she found her sanctuary. "J.T. don't leave me, okay?"

"I won't."

Barnaby heard the exchange in the back seat and felt his soul begin to tear. What was he doing? Would this really help? Why not move on with life and put the past in the past? These two children, the tall boy with the vacant expression and the smaller girl, vibrant and energetic, had their whole lives ahead of them. In that moment, he remembered what it was like to be young and innocent, secure from a world that would soon rip his guts out.

He knew he shouldn't be doing this. These kids were innocent like he was. But Gustav wouldn't quite release his grip.

"Look," Gustav said as he turned right and drove towards Clancy, "I'm sorry that I had to use you kids, but someday you'll understand."

Chapter 17.

Gustav pulled the car into his driveway and shut off the engine. Now almost immobile with fear, the two children fell out of the car and into the snow when he opened their door.

As Gustav reached down to grab her shoulders, Murgatroyd slapped his hand away. Instead, she reached out to J.T who helped her. Following Gustav to the house across crunching snow, J.T. memorized their surroundings and where they were. He was hopeful that the information might come in handy later on. Tall, white, two-story house, three bushes in the front. On the mailbox was a 251. Turning his gaze towards the street sign two hundred feet in the distance, he focused on the street name: Humboldt.

Three streets away, he saw a young couple carrying bags of fast food: Hardees. J.T., with the thought of food, felt his stomach turn over. He was hungry.

Above them, the moon's belly was half-full, or at least that's what his dad used to call a half moon; a glittering handful of stars twinkled brightly. Christmas was just around the corner. Gifts and presents were stacked under the trees and hidden in crevices around the house. Would they be able to open them?

As they walked, he suddenly remembered the hidden present in the belltower of the church. What could that be?

Then, they were inside the house. Barnaby dropped the keys onto a desk in the front alcove. The children, still holding hands, made their way into a darkened living room where Gustav flicked the switch and light flooded the room. The sparse furnishings were in stark contrast to the children's homes. J.T. glanced to where Gustav had entered the kitchen.

"How long are we going to be here?" Murgatroyd asked J.T.

He shrugged.

"Are you hungry?" Gustav asked them.

"Yes," they answered simultaneously.

"I've got some bread, peanut butter and jelly."

The children stood in the kitchen entrance. J.T. noticed the lack of decor in the kitchen. No pictures – nothing on the walls. "How long have you lived here?" Murgatroyd asked.

Son of a Butcher

"Quite a while." He busied himself with the plain white bread spreading peanut butter across it creating holes and smears.

"It smells in here."

He ignored her comment.

"It smells like an old person."

Jelly. The knife made a tinkling sound on the jar and echoed in the room

"And like moldy cheese. Maybe that's the same thing."

More jelly.

"Do you have any family?"

"No."

"Your parents are dead?"

He shrugged and handed a shredded sandwich to her.

"What am I supposed to do with this?" She opened it. "This isn't a sandwich. It's two pieces of toilet paper with a…"

"Look, kid. Just eat it."

She grimaced and took a bite in silence.

"What about you?" Gustav spoke to J.T. "Do you want a sandwich?"

He nodded.

"You didn't answer my question about your parents. Did they die?"

"No, yes, but I have been dead to them for a long time."

"Because of your rape?"

Stopping, he pointed the butter knife at her. "I didn't rape anyone," he growled.

"It seems like a natural deduction." She took another bite.

"You're a strange little girl."

"I've been told that before."

Gustav handed the next mutilated sandwich to J.T.

"So they don't talk to you anymore?"

"No, they don't."

"They're embarrassed, aren't they?" Murgatroyd pushed.

His face reddened and he shrugged.

"Do you miss your mum and your da?"

Chapter 17.

His jaw moved up and down. The question was so out of left field, something he hadn't thought about for so long, he was speechless.

Before he could answer, Murgatroyd launched into her own story. "I never got to know me da. He was a slippery bastard, or so Mum said, and he certainly didn't want anything to do with me. There have been lots of blokes in me mum's life, but I wouldn't put any of them in the category of father material. I do have a good mum, though, don't you think?"

Gustav was quiet.

"Tell us about your mum and dad. At least until you've decided when to trade us."

"I already said I was sorry." He moved past them into the living room.

"Well, *now* I feel better."

The children followed him. When he sat down, the kids sat opposite him. J.T. still munched on his sandwich while Murgatroyd wiped her hands on her shirt.

"Come on," she insisted, "tell us your secrets."

"You are ridiculous," he responded.

They waited. Murgatroyd cupped her chin and rubbed her non-existent whiskers. "Tell me about your mother. I saw that in a show about Cinnamon Freud."

Barnaby rolled his eyes "It's Sigmund, not Cinnamon."

"It is?"

"Yes."

"Okay, we're ready. Tell us a story. As long as you've got a couple of kids held hostage, you might as well entertain us while we wait."

For Gustav Keller, this was a strange, unexpected turn of events. Surprisingly, almost miraculously, Gustav felt a sudden urge to share his story and his reasons why they were in the current predicament.

"In the fall after graduating from college, I left my parents' business, a restaurant on the eastern shore of Lake Michigan. They were hard workers, but they weren't great at talking. I spent a lot of time with my friends." He studied Murgatroyd's surprised expression. "Yes, I had a lot of friends, actually. I didn't always look like this."

Son of a Butcher

"Go on," Murgatroyd motioned with her hand.

"That autumn, I met a woman," his eye strayed towards J.T. but he couldn't have known that J.T. could see it. "She was beautiful. It was a chance encounter. A wonderful night turned into a nightmare. You're too young for me to explain the details, but soon after she left, my life was ruined. I remember the smell of the police car, the rough feel of the cuffs, the horrified stares of my neighbors who had suddenly pegged me as either a drug dealer or murderer."

"I had one phone call. I called my parents. I told them the truth, but once accused you are guilty until proven less guilty. They were shocked and saddened and horrified. My mother told me 'That's not the way we raised you,' to which I asked her if she'd heard a word I said. I ended up slamming the phone down. I remember that sound too. It was final."

"They showed up at the trial but left before the final verdict was read. I couldn't prove my innocence. I couldn't prove anything. But the woman got away free. She's free! And I lost everything in jail!"

"On the bus to the prison, I began to understand about unfairness and injustice. My life as a normal member of society, one with hopes and dreams, a life with a future, was now finished. No hope for me. Your mother had taken it all from me."

It didn't resonate with Gustav that he'd just injected a large piece of information into the monologue until Murgatroyd's face scrunched up.

"Me mum? Are you mad? We've only been here for a few months."

Gustav shifted his gaze. "Not yours. His."

J.T. ultimately understood then that there were many things he could see, whether the number of spiders in the room, the dead flies in the ceiling lights, the boxelder bugs on the floor, but he couldn't see the deepest dark in front of him.

"It was Rhonda Redman. Your mother flushed my life down the toilet."

Chapter 18.

By seven o'clock, Glory and Rhonda sat nervously in Rhonda's living room, hysteria edging closer.

"Okay, well," Louise's breath blew out, "if they're not home in an hour or so, we'll call in the State Police."

"An hour?" Glory said. "That seems like a very long time. A lot could happen in that hour."

"If they're out at someone else's house, or they've gone to the gas station – we don't want to call the troopers in if we can help it."

"So we just wait?" Rhonda said quietly.

Louise nodded. "Do you have any coffee, Rhonda? Can I make some for everyone?"

Rhonda pointed to the coffee pot. "I don't want any, but you can all have some."

As the uncomfortable emptiness filled the room, Glory sniffed and blew her nose loudly. Rhonda couldn't take it anymore. "Glory, tell me some things about England, about your life there that's different than Amicable."

Glory looked up at the ceiling before she spoke. "Life always seems easier when you look back." She smiled ruefully. "Anything would seem easier than this right now, I guess. But in Chigwell, the people were always too busy, not just for talking, but for everything. It's like life was one of those motorized walkways at the airport and you just stand on it. As it moved, you chose a job, or a partner, some entertainment here or there. Then, suddenly, you're at the end of the line and when you turn around, everybody else is gone. You've spent your whole life moving but never going anywhere."

"My dad left when I was little, and when we finally connected again, it wasn't pretty. He had gone somewhere, you know? The man that I had built up in my mind as the prototype for a dad was a machine. He still looked kind of the same, twitchy, like he was trying to understand who I was and how I could possibly share DNA with him."

"Before Murgatroyd and I left England, my mother told me that he wanted to see us – to meet Murgatroyd. I didn't want to do it. It was hard enough seeing him in that bar, with his wild eyes and puffy cheeks. My mother, though, said that it might be the last time. So, we met in a park."

"It was springtime in London – he couldn't bear the thought of coming out to Chigwell again, so we took the train in. Springtime in London is very similar to here. But the city was grey and dull, depressing, you know? People scurrying everywhere, scrounging around in the bins of everyone else's rubbish hoping to find some treasure where there wasn't any before."

"He was sitting on a park bench feeding pigeons. He looked sad and lonely, like the motorized walkway had finally stopped and he realized that he was never going anywhere. When he looked up at me, I realized we felt the same way. For a long time, he just stared at Murgatroyd who stood there and held my hand. She asked who the sad man was, and I said that he was nobody."

"I saw it in his eyes, the hurt and the despair. I wanted to tell him that I was sorry, and that I didn't mean it, but I did. I wanted him to hurt too. He deserved it."

"As we turned to walk away, he called out to me and he said, 'Glory, if I could do it all over, I would have taken care of you.'"

Glory sighed. "It was that sentence that hurt me more than anything. Why would he begin to assume I needed to be 'taken care of?' I only wanted a father who would love me. A father who wanted to be there with me through all things, but certainly at the birth of my beautiful baby girl."

"I went back to Chigwell and cried for a week."

Glory leaned back and ran her hands through her hair before puffing out her cheeks. "I was tired of the moving travelator. I had a daughter, but no time. I had a house, but no home. I had things, but no love of them."

"How did you end up in Iowa?" Louise asked.

"One day after being bullied at school, Murgatroyd came home and said, 'Mum, I don't like my life.' This was from an eight-year-old girl, mind you. I remember the sad expression on her face as if the weight of the world had settled on her small shoulders. We cried a little bit, then Murg said, 'What'll we do about that, Mum?'"

Chapter 18.

"I settled her across my lap, something I hadn't done since she was a wee girl – I never had time, ya see – and I asked her, 'Where would you like to go? If you could choose anywhere in the world?'"

"She said Iowa?" Leslie asked incredulously.

"No," Glory smiled sadly. "She actually said New York. But I didn't think that was such a good idea. London was bad enough."

Rhonda shook her head sympathetically.

"We found a fold-out map of the United States at some cheap tourist shop. Spreading it out, we pinned it to an old corkboard. I handed a dart to Murg and said, 'Throw it. Where it lands, that's where we're going.'"

"It landed on Amicable?" Louise asked.

Glory snorted. "Do you think Amicable would be on an American map we found in London?"

"I guess not," Louise responded.

"Her throw landed directly left of a place called Des Moines. I'd never heard of it. Sounded French if you ask me, and I'm not too fond of Frogs."

"I explained to Murgatroyd that we were moving to the exotic locale of a place called Iowa." She lengthened the word. "And that we'd have a happy life, and we'd grow old together, far away from the problems of jolly old England, and we'd…" Glory found that she couldn't finish the sentence. Her mind turned back to her missing daughter.

"You found us," Rhonda said quietly. "And we got you."

"Yes, well, that's one way of putting it." Glory struggled to keep her emotions under control. "Where the dart hit, there was nothing on the map. No mountains or lakes or even rivers. It was the plainest of places, which suited us just fine. I called my mother and stepfather to let them say goodbye to us. It was awkward and unsettling – my stepfather was quite happy to see his misfit stepdaughter and similarly misfit step-granddaughter go to where all the misfits end up – America. My mother tried to cry, but she failed. Once they had waved their goodbyes, they toddled off to the airport bar for a few gin and tonics."

Glory wiped an eye before it became a mascara streak. "And now we're here in Iowa where it's calm and nothing ever goes wrong," she mused ironically.

"Do you regret coming?" Leslie asked.

"A little. But we found some happiness. I've never seen Murgatroyd so accepted. J.T. is a marvelous young man. I hope that they can stay friends for a very long time."

"We'll find them, Glory."

For the next minutes they sat in resolute hope waiting for a phone call, or simply for the front door to pop open and J.T.'s face to emerge from the darkness. A small grin would cross his face and then he'd walk to the fridge to get something to eat. That was the routine and Rhonda desperately wished for it.

A text came in.

It was from Murgatroyd's phone.

Her voice caught. Rhonda noticed the words at the beginning:

You have one hour. I have him and the girl. If you show anyone this text, bad things happen. Respond with a yes and I will give you directions.

"He… it's not them…" Rhonda said.

"Who is it then?" Leslie asked.

"Uh… Linda Harmsen. She was asking about… uh… something to do with my hair appointment."

"At this time of night?" Louise was dubious.

"She does that sometimes." Rhonda rose and walked to the kitchen. The others watched her. Surreptitiously, she put the phone on silent and typed.

Yes.

Tensely, she waited for the response. It came seconds later.

Meet me at the wax. Then, I'll let them go.

The wax?

Chapter 18.

I don't understand. What does that mean?

Where your husband is melting.

The lightbulb turned on in her mind. The kidnapper had an intimate knowledge of Amicable. To meet in the cemetery, as morbid as that was, meant that the man was a local. Thankfully, he wouldn't be taking them far away.

Midnight.

Rhonda glanced at the time. It was almost eight o'clock. Four hours to go, but she'd have to get rid of her guests. As much as she wanted to include them in the effort, the kidnapper insisted that it be only her.

I'll be there.

Alone.

At 8:00 p.m. Louise called the State Police and gave them the details. In an hour, they would be at Rhonda Jensen's house. She would not show them her phone.
That would be unfortunate.

* * * * *

Murgatroyd was getting antsy. And tired. As it was almost ten o'clock, she yawned loudly. Even on her longest nights, ten o'clock was really pushing it. When Barnaby told them they'd be on the move at 11:30, she wasn't particularly impressed and she let him know it. He told her that if she kept her mouth shut, she would be home and in her bed by morning.
    He did *not* tell her what he had in mind for J.T. and Rhonda, though.

Son of a Butcher

As Murgatroyd's head began to nod off in exhaustion, J.T. also showed signs of losing the battle with sleep.

"I'm really sorry, kid."

Gustav wasn't sure why he said it. The reasoning sounded hollow, but he felt sorry nonetheless.

"I know."

Surprised by the response, Gustav shifted in his. "What does that mean?"

"I can see it."

"See what?"

"I see all sorts of things. It's hard, though, with you. Your glasses make it difficult."

"My glasses?"

He nodded. "People said my dad had a gift. They said he could see through people. Of course, he couldn't, but he showed me how to do some of it. It's almost always with the eyes."

Barnaby waited.

"I've got good eyes and ears. I can see and hear almost everything. I've already memorized your house and the things that you've said. I know that you were messaging my mother and I read it."

"There's no way you read what I sent. You're way over there."

J.T. shrugged. "Test me."

"How many windows are in the house?"

"That's easy." J.T. closed his eyes and counted. "On this side of the house there are four."

"Wrong," Barnaby said.

Opening his eyes, J.T.'s gaze seemed to swallow Barnaby. "There are two downstairs and two upstairs. There are twenty-seven rows of siding. Seventeen squares of cement in your front walk. You have twelve cupboards in the kitchen."

Barnaby frowned.

"When you texted my mom, you wrote, 'You have one hour. I have him and the girl. If you show anyone this text, bad things happen. Respond with a yes and I will give you directions.' That one scared me a little bit. What bad things might happen?"

"You don't have to concern yourself with that."

Chapter 18.

"I already have."
"It won't come to that, kid. Your mom will come."
"I know."
"You know that I won't hurt you?"
"Yes."
"Tell me how you know."
"I can tell when people are lying. It's in their eyes."
"But you can't see my eyes."

Murgatroyd shifted on J.T.'s arm and she slid down onto his lap. He put his arm over her shoulders in a tender, brotherly way. "I know that you don't *want* to hurt us. When you were texting my mom, your pulse quickened. My dad told me that's one of the ways to tell if people don't like what they're doing."

"What if I was excited?"
"Then you would have started sweating, which you didn't."
"So you can tell if I'm lying?"
"I can try. But you'll have to take off your glasses."
"You aren't afraid of me... er, my looks?"
"Why would I be afraid of that?"

What Barnaby meant was that he was afraid of himself. He was afraid that the kid would be able to see through him, to see his inner anger which truly wanted to hurt his mother. He really wanted her to *feel* the torture of loss. His greatest fear was that he would lose himself to Gustav and never return.

Slowly, Gustav receded farther into the background and Barnaby stepped forward. He removed his glasses. Even in the light of the living room, he squinted. His injured pupil did not dilate properly. The poorly functioning facial muscles around his ears couldn't quite close his eye enough and he winced. He put them back on.

"You can turn off the lights, if you want."
"Then you won't be able to see me."
"I will. Light and dark are the same to me."
"Ridiculous."
"Test me."

Replacing his sunglasses, he stood up, keeping his eye on J.T. and moved to the doorway and flipped the switch. Light extinguished, the house was pitch black save for the small amount of light streaming through the slatted blinds. It took a few moments for Barnaby's eye to adjust.

"Okay, how many fingers am I holding up?"
"Three."
That was too obvious.
"And now?"
"One. Four. Seven."
Barnaby lowered both of his hands.
"Now you can take your glasses off and it won't hurt."
Slowly, Barnaby removed his glasses. In the dim light, the boy seemed vulnerable and soft, something to be protected. Barnaby felt a weight of guilt settle over him and he wanted to put his glasses back on.
"Tell me three truths and a lie and I'll pick the lie."
"That's your test?"
"Write them down then and I'll pick."
Without speaking, Barnaby turned to the living area. Holding out his hands to guide him, he stumbled slightly on a dining chair. Eventually, he found the bookshelf.
"To your left a little," J.T. said. "There's a pencil and some paper."
This is a little too eerie, Barnaby thought.
"You can stay there at the table and write them. I can read it just fine from here."
"Yeah right. In the dark from ten feet away."
"Try."
Barnaby scribbled down four things:

I have two brothers and no sisters.
My first car was a Datsun pickup.
I have been to Disneyland.
Jacob was the name of the person who took my eye.

He lifted the sheet of paper up. "Okay. Try away."
J.T. followed Barnaby's eyes to the first statement. Obviously, this was the lie. "You don't have any brothers or sisters. The first one is a

Chapter 18.

lie."

The paper in Barnaby's hands shook. "How…"

"I don't know other than I watched your eye rest on the first one. I want to go to Disneyland someday too, but I don't know if it's going to happen."

"What about the last one?"

"How long were you in prison when it happened?"

The boy was a savant.

"So you know when I'm lying. Even in the dark. But what about if I tell you something. Can you tell if it's true or not?"

"I hope so."

Barnaby stared at him. "I'm not going to hurt you."

Silence filled the room. Finally, J.T. spoke. "I think you're telling the truth."

He was. But if Gustav surfaced again, perhaps not.

"Barnaby, someone is coming."

Barnaby's heart thumped with adrenaline. "What do you mean?"

"Out there," J.T. pointed out the front window. "There is a fat man walking towards us. He has a package. And your name is on it."

Danny.

Sidling away from the table, Barnaby moved to the front door. "Do not make a sound. If you do, I'll have to hurt her."

J.T. could see that this was truth.

* * * * *

Danny felt his breath coming in gasps.

He had decided to walk across Clancy on Christmas Eve eve and hand-deliver Barnaby's Christmas present.

Barnaby had been acting stranger than ever. It was as if he was watching the end of a close football game – he was tense and jumpy, as if he didn't know how it was going to end. When Danny had stopped a few weeks before, there had been a sheet covering the table. Danny had asked him about it, but Barnaby had responded that it was none of his business. Naturally, this made Danny suspicious, but he still liked Barnaby. He felt sorry for him.

Son of a Butcher

That was why he walked over with a Christmas present. Danny didn't know Barnaby's plans for Christmas, whether he had family or friends or if he was going on a vacation. Now that Danny thought about it, he realized that Barnaby didn't really talk about himself. Ever. Danny was always the one doing all the talking. Still, Danny didn't want to intrude on Barnaby's private life. Frankly, Danny was going to be busy visiting nieces and nephews so there wouldn't be much time for Barnaby anyway.

Pausing at the end of the walkway, lightly covered by a dusting of new snow, Danny caught his breath. Steam rose into the air from both his exhalations and the heat from his body and he knew that if he took off his coat, the sweat would show.

There were no lights on in the house, yet Barnaby's car was parked in the driveway. Strangely, there were smaller footprints in the snow. *What in the world?* As he approached the house, the front door opened, and Barnaby stepped out.

"Merry Christmas, Barnaby!"

"What are you doing here, Danny? It's late."

"I thought I'd bring some Christmas cheer." Danny handed the package to Barnaby, who merely stared at it. Danny slowly pulled it back. "The polite thing would be to say, 'Merry Christmas.'"

"It's late, Danny. I… appreciate the thought, but I've got a big day tomorrow."

"Spending some time with a niece or nephew?"

"What?" Barnaby's voice raised an octave.

"There's a set of small footprints in the snow," he pointed, "and I thought maybe you had a brother or sister and their child with you. Is that why the lights are out already? They're sleeping?"

Barnaby glanced down at the ground and swore.

"No, no one is staying with me. It must have been a neighbor kid running through my yard."

"All the way up to the door?"

Gustav ground his teeth. "Merry Christmas, Danny. I'll talk to you after the holiday." He began to close the door.

"Wait," Danny took a step forward, "don't forget your gift." He reached out with it again.

Chapter 18.

Receiving the gift with one arm, he nodded and waited for Danny to leave. As Danny turned, he caught a glimpse of a face in the window, someone peeking through the blinds. Or at least that's what he thought it was. It might have been a shadow.
He hoped it was just a shadow.

Chapter 19.

At 11:30, Rhonda's phone dinged. The others had left, even the State Troopers. They were going to coordinate with Louise at the station, while Glory and Rhonda waited.

You have thirty minutes.

Heart racing, Rhonda packed up her handbag, put on her coat and boots, and pulled the door shut behind her. She stepped into the winter air. As the door clicked, her phone beeped again.

Do not bring your car. Walk from your house.

It hit Rhonda that this person knew who she was and where she lived. That she would walk to the cemetery by herself was frightening. Would he be watching her? Would he be following her? What would happen when she saw J.T.?

Walking briskly down the sidewalk, she turned right. Large snowflakes were beginning to fall. A few fell on her face, her nose and cheeks. They felt like melting feathers. The houses she walked past, although dim, were lit with Christmas lights. From the outside, each appeared festive and cheery. Thankfully, no one saw her walking.

She turned left by the football field. Her pulse quickened. Either she would see her son and Murgatroyd, or she might suffer the agony of not knowing what happened to them.

We're waiting at your husband's grave.

Chilled to the bone, both literally and figuratively, Rhonda entered the quiet sanctuary of the cemetery and stepped past the graves of people she had known for years. Beautiful, kind people who had helped shape her life and the lives of so many around her. She prayed that these saints would protect her and guide her on the way.

Chapter 19.

Near the back of the cemetery, she saw Butcher's monument. Just as in daylight, in the darkness, the sculpture was a shadow over her life. In the years since Butcher's death, she had not returned often because the melting wax saddened her. She wanted to avoid seeing the last remnants of her beautiful husband dripping onto the ground.

The dim streetlights illuminated the low clouds surrounding the town. Snowflakes flew under their glow. They appeared like slowly dropping stars.

Her husband's gravestone loomed. She sensed the great despair of approaching this moment feeling dreadfully alone. To have him with her. To hear his voice. It would have made all the difference in the world, but it was not to be.

There was movement behind the grave. It was Barnaby Koppel.

"You seem surprised."

"Barnaby! How? Why?"

"You really haven't figure it out, have you?"

"I don't understand. Where are the kids?"

"They're safe." Barnaby had left them in his car with a warning that if they tried to run away, he would hurt their mothers. Both of them.

"Where are they? You said that there would be an exchange. You said…"

"SHUT UP!" Without conscious thought, Gustav arose from the shallow grave of anger and erupted with pent up, volcanic rage. "YOU BROUGHT THIS ON YOURSELF!"

Terrified, Rhonda took a step backwards and tripped over a grave. Falling onto the ground, she crabwalked backwards away from his looming shape. His eyes hidden by sunglasses and his scarred face were more frightening in the dark. "Please. I don't…"

"I was there when he died. You didn't know that."

Rhonda's heart failed and her lip began to tremble. "What?"

"I was standing at the foot of the dock. I saw the wheelchair fall in. I could have saved him, but it felt so good to see that part of you suffer. He's probably in hell now."

"Don't, please."

Son of a Butcher

"The elevator explosion? Guess who placed the incendiaries underneath the grate. It only took a little spark and..." Gustav's face lit up as he made a silent 'boom' with his mouth and hands.

Rhonda was shocked to the core.

"But... why?"

He edged closer and leaned down over her. "You don't recognize me?"

"No. I've never met you before. So why me?"

Furiously, he grabbed her arm and lifted her from the ground with superhuman power. The pressure was painful and she cried out as he forced her forward, away from her husband's grave, through the falling snow and out of the cemetery.

"What about J.T. and Murgatroyd?"

"You should be worrying about yourself."

"Where are you taking me?"

"You'll see."

Gustav continued to hold on as he pulled her along the sidewalk to the east. Through darkened streets, beyond the consciousness of Amicable, Gustav took her to West First Street where he turned left. Looming on the corner was St. Clements. Now, almost dragging her, he forced her to the front stoop and grabbed the door.

"The church? Why the church?"

"You are about to witness the last destruction of your precious town. After this night, Amicable will be no more."

Cold fear gripped her heart. "What are you going to do?"

Throwing open the door, he hauled her up the stairs and into the sanctuary. In the glow of the Christmas lights, they staggered to the apse where he threw her down at the foot of the altar. "You will be my sacrifice, Rhonda. Merry Christmas!" The crazy look in his eyes was horrible.

"Stop. Please. Can we talk about this?"

"We can talk." If she could have seen his eye, it would have shone with a maniacal fury. "I thought about what would hurt you most. Certainly, hurting your kids would affect you, but that would have been hard, even for a vengeful guy like me. I could have wrecked your husband, but he checked out early." His grin was eerie. "What about the

Chapter 19.

town? I thought the elevator's destruction would crack the town in half, but it only seemed to galvanize the citizens. But what about the heart, mind and soul? What about if all three were to go up in flames?"

Rhonda's panic intensified.

"The heart of the community revolves around that stupid bowling alley. That ridiculous dance the other night – to feel your hand in mind. It was unbearable. To feel your body heat, to see you as a princess."

"Why do you hate me so much?"

He ignored her. "The mind of the town? The school has been a source of safety for kids over a hundred years. If it's gone, does Amicable go down? I hope so."

"Not the school…"

Grinning malevolently, he continued. "And the soul?" He lifted his face to the ceiling where the church's decorating committee had strung white stars from the rafters. They moved slightly in the small drafts eddying through the upper reaches. "This building. If this were to go down, perhaps then, everything you held dear, would finally be taken from you."

"What have you done?"

"It's amazing what a man can learn when imprisoned. During the years I was locked up, I learned how to burn things. I couldn't put it into practice, but I dreamed about the moment when I could put it into action."

He took a shuddering breath as he stood above her.

"I've lived in Clancy for five years. In Iowa. Do you know how difficult that is? Of course you do. You've lived here your whole life except for that short time after high school."

Suddenly, something clicked inside Rhonda's mind. "No, it couldn't be."

"You're finally getting the picture, aren't you? It was *you*, Rhonda, who sent me to prison, *you* who gave me the scars that I must wear and bear. It was *you* who made me like this, an enraged, bitter man with very little to live for. If *you* weren't such a deceptive witch, Amicable wouldn't have to suffer like this. When everything is done, you will have only yourself to blame."

"Gus?"

"Ding, ding, ding. The Price is Right! You win the prize. Now you see me."

Tears began to stream from Rhonda's eyes. "I thought you were dead. You sent me that letter. That note."

"I have been dead to you. In fact, I haven't lived in a long time, not until this very moment."

"How...?"

"I had a cellmate who did me a favor by planting a headstone with my name etched in it. When you and your husband visited that grave, I was dead – dead to you. But now?" He grinned maniacally. "How did I get here? They released me from prison. You should have received a message, but it might have gone unnoticed in your happy life. I'm so grateful that you were blissfully unaware of me until this moment. Do you like the disguise? The beard? The extra pounds? And the irony – I learned how to be a butcher. Just for you."

"What are you going to do?"

"It's all going to come down. All of it." He reached inside his shirt and produced what looked like a remote car starter. "In a few moments, everything – the Amicable school, the bowling alley, and St. Clements church – will burn. I stashed incendiaries in a locker at the bowling alley. Glory unknowingly delivered one to the third-grade room. And above us," he pointed to the ceiling, "a beautiful Christmas present lies in the bell tower."

"What about the kids?"

"WHAT ABOUT ME!" Gustav shouted at the top of his lungs. He stepped back and dramatically raised the starter above his head. "Lying will never get you anywhere." He depressed the button and above them, a muffled boom sounded.

Frightened, Rhonda tried to scrabble to the side, but he grabbed her and fell on top of her. "I didn't do it the first time and I won't try the second time, but we're going to be here until the end." As he finished speaking, a muted crackling sound could be heard above them. Some smoke began to leak in through the cracks of the wooden ceiling.

Within moments, hell would appear from above.

Chapter 19.

* * * * *

"J.T." Murgatroyd whispered, "what are we going to do?"

"I don't know."

"I think we should get out of the car. We should find someone."

"He said he would hurt our moms."

"He's already got your mum. We've got to save her."

"What are we going to do?" J.T. asked. "We're just kids."

Murgatroyd opened the car door. She was very cold and cranky. "Come on, Boyo. We've got to go."

She tugged on his arm and pulled him from the car. "Now. Where did they go?"

J.T. glanced around. He had seen them leave the cemetery and walk east, but they could have gone anywhere. Then, J.T.'s eyes saw a glow. Not only that, but he could also see smoke rising from St. Clements. He realized at that moment, the package they'd seen in the bell tower was *not* a Christmas present. *Neither were the ones in the bowling alley and the school!*

"Come on, Murgatroyd! The town is on fire!"

They raced down the midnight street toward the infant infernos. There was no one stirring yet, but soon, Amicable would be alive trying to save its heart, mind and soul.

When they turned the corner, the bell tower was alight. The silhouette of the bell stood in contrast to the low-lying clouds above the church. Snow continued to fall as the flames continued to rise.

"J.T.! The church! And look, the bowling alley has smoke coming out of it."

They pulled up short at the intersection of the three burning buildings. "And the school, Murg. And the school. It's all on fire."

"What are we going to do?"

J.T. glanced at the Deakins' house. "We need to get Unca John." The kids raced to the front door and pounded on it. The lights turned on just before John and Leslie appeared at the door. "J.T.!" John grabbed him and hugged him tight. "Where have you been?"

"Unca John! The church!"

Son of a Butcher

John followed J.T.'s pointed finger. His face began to reflect the flickering lights above him. "Oh, God help us!" He grabbed the kids and pushed them inside. "Leslie, take care of them and call the fire department and the police. I need to get over there!"

"Wait! Unca John! Mom is in there. He's got Mom!"

John grabbed him by the shoulders. "Who? Who's got her?"

"Barnaby."

John's heart leapt into his throat. Running out the door, John raced to the church and threw open the front door. He stumbled up the stairs and peered through the sanctuary windows.

"Rhonda!" he shouted. "Where are you?"

A scream came from inside. "In here! John! Help!"

Taking the stairs two at a time, the smoke grew thicker the farther he ascended. As he entered the sanctuary, he saw the silhouetted forms of two people near the altar. Covering his mouth with his bathrobe, he charged up the center aisle. Above him, the world was ablaze. Pieces of the roof were crumbling, and smoldering embers landed around him. When he reached the altar, he found Barnaby Koppel sitting astride Rhonda Jensen. Her eyes were wide with fear, and they were both coughing.

"Barnaby! What are you doing? Let her go!"

"My name is Gustav Keller. This woman sentenced me to a life in hell a long time ago."

The crackling fire above them almost drowned out the words. John struggled to hear him. "We have to get out of here! Everything is coming down!"

"I know!" Gustav began to laugh crazily. "I know!"

Without hesitation, John charged Barnaby and tackled him. Rolling to the side, John found himself under the altar wrestling with Barnaby. "Rhonda," he grunted. "Get out! Get help!"

Needing no further words, Rhonda pulled herself from the ground and ran down the center aisle. The organ was beginning to catch fire in the balcony, and directly above her, paper stars were lighting up like meteorites and flashing out of existence. Smoke stabbed her coughing lungs as she stumbled out of the sanctuary and down the stairs. She fell in a heap and crawled to the front door.

Chapter 19.

Time was running out. She had to hurry.

* * * * *

After Aunt Leslie closed the door, J.T. couldn't stop thinking about his mother. He had to get to her. While Leslie took Murgatroyd into the kitchen, J.T. ran back to the front door and threw it open. He heard Leslie shout after him, but he did not stop.

Arriving at the east side of the church, J.T. heard sirens. Soon, the volunteer fire department would arrive, but they would not have enough manpower for all three fires, not even for one of them. Suddenly, his mother streamed from the front doors of the church. Her hair was smoking.

"Mom!" he screamed and ran towards her.

Shrieking with relief, she found him and fell to the ground. The snow felt good on her warm arms. "Sweetheart," she grabbed his face and noticed, maybe for the first time, how much he looked like his father, "you have to wait here. I've got to find help. John is still in there!"

But Unca John was still inside.

Instead of following his mother's wishes, J.T. pulled himself up from the snowy ground and walked zombie-like to the front doors. As he pulled them open, one of the stained glass windows exploded and smoke began to billow out. In spite of his fear, J.T. walked into the narthex and up the steps. When he looked across the sanctuary, he saw Unca John under the altar. Near him, Barnaby was pinned to the floor by a fallen beam.

"Unca John!"

"J.T.!" John shouted to him. "Don't come any closer! Get out of here!"

J.T. looked up at the ceiling and focused on the exposed beams. Fire had destroyed most of the roof, and ash was settling like snow across the sanctuary. It was hot and it stung his arms, but he knew that he had to get to John soon. "I'm coming!"

Awkwardly, his long legs loped rather than ran. He dodged falling embers and made his way to the front. Quickly, he crawled under the altar with John. They both covered their faces with their shirts. When

Son of a Butcher

J.T. looked over at Barnaby, he winced. Embers had fallen around him and were beginning to burn his clothes. Soon, he would catch on fire.

"Barnaby," J.T. reached out, "we'll save you."

"Don't even think about it! I did this! This is my punishment!" His glasses were broken, and his eyepatch had fallen off. Here, Gustav Kellar was vulnerable, trapped under a crossbeam, crucified in his vengeance.

"No, we'll get you!"

"J.T." he said, "you're a good boy. Tell your mother I'm sorry. I was wrong."

Flames dripped from the ceiling landing on Barnaby's collar. When the fabric began to burn, searing his chest, he began to scream. Then, Barnaby's beard caught fire. As he flailed at it, he heard J.T. shout, "Unca John, help him!"

John scrambled out from under the altar and raced to the sacristy. Opening the cupboard, he grabbed the large bottle of communion wine and ran back to Barnaby. "Son of a…" John shouted as he broke the top of the bottle on the altar and poured it over Barnaby's face. The wine sizzled as it hit him and extinguished the flames. For good measure, John Deakins poured the rest of the bottle over his body. Barnaby sputtered.

"J.T.," John coughed, "we need to lift the beam."

John and his godson stood at the end of the beam. They attempted to raise it, but it was too heavy.

"I wish I was as strong as my dad," J.T. shouted.

"We can do this!"

Just as J.T. Jensen was about to reach down one more time, he suddenly felt a strange sense of calmness, as if his father was with him. With a renewed sense of power, J.T. glanced up to see one last star hanging above the clerestory, dancing in the fury of the smoke and flames. As the star danced, a brief thought entered J.T.'s mind and he wondered if *he* was Starman.

J.T. felt a miraculous strength surge through him. Squatting, they lifted the beam. "Unca John, I got this. Pull him out."

John saw the supernatural, furious light in the boy's eyes, and heard the voice of Leo Jensen issuing from his mouth. He nodded. The

Chapter 19.

weight of the beam was almost too much for J.T. but he held on. John Thomas Deakins grabbed Barnaby Koppel under his arms and dragged him out. Only then did J.T. let the beam crash to the floor.

John and J.T. each grabbed an arm and started dragging Barnaby down the center aisle towards the back of the church. Just as they were about to pass out from exhaustion, heat and smoke inhalation, they paused under the balcony. Barnaby grunted something and John leaned over him.

"What did you say, Barnaby?"

"I claim sanctuary. Please." His eyes closed and he passed out.

John and J.T. felt arms encircle them. They were pulled from the burning wreckage of the church.

Chapter 20.

It took two months of convalescence before the Reverend John Thomas Deakins was fully able to speak and understand all the things that had happened on that fateful Christmas Eve night. After a few weeks, he had attempted to speak, but Leslie had patted his arm and shushed him. Instead, she related the tragedy, withholding only a few details until he would be able to bear the full force of the news.

The damage to the buildings was catastrophic. Stedman arrived back in Amicable to assess the devastation. The three buildings had suffered immense structural damage, especially the church. Because the church was predominantly built of wood, the inferno had been the greatest and the highest. All that was left of St. Clements church was a shell. The bowling alley and the Greedy Pecker would have to be rebuilt from the ground up. The school, though mostly made of brick, would need complete restoration. Its destruction hit the community the hardest.

One person from Clancy, an overweight man named Danny Thul, opined on Channel 10 news, that Amicable seemed cursed.

When John was able to keep his eyes open for more than ten minutes at a time, Leslie delved into the harder topic of Barnaby Koppel.

"Do people know that it was him?"

Leslie's mouth hardened. "He was charged, yes."

"I can't see how he won't be thrown back into prison."

"Do you know anything about his relationship with Rhonda?"

"Rhonda? What does she have to do with it?"

Leslie let him in on the confidential, terrible history between the two and how it had been carried forward to the present. At the end of the narrative, John began to weep. "Why does God allow this all to happen?"

"That's the question we all have, isn't it?"

"What are we going to do?"

"I was going to ask you the same thing," Leslie said as she stroked his arm where the hair was growing back. He had scald burns all

Chapter 20.

over his body, but they were less devastating than the smoke damage to his lungs. Thankfully, they also were beginning to recover.

"Can we help him?"

"Who, Barnaby?"

"Yes."

"He deserves what's coming to him, you know."

"Does he? When he was caught under the beam, he told me that he was Gustav Keller. Maybe he was insane? Maybe that was his defense?"

"Seems tenuous at best."

"I'd like to stand for him."

Leslie's eyes widened. "How do you think Rhonda will react?"

"I don't know. I'll have to talk to her too."

"And J.T.? How is he getting along?"

"He's visited you a few times. He doesn't say much. The trauma seems to have taken him backwards a step, but Murgatroyd is helping."

"That's good. How is Glory?"

"Hmm, that's a tough one. I think she wants to leave, to run away. Even though she couldn't have possibly known what Barnaby was capable of, she still feels guilty. People have been very supported, so we hope she makes the decision to stay."

"I'm glad she's okay."

* * * * *

Now that a few months had passed, John continued to recuperate at home. Slowly, his endurance was coming back. Although he coughed all the time, he could now breathe deeply. He had to be able to speak well because his first church council meeting since the fire was occurring that night. As he walked by the burned-out shell of his church, past the remnants of the bowling alley and onwards to the city council chambers where they'd been allowed to meet while the church was in ruins, he pondered what he was going to suggest for St. Clements.

Over the last years, since Butcher's death, John had begun to question the function and focus of both the church and his vocation. As the years had passed, John was beginning to recognize a different calling for the church and himself. He didn't want to leave, but certainly, the call to share faith extended well beyond the walls of the building. Now that the walls had burnt down, both literally and symbolically, the church had to find a way to get out.

Opening the door of the city council building, he found the council members sitting around a table drinking coffee and chatting amicably. These were good and faithful people, kind and understanding. They understood that all things must change. Butcher had taught them that. Now it was John's turn to remind them.

The council clapped as he entered. He smiled and waved them to their seats. After the meeting was called to order, they prayed, and John was given the floor.

"It's been quite a few years, hasn't it?"

Polite laughter.

"Physically, I'm doing well. Emotionally," he waggled his hand, "and spiritually, I'm struggling." Now, there were concerned faces. "I'm not in danger of losing my faith, only frightened by its evolution. Tonight, I wanted to share a few of those thoughts with you, if I may."

The chairperson nodded.

"While lying in bed these last two months, my mind has been very active. I've realized, not for the first time, that the church is not a building, it is the people."

"Yes, we've heard that before, Pastor," one of the council members said.

"But the school, also, is more than a *building* and so is the bowling alley. Every business, every home, every area of community life has always been for people and about people. Without the bowling alley, we will still gather; without the school *building*, the kids will still learn; without the church *building*, the people will still celebrate their faith. It's not that the *buildings* aren't important, but they aren't the most crucial thing."

He glanced at the council noticing their confused looks. "The word crucial, has the basis of the word 'cross' in it. At the crucis, or crux, of the future, is a genuine hope that at the heart of everything we do in Amicable, we should be thinking about the people first."

Chapter 20.

"As I thought about the people," he continued without pausing for questions, "one person in particular came to mind. You might think I'm crazy, but that person was Barnaby Koppel." Mumbles of displeasure. "In some ways, the church failed him."

"What! That's insane. He burned down half the town!" One of the council members was irate. "He's crazy. He belongs in prison for what he did to us."

John sighed. They were good and kind people, but he hoped they could see where he was going. "He'd already been in prison for a long time. A personal prison. A hellish one that we wouldn't want inflicted on anyone else. No, Barnaby Koppel certainly does not need any more prison time."

"Then what are you suggesting?"

"That the church cares for him. You don't know this, but his last words to me, as we were pulled from the church were, 'I claim sanctuary.' Do you understand what he was asking for?"

Confused looks.

"Barnaby Koppel is asking for a reprieve from the life he had been living. Our traditional church sanctuary had always been a *place* of safety and security for members and Amicableans who have needed a nice place to spend an hour on Sunday mornings. As I pondered during these last months of recuperation, I asked myself, 'Isn't this wasteful?'" More frowns. "I'm not saying that worship or gathering is a waste of time, but is it a waste to only use the church building a couple of times per week?"

He took another breath. "When Barnaby claimed sanctuary, he claimed something a little deeper inside of me. He staked a claim on what I truly believe. Do I value a building and Sunday morning worship more than I value the people that truly need sanctuary, those who have been marginalized, hurt, discarded or abused? Do I value this hour of catching up on Sunday mornings with like-minded, like-faithed people more than I value making a difference in the world around us?"

"The short answer is, 'no.' I came to the realization when Barnaby made this claim on my faith, I can no longer be a pastor who serves a church building, but a pastor who serves the church – the people outside the building."

"You're not going to be our pastor anymore?" one council member asked.

"You're not listening,' John responded kindly. "To be a pastor simply means I help lead people to know who God is. What better way to do that than outside the traditional walls?"

"Who's going to do worship for us, then?"

"You will. We all will. Wherever we are. Remember God's command on the people of Israel, teach your children at all times, when you sit at home and when you walk along the road, when you lie down and when you get up. Imagine if we all did that. Imagine if our worship gathering was along the road, at the bowling alley, at school, before we went to bed, walking in the park, at funerals and weddings. Imagine if our faith was something lived, not timed."

"What do we do with the church building then?" a member asked.

John ran a hand through his hair. "You can disagree with me, but I believe the future of the Church will be like this: to be transformed from a building *with* a sanctuary into a building that *is* a sanctuary. We recondition it to be an ark, if you will, for people who need to be rescued. We take in the widows, the orphans, the refugees, the downcast, the downtrodden, heck, all the down and outs and we give them sanctuary. We will just naturally say to people who have suffered like Barnaby, 'Come on in. We'll take care of you.' Do you see where I'm going?"

"Yes," one council member said stubbornly, "but who's going to be our pastor?"

He sighed and looked down. "I am. You are. Barnaby Koppel is. Glory MacDonald is. Murgatroyd and J.T., Louise Nelson, the Peterson twins. Every Amicablean will be pastoral and will have a part of the sanctuary."

"Won't it be dangerous to bring in all these people?" One said honestly. "We're talking about some severe mental health issues among them, aren't we?"

"Let's talk about those details as we dive deeper."

"Are you sure about this, Pastor? This seems... dangerous. And... and... full of risks of lawsuits. Do you really think people will

Chapter 20.

pledge their time and money to it?"

"If I'm reading my Bible correctly, not only will they pledge to that, they'll see a magnificent change in the world around us."

* * * * *

While John Thomas Deakins attempted to explain a different future, J.T. Jensen and Murgatroyd MacDonald were bundled up in the backyard of her house staring up at an elm tree. J.T.'s lungs had recovered quickly. Because of his youth and health, he was soon back to running the streets of Amicable after school with his best friend.

"How big should we make it?"

"Bigger than yours," Murgatroyd said.

"Why is that?"

"Because I deserve it. I saved you."

"What? That's ridiculous."

"If I hadn't pulled you from the car, you would have stayed there like a frightened little baby."

"Bollocks," said J.T.

"Now you're getting the hang of it." Murgatroyd punched J.T. in the arm.

The End

Son of a Butcher

Dearest Reader,

It feels like the end, doesn't it? As I finish penning the last words to this tale, I sit in my study (John still thinks it's his, but it's not), looking out over the reconstruction projects. As they are transformed from something old into something new, I still feel a stab of pain that the old will no longer be with us. Only memories we have of what used to be. They are bittersweet, lacquered with sentiment and nostalgia, but good enough for now. The future will hopefully be more sweet than bitter.

I've just written the words THE END. I want to erase THE END, but I can't.

As with almost all of life, there is no such thing as a happy THE ENDing, only one with meaning.

The Amicable High School still looks the same from the outside. Dark red bricks rise upwards, solid, yet they are a façade of what has occurred within it. The school has been gutted. All the things that were, have been burnt. A few Amicableans have watched as the ash and the debris have been pulled out like cremated remains. I have not watched that closely. I am more interested in what will be put back in the school. What kind of education will be taught in this new age? Will children learn to think, or only to watch? I don't know. I worry about that.

The bowling alley and Greedy Pecker have been razed and raised in quick succession. Maybe not so strangely, as the town returns to normality, the people have needed their place to connect. In this social center of Amicable, we soon will hear the same sounds, the laughter, the rolling of bowling balls, the good-natured shouting and ribbing. I look forward to that, even if the surroundings won't look the same.

As for St. Clements? At first, the congregation members balked at not rebuilding as a church but as a sanctuary for the disadvantaged, the isolated and the outcast. Many arguments ensued over the months until John was able to accurately depict what he believed George, Butcher, Anne and so many others would have wanted for the life of the community. As the Sanctuary is being created, so, too, is the sense of goodwill and generous growth amongst the town. Amazingly, we find people living and speaking their faith outside of the walls. People thank God for everything. I'm thankful for that.

Chapter 20.

As for Barnaby…

His wounds were too great, and he succumbed to the results of Amicable's fires. In the end, his claim for sanctuary was granted. We are all quite certain that the fires of his pain have been quenched in a place far, far away from the hell he'd been living through.

Glory, of course, was inconsolable, but she is determined to stay and soldier on as an Amicablean. More for Murgatroyd's sake than for her own. We are happy.

And for me…? I feel my son kicking inside me unhappy about being pent up in the sanctuary of my womb. As I rub his back through my belly, I say to him, 'Leopold Butcher Deakins, be patient. The world isn't quite ready for you.' There could have been no other name for him, right?

In THE END *we all must find our sanctuary. For me that has been Amicable. For you? That's for you to figure out. May God bless you on that journey.*

Leslie Deakins

www.ingramcontent.com/pod-product-compliance
Lightning Source LLC
Chambersburg PA
CBHW051424290426
44109CB00016B/1430